Best Answers to 202 Job Interview Questions

Expert Tips to Ace the Interview and Get the Job Offer

Daniel Porot and Frances Bolles Haynes

Manassas Park, VA

Best Answers to 202 Job Interview Questions

ISBN (10-digit): 1570232717

ISBN (13-digit): 978-1570232718

Library of Congress: 2005929762

Publisher: For information on Impact Publications, including current and forthcoming publications, authors, press kits, online bookstore, and submissions, visit our website: www.impactpublications.com.

Publicity/Rights: For information on publicity, author interviews, and subsidiary rights, contact Media Relations Department: Tel. 703-361-7300, Fax 703-335-9486, or email: query@impactpublications.com.

Sales/Distribution: All bookstore sales are handled through Impact's trade distributor: National Book Network, 15200 NBN Way, Blue Ridge Summit, PA 17214, Tel. 1-800-462-6420. All other sales and distribution inquiries should be directed to the publisher: Sales Department, IMPACT PUBLICATIONS, 9104 Manassas Drive, Suite N, Manassas Park, VA 20111-5211, Tel. 703-361-7300, Fax 703-335-9486, or email: query@impactpublications.com

Contents

Introduction 1

1 Ice Breakers 16
2 Self-Evaluation 36
3 Personality, Personal Characteristics, and Style 62
4 Competencies and Skills 88
5 Problem Solving and Decision Making 118
6 Education and Learning 140
7 Work Habits 166
8 Likes and Preferences 194
9 Professional Goals 218
10 Motivation 238
11 Previous Professional Experience 280
12 Organizational Hierarchy 316
13 Workplace Relationships and Communication 340
14 Vision 372
15 Job Hunting 386
16 Salary 412
17 Trick/Delicate Topics 430
18 Social Status 472
19 Behavioral Interviewing 494

By Daniel Porot and Frances Bolles Haynes

101 Salary Secrets: How to Negotiate Like a Pro
101 Toughest Interview Questions: And Answers That Win the Job!
Best Answers to 202 Job Interview Questions
Winning Letters That Overcome Barriers to Employment

Introduction

Y OU'VE MADE IT TO the interview stage! Congratulations! Perhaps you just started looking for a job two days ago and already have your first interview, or perhaps you've been working at it for months on end with little success. Whatever your path has been, you now face that last big hurdle to get the job.

So, what do you do? Put on a new suit and just show up, hoping that your personal magnetism and good qualities will win the day? It's possible. But if you want to put all chance (which means 99% preparation) on your side, you have to do your homework before you step one foot into any interviewer's office.

Simply put, there are four things you must know before you go!

First: Know Yourself

Good old Socrates (at least some credit it to him) said "Know thyself." It was good advice 2,000+ years ago and it's still good advice today. In fact, it's fundamental if you want to do well in your job-hunting efforts. It's hard to write a resume, respond to an ad, or write an unsolicited letter if you don't know what you most want to convey to someone else about yourself (and what they most need to know to make a decision). It's even harder to interview if you haven't done your homework on yourself because you are face to face with someone who is watching, listening, judging, and paying attention to what you say, don't say, do, and don't do. There are no second chances, no re-do's and no way to grab words that come from your mouth and stuff them back in. You either know what you want to say or you don't.

It's a safe bet that you won't know what you want to say if you haven't taken the time to sit down and really think about what you might reasonably be asked in an interview and how you can best respond to show your skills, knowledge, enthusiasm, personal traits, and experience.

If you haven't given thought to the questions you might be asked, and how to address them, it's a pretty safe bet that you'll ramble on and on while you try to organize the thoughts in your head. Eventually you might get to a good answer, but the road to get there has taken you through forests and valleys, over mountains and into rivers and lakes, and your interviewer will be so confused by the passing scenery, he/she might miss the end point.

So, what do you do to make sure you know what you need to know about yourself?

1. Make a list of 15-30 achievement paragraphs. Include the following information to make sure your statements are complete:

   - The task
   - The means you had at your disposal to achieve it
   - Where you did it (company/place)

- Your job title and responsibilities
- Did you do it alone or with others
- What made the task difficult (if anything)
- How you overcame the difficulty
- Tangible proof of your results using quantifiable facts and figures

2. Make a list of your preferred working conditions.

3. Make a list of your values as they relate to your work.

4. Make a list of the characteristics you look for in your:

- Superiors
- Colleagues
- Subordinates
- Customers/Clients

5. Make a list of your core competencies and preferred skills.

6. Think about your decision-making style and come up with several sentences about how you make decisions under specific circumstances.

7. Make a inventory of your educational background, including courses and training you have undertaken during your career.

8. Make a list of your former bosses and what you have learned from each one.

9. Make a prioritized list of what motivates you to do a good job.

10. Make a list of your professional goals and why you want to achieve them.

11. Make a list of the questions you would most prefer **not** to be asked, and then answer them in writing.

12. Write down your salary expectations, including your bottom-line figure and benefits you would like.

13. Make a list of your leisure-time activities and why you like them.

14. Write down what your dream job would look like. Include everything you want in a job (don't edit yourself because you think it is not possible to get what you want).

If you do this homework on yourself, you will be ahead of most job hunters. You will have gathered pertinent information that will be at your fingertips when you need it. You will be prepared to talk about yourself without feeling self-conscious, embarrassed, or insecure. There will be no need to be nervous. You will be ready.

Second: Know About Interviewing

It's not enough to know about yourself. You need to invest some time getting familiar with the questions you will be asked in an interview. There are about 2 billion Internet sites and books that can tell you the frequently asked questions for most interviews. It's good to know these so you aren't surprised.

But what's most important about the questions you will be asked is not the form they will take, but the reason they are being asked. Most questions, with the exception of some "icebreaker" questions (so you and the interviewer can shake off the first two minutes of awkwardness) have deeper meanings and are asked to elicit very specific information.

Interviewers have reasons for the the questions they ask. Most good interviewers know how to get at the information they want from you.

In our book, *101 Toughest Interview Questions* (Ten Speed Press, 1999), we identified the four concerns interviewers have when they talk with a candidate.

They want to know:

1. Can you actually do the job? Are your experience, education, aptitude, and interest sufficient so you will be productive in this job?
2. Who are you? What are you like? What characteristics and traits do you possess?
3. Will you fit in with the others in my company/organization? Will you be part of a problem or part of a solution?

If you can satisfactorily address these three concerns, then the final concern of the interviewer is:

4.   How much will you cost me?

Your job as a candidate is to understand what information the interviewer is trying to elicit and then develop an appropriate response.

You need to answer questions by:

- Asking questions for clarification
- Defining terms so communication is clear
- Describing your accomplishments
- Detailing specific accomplishments to show your worth
- Discussing past experience
- Focusing on job-related issues
- Giving examples of personal growth
- Giving precise answers
- Listing activities and interests
- Listing examples of your skills and abilities
- Listing personal achievements
- Listing tasks you have done/can do
- Listing time frames
- Listing your interpersonal skills
- Outlining your knowledge
- Pointing out your strongest skills
- Postponing discussion if necessary
- Showing methods you have used to deal with people
- Showing your passion
- Stating negative information succinctly and moving to another topic immediately

- Suggesting an exchange of ideas on job-related topics
- Suggesting strategies for dealing with problems
- Talking about others in positive terms only
- Using comments others have made about you
- Using facts and figures
- Using quantifiable examples from your past experience
- Using ranges whenever possible for salary discussions
- Using statistical information

Once you have done your homework on yourself and understand the reasons certain questions are asked and the form they are likely to take, you can formulate strategies to make sure you respond in a way that is going to give the interviewer the information he/she needs to make an informed decision whether to hire you.

So, how do you get ready?

Start by practicing. Then practice some more. Then practice one final time. You might like to start by making a list of 20 to 40 questions you want to fine-tune. Write them down and then practice your answers in front of a mirror. Once you feel comfortable with that, ask a friend or family member to practice with you. It's important that you practice with someone else—so there is the give-and-take aspect that you would find in a real interview session. If you only practice alone, you will not get needed feedback and interaction that is a must if you are to know how you really come across to someone else.

The more you practice, the more comfortable you should become. It's important to do this so your real self shines at the interview. You want the "real you" present at the interview—not someone else who doesn't reflect your ideas, values, and accomplishments. You need to be real. If you're funny, let your humor shine through. If you don't understand something, feel comfortable enough to ask for clarification. If you are good at using metaphors, use one or two. Use your strengths. Make the most of your assets. Confidence can do that for you. Confidence you will have gained from knowing you can handle any question put to you.

Don't forget the basics of interviewing. These seem pretty self-evident to most, but to make sure we are all on the same page, we'll go over them here!

- Make eye contact. Maintain eye contact. You need to show you aren't uncomfortable looking into your interviewer's eyes. (If you are, look at their eyebrows!)
- Have a firm handshake.
- Smile!
- Dress appropriately.
- Don't be late (go the day before as a practice run if you are worried about this).
- Introduce yourself in a courteous manner.
- If you have to wait, read the company materials.
- Watch your body language. What is it telling the interviewer?
- Thank the interviewer (and anyone else who has been kind enough to help you) both verbally and with a thank you letter.

Third: Know The Job and the Company

The Job

You need to make sure you understand exactly what the particular job you want is all about (the job content). Most interviewers ask job-specific questions during the interview. These questions are usually about:

- Transferable skills
- Duties/tasks
- Responsibilities
- Job functions
- Education
- Training

- Special knowledge
- Personal characteristics (personality traits)

These questions are very specific to a particular job/industry/field and are asked by the interviewer to know:

Can you actually do the job? Is your experience, education, aptitude, and interest sufficient so you will be productive in this job?

It's impossible to write an interview book that can address the job-specific questions that would be asked for every job. That is why you must be familiar enough with the kind of questions that may pertain to your specific field and job to be able to answer properly. These questions can be highly technical and are often asked in the form of behavioral-based questions.

Let's say you are applying for an administrative job. You may know some of the questions likely to be asked of an administrative assistant, but you need to make sure that what you think the duties and requirements of the job match what the interviewer thinks they are. What you might call an "Administrative Assistant" might be what they call a "Marketing Coordinator."

Before you head off to your interview, try to find out as much as you can about the job you are interviewing for. Check the company's website to make sure you have mined it for all the information you can about the job. If you don't see the job listing on the company's site, try other sites that contain job-content information. The great thing about the Internet in this regard is that job listings are often very detailed and descriptive and will allow you to match up your qualifications with the job-content required. This will allow you to know what kind of questions are likely to be asked about the specific job content for your position.

The Company

Gone are the days when you could show up for an interview without knowing something about the company you are interested in joining. You need to research a company before you arrive for an interview. Employers expect that candidates will know about their organization. Employers often see a candidate's efforts at researching their company as a crucial factor in determining the candidate's true interest and enthusiasm for them. It also makes it easier in the interview to have a common base of knowledge from which questions can be asked and to which information can be added, if both the interviewer and candidate are equally knowledgeable—no time has to be wasted explaining the company's goals and strategies if the candidate has done the homework. Employers are unimpressed by candidates who know nothing about the company, what the company does, or the position being offered. Don't be one of those (roughly estimated to be about one out of five) candidates.

At the very least, look at the company website. Most companies with over 10 employees have a website now. Check it out. Look for articles written in the press about the company. If you know anyone at the company, talk with them if you can before going to the interview. Ask them what the interviewer is likely to ask and how you might prepare.

Get clever and figure out ways to research companies. Google (or use another search engine) to find out what comes up when you type in the company's name.

The things you might try to learn about a company include:

- The company's main product or service
- Secondary products or services
- Leadership (try to find out who the CEO, CFO, COO, and board members are (if applicable)
- Major customers, clients, suppliers, vendors
- History
- Recent transactions
- New developments
- Size in employees and locations
- Hiring practices
- Competitors
- Annual and quarterly reports (for review)
- Mentions in the press

- Awards and recognition
- Earnings and current stock price (if publicly traded company)
- Mission statement

If you don't have access to your own computer, try your local library. They have computers you can use by the hour and volumes and volumes of information on companies.

Fourth: Know Your Strategy

You're all set. You know about yourself, the interview questions likely to be asked, the job content, and the company information. What's left?

You need to think about your strategy. How will you respond to certain questions?

Some responses are more effective than others for different questions. You will need to evaluate the best strategy to use, question by question. Balance your strategies so you don't seem like a "one-note" person. Don't use humor all the time, but don't be too serious either.

First things first!

Listen

Listen to the actual question that is being asked. Take one or two extra seconds to frame your answer before you begin speaking. Make sure you answer what they have asked. It's a big mistake people make. They are so eager/nervous about the question that they don't really address what's being asked. They don't listen to what the interviewer says because they are busy arranging the answer in their mind. Stop! Listen! Answer what is asked. Sometimes a question will ask you about a certain situation and they tack on "Why?" at the end. Most people only listen to the first part of the question and don't answer the "Why" part. Make sure you answer all parts of the question. If you aren't sure you've done it, ask the interviewer, "Did that answer your question?"

Provide the Most Relevant Information

When you are asked one of those questions like "Tell me about yourself" or "What makes you tick?" or "Why should I hire you?," think to yourself, "What is the most important thing I want this person to know about me?"

When asked these kinds of questions, think of the one or two most important facts about yourself that might make the interviewer want to know more about you and talk only about them. Pretend you only have this one question to answer and make it good. It would be nice to tell them you were born in New York City or that you played varsity ball, but will that make the difference in their mind to hire you? Probably not. So, don't waste your chance to jump on every question as if it were the only information you were going to be able to give to make your case about why you should get the job.

Communicate More Than One Thing With Your Answers

Use your answer to give the most information you can. Use some answers to not only talk about your job skills but to highlight interpersonal traits. By emphasizing specific examples of knowledge-based skills learned through education and experience, transferable skills, and personal traits, you can reveal a summary or snapshot of yourself in one answer.

Don't Volunteer Information That Isn't Needed

Giving too much personal information isn't always a good practice. Some things are illegal to ask (although they may get asked anyway). Information that is considered off limits can be kept to yourself. You don't have to tell the interviewer that you have five children. Be careful of giving information that is too revealing or not relevant to the question asked.

Be Concise

Don't ramble on and on. Your answers should run from 30 seconds to 2 minutes (for more technical questions). If the interviewer is interested in what you have said, they will ask more questions to get more information. Let them reveal (by their questions) what has caught their attention.

Rephrase the Question or Ask Another One

Sometimes it's perfectly appropriate to wait to answer a question, particularly when, by waiting, you will have more information and know exactly what kind of information they are seeking. You can say, "I'd be happy to answer that, but first may I ask you _____ ?" It's also appropriate to ask for clarification when a question has been worded vaguely. It's better to ask for clarification than to answer a question that has not really been asked.

Provide Concrete Examples

Anyone can claim anything. Adjectives are cheap! You can say you are good at something, but the best way to make your case is to use concrete examples of things you have done. Come prepared with your achievement statements so you can answer in specifics and not use generalities. Use strategic examples that show how you match the job's responsibilities and requirements. You can say, "Yes, I have done that before. Here's an example of how _____."

When you talk in generalities, the interviewer does not get a big picture of your abilities.

Use Humor

Some questions lend themselves to an answer that is lighter in tone, especially when a rational answer will not reassure your interviewer. By using humor, you can sometimes demonstrate to the interviewer that the question and the underlying issue it addresses are not a problem for you. You have to be careful how you use humor so that you don't offend or make the interviewer think you are not to be taken seriously. Humor is best used when you have built up rapport with your interviewer and you feel safe that you will not be misunderstood.

Be Honest

In some ways, the biggest mistake a candidate can make in an interview is to lie or somehow try to hide the truth. It's a mistake, if discovered, from which you will not recover. If you lie and are hired and your lie is found out, most companies have no choice but to fire you, even if they like you. If you try to dance around difficult questions you rarely dance fast enough or good enough to fool the interviewer. They know you are avoiding something, and they will keep probing until they get to the bottom of it. You are much better off admitting the truth and then moving swiftly onto another topic.

Control Your Body Language

It's easy to betray yourself with your nonverbal language. This is often an immediate and unconscious response. Some people, when faced with a question they find difficult or embarrassing, respond by coughing, blushing, looking down at the floor, playing with their hair, wringing their hands, etc. Interviewers are good at noticing these moves, even the less obvious ones like tensing your muscles. The only way you can combat this unconscious behavior is to practice ahead of time so these questions don't throw you off your game.

Stay Professional

Some interviewers are serious and you know immediately who you are dealing with. Others are more informal and relaxed and put you at ease right away, which can relax you right into giving away things you don't mean to. Keep your guard up and remain professional. Don't cross the line by thinking that you can tell your interviewer anything. You can't. Don't give away the baby with the bath water.

Use a Proactive Approach in Your Answers

Through your answers, show that problems are secondary in comparison to how you handled and resolved them. Whenever you can tell a success story, you are revealing a past behavior as an indicator of future success. The interviewer thinks, "If you did it for someone else, you could do it for me."

Smile, Relax, and Look Happy!

Nothing is more powerful than a smile. Use it often. Look directly into the interviewer's eyes and let them know you are relaxed. You can master this technique with practice, just as you can with your body language. If you act like there is no question you would rather answer than the one you are being asked, it will be hard for the interviewer to remain neutral about you.

Ask Great Questions

Finally, as you head into that last part of the interview, you'll be aware that tables will be turning and the interviewer will ask if you have any questions. This is it—your chance. Don't lose your opportunity to show your interest in the job. Ask good questions now! Little is more disappointing to an interviewer than a candidate who says, "No, I think you answered everything I wanted to know."

So, in your preparation, think about what you want to know about the job, company, interviewer, or process. Write a list of questions. Ask something that takes some courage—ask a well-thought-out question that shows you know the business/field or that you know their company to some extent. Let them see your enthusiasm and your interest in the job. Let them see that you are thoughtful. Let them see your curiosity. Let them see that you really listened to them during the interview.

How We Organized This Book

This book was written to help you prepare for your interview. Its comprehensive look at 202 of the most frequently asked interview questions should prepare you for whatever is asked in most job interviews.

We have arranged these questions into 18 clusters with an introduction about each cluster and the kind of information the interviewer is looking for by asking the particular questions within the cluster.

We have delved into six different areas on each question to give you the most help possible. We didn't stop by listing sample responses you might give to each question, but have broadened the information for each question to include the most thorough look possible.

We've included a mini-quiz for each question to help you focus on the issues being addressed. At the end of the discussion of the question, the best answer of the five is given. Many of these answers (some are unbelievable!) were taken from actual responses given by candidates.

We've also included a section about what the interviewer is really trying to find out. Each one offers three different questions that help you understand what kind of information the interviewer is trying to elicit from you. These can help you formulate your responses so you are sure to address the real issue(s) about why the question was asked.

Four other sections for each question are designed so you:

- **don't do** the wrong thing.
- **don't say** the wrong thing.
- **do** the right thing.
- **say** the right thing.

In addition to these questions, each presented graphically for ease of reading, we have included a chapter on behavioral interviewing and the kinds of questions you might be faced with should your interviewer use this style of interviewing. This technique uses your past experiences and behaviors as an indicator of your future success. Answers are almost always in the form of stories, which illustrate concrete examples of how you behaved in certain circumstances.

Feel free to start wherever you need the most help. There is no real beginning or ending point for the questions. You can flip through them for a quick glance and come back to those you want to go into more detail.

1

Icebreakers

I CEBREAKER QUESTIONS are used to start off the interview and are meant to be fairly easy for the candidate to answer. They are designed to put both the interviewer and candidate at ease and gently move into a more formal conversation. If done well, they can establish a basis of rapport between the interviewer and candidate. Since most candidates are generally a bit nervous at the beginning of an interview, these questions serve as a buffer zone to take the edge off and let the candidate find his/her footing. Icebreaker questions should only take a couple of minutes—they are usually not meant to take too much time away from the more important questions an interviewer must ask to judge a candidate's qualifications for the job.

These questions don't usually probe too deeply—they are more likely to be of a superficial nature, such as "Did you have any trouble finding us?" or "Would you like a cup of coffee?"

Icebreaker questions included here are:

- Did you have any trouble finding our office/factory? Was your train/plane/bus on time? How is your hotel?
- I see you are driving a (car make/model). How do you like it?

- I see you read (newspaper or magazine). Why this one?
- Could I have your business card?
- What do you think of our office/place?
- What do you think of our city?
- What do you think of the weather we're having?
- What is your opinion on _____ ?
- Would you like a drink?

What the Interviewer Wants to Know About You

Because icebreaker questions can be so varied, it's hard to know what an interviewer is really trying to discern by asking them. Although there usually isn't a hidden agenda from an interviewer with these kinds of questions, it would be foolish to let your guard down so much that you think your responses won't be judged. They will, and some interviewers use these seemingly simple questions to see if candidates will tip their hat and reveal something of their true personality.

How to Answer

When answering, keep a positive tone—don't start off by complaining about anything (traffic, directions, weather, etc.). Keep your answers short. Answer only what has been asked. This isn't the time to take three or four minutes to launch into a response that deals with far more than the question asked or intended. If you do this because you are nervous, you will most likely be penalized in the mind of the interviewer.

Remember, if asked a question like "Tell me about yourself" (which is often used to get the ball rolling), keep your answer related to the job you are interviewing and don't use all your best points on it, as it's just the opening question and the interviewer probably won't be taking in all you say just yet. There will be sufficient time in the interview to really make your case!

Did you have any trouble finding our office/factory? Was your train/plane/bus on time? How is your hotel?

✓ Choose the Best Answer

- ❑ I had a little trouble finding you, but I finally made it.
- ❑ I drove around in circles for a while before finding a parking place.
- ❑ I'm a bit tired. The hotel was loud, and this morning I didn't see any signs to tell me where I was. Your office seemed hard to find.
- ❑ Yes, it's not well marked so I had to call for better directions.
- ❑ Everything went well. Your directions were very clear. Thank you.

? What They Really Want to Know

- ▪ Are you well organized? Do you plan ahead?
- ▪ Is our company well placed?
- ▪ Do you have a good sense of direction or know how to figure things out?

! Watch Out!

Don't:

- ▪ Arrive late.
- ▪ Give a negative answer—show that you had difficulty finding the place.
- ▪ Complain about the directions you were given/used.
- ▪ Try to justify being late (if this is the case) by saying you didn't know where the office/factory was located.

Don't Say:

- ▪ I had trouble finding you, even with a GPS.
- ▪ I missed the train/bus.
- ▪ I ran into problems following the directions I had to get here.
- ▪ I'm exhausted from looking for the office/factory! I guess I should have come here before the interview to figure it out.

- Awful, thank you!
- Yes, I had problems finding you. It was more complicated than I thought it would be.

Try This!

Do:

- Be sure you have done sufficient homework (including a trial run if need be) to familiarize yourself with the location of the office/factory.
- Allow plenty of time for contingencies (late bus, wrong turn, etc.)
- Stick to the point and don't give too many details if you had trouble.
- Demonstrate that you allow for the unexpected.
- Remain positive.

Say:

- I had checked where your office was before leaving, so I had plenty of time to find it.
- This is an area I am familiar with, having been here many times in the past.
- Thanks, I got here fine.
- No, since the directions were so clear.
- Yes, the hotel was quiet so I had a good night's sleep.
- Fine. Thanks for asking.

BEST ANSWER

Everything went well. Your directions were very clear. Thank you.

I see you are driving a (car make/model). How do you like it?

✓ Choose the Best Answer

- ❑ It gets me where I'm going.
- ❑ I like it, but I wouldn't buy the same one again. My next new car is going to have more special features. I made a bad choice this time.
- ❑ I believe one's car defines one's personality.
- ❑ At 65 mph on highways, the mileage per gallon is excellent. It was a good buy for me.
- ❑ You don't like these hybrids? You prefer those gas-guzzlers?

? What They Really Want to Know

- How do you judge things? Do you tend to make positive or negative comments?
- What are your real values?
- Are you good at making your case?

! Watch Out!

Don't:

- Criticize another make of car. It may be the one the interviewer drives!
- Gloat over your car.
- Elaborate on its performance.
- Act overly attached or emotional about a car.
- Talk about your car in monetary terms.
- Point out the car's negative points only.
- Brag about the way you drive.

Don't Say:

- A modest car means a modest person!
- Well, it's better than an old used car!
- I didn't choose it. My spouse did.

- It cost me $_____. Taxes and insurance come to $_____. A full tank costs me $_____. This car is just one big money pit.
- Do you think I'd buy a car I didn't like?
- I'm planning on getting rid of it as soon as I get a job and buy one that I like more.
- I couldn't afford anything better.

Try This!

Do:

- Describe your criteria for deciding to buy this car.
- Explain that you looked at several different models and that you are satisfied with your choice.
- Stress the advantages of this kind of car.
- Show that your purchase was based on serious consideration and wasn't an impulsive decision.
- If you have a car that particularly stands out, park it out of sight if possible.

Say:

- It's an economical car and I like it.
- It's practical and useful and I can count on it to run well.
- I studied all the hybrids made and chose this one because it was made by (name company) and I trust them.
- I have always wanted a (car make/model) and last year was able to get it. I feel it was worth the money.

BEST ANSWER

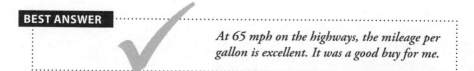

At 65 mph on the highways, the mileage per gallon is excellent. It was a good buy for me.

I see you read (newspaper or magazine). Why this one?

✓ Choose the Best Answer

- ❑ There's a very interesting article by the union on employees' sick leave rights.
- ❑ I buy this paper regularly. It has informative articles on subjects that interest me. Just now I was reading a comparative study on _____.
- ❑ I'm reading an article on the world's largest fortunes. I am amazed that those people are so selfish. What about all the poor starving people in the world?
- ❑ I bought it because I like the photographs.
- ❑ I wanted to see if there were any job ads. But, as usual, there's nothing!

? What They Really Want to Know

- ▪ Do we have similar areas of interests?
- ▪ How good are you at analyzing and summarizing?
- ▪ What things interest you?

! Watch Out!

Don't:

- ▪ Admit that you don't read much.
- ▪ Criticize what you are reading.
- ▪ Shrug your shoulders as if to say, "It's okay."
- ▪ Indicate that what you are reading is not a deliberate choice.
- ▪ Put it away or try to hide it, feeling embarrassed.
- ▪ Give the interviewer a surprised look that he/she noticed what you were reading.
- ▪ Act fanatical about what you are reading.
- ▪ Show any vulnerability or defensiveness and try to justify your choice of reading material.

Don't Say:

- ▪ I just read this to pass the time.
- ▪ It's just to keep me busy, because interviews stress me out.

- As a matter of fact, I've only read this paper once before.
- Believe me, there's nothing of interest in it.
- I was told I should mention my hobbies on my resume, so I put "reading."
- I like shock reporting and I love the tabloids.
- I spend my time reading all kinds of papers. I'm a real news junkie.

Try This!

Do:

- Focus on the paper's/magazine's qualities.
- Lay it down purposefully on the table.
- Mention your interest in an article as a subject you are knowledgeable about.
- Show that you consider it important to keep up with news.
- Link your reading material to your potential position.
- Link one of the interview questions to something you read in your paper/magazine.

Say:

- This is one of three papers I read regularly.
- In this magazine, the _____ section is always worth reading.
- In this magazine, I often find interesting information relative to my work. For example, _____ .
- I always take advantage of waiting periods to catch up on the news.
- I was looking to see if I could find your ad.
- I just found an interesting article on _____ .
- Yes, and I appreciated the article on _____ .

BEST ANSWER

I buy this paper regularly. It has informative articles on subjects that interest me. Just now I was reading a comparative study on_____.

✓ Choose the Best Answer

- ❏ I'm afraid I don't have any with me, as I just ran out of thick paper to print out my cards.
- ❏ I am out of work, so it doesn't make sense to carry a card right now.
- ❏ Of course. May I ask for yours also?
- ❏ You've got everything you need to know about me on my resume. I can't see that you need one.
- ❏ Here you are, although it is out of date. I'm no longer at this company, but the cell phone number on the card is correct.

? What They Really Want to Know

- ▪ Do you have a good sense of business etiquette?
- ▪ How do you react to an unexpected question?
- ▪ Are you careful about your image?

! Watch Out!

Don't:

- ▪ Forget to take your cards with you.
- ▪ Feel you have to justify whatever functional title you use on your card.
- ▪ Offer a card from your previous job.
- ▪ Offer a card with obsolete or out of date information.

Don't Say:

- ▪ Oh, I forgot to bring some, but everything's on my resume.
- ▪ I'm embarrassed to admit that I didn't think to bring one.
- ▪ I just gave away my last one.
- ▪ Sorry, but I don't use business cards. Will a post-it do?
- ▪ Could I please borrow your pen?

Try This!

Do:

- Be sure to come prepared with up-to-date cards.
- Offer only professional looking cards.
- Offer two cards: one for the recruiter/interviewer, another that can be circulated.

Say:

- I'm afraid I don't have a card on me at the moment, but here's where you can reach me. I would be delighted to answer your questions or meet again with you.
- I will give it to you now and confirm by email and/or letter.
- Here's my card. Please do contact me for any additional information you might need.
- Here's my card. By the way, where do we go from here? What is the next step in the recruitment process?
- Of course. Here it is.

BEST ANSWER

Of course. May I ask for yours also?

What do you think of our office/place?

✓ Choose the Best Answer

- ❏ It's not exactly next door! I live on the other side of town, and there is construction work going on in the tunnel, which of course slows up the traffic. I'm certainly glad to be here, though.
- ❏ I was held up by security. It seems to me they are a bit overly cautious.
- ❏ Does everybody wear a uniform here?
- ❏ At first glance, it's a bit overwhelming. The premises seem extremely complex to me. But I'm sure when I get to know your company, I'll be fine.
- ❏ It's a vast complex, but seems particularly well structured and friendly. I would enjoy working here.

? What They Really Want to Know

- Would you like working with us? Do you feel at ease?
- What kind of working conditions do you want in your job?
- Are you really interested in our firm? Are you attracted by it?

! Watch Out!

Don't:
- State that you find the firm a little too far away.
- Admit that the premises seem pretty complicated.
- Make a negative comment, even about a minor detail.
- Give exaggerated compliments.
- Indicate that their literature/material is a little obsolete.

Don't Say:
- I hope I'll be able to feel at ease here. We'll see.
- I'd rather have my own office [if you would be working in an open space].
- Is the cafeteria on this floor?
- Are the premises always this crowded?

Do:

- Affirm that the office is attractive and friendly.
- Assure them that the atmosphere corresponds to the company's style.
- Show enthusiasm for the office space and materials.
- Make it clear that you already have read quite a bit of information about the company. Indicate that you are going to be able to fit in easily.
- Point out a precise and positive detail that you have noticed.
- Use the opportunity to ask if you might have a guided tour of the premises.

Say:

- This is just the kind of place I like because _____ .
- It's well organized.
- I like the decor and style of the offices.
- I feel comfortable here.
- It's very nice.

BEST ANSWER

It's a vast complex, but seems particularly well structured and friendly. I would enjoy working here.

What do you think of our city?

✓ Choose the Best Answer

- ❑ To be perfectly honest, I don't really know it too well. I have never come here before.
- ❑ It has its good points and its bad points, like every city.
- ❑ I'm afraid if I tell you, you might not hire me!
- ❑ I prefer big cities (if it's a little one)/I prefer small cities (if it's a big one).
- ❑ It's a great/magnificent city. It has so many things going for it and you can find anything you want. I (would) enjoy living here.

? What They Really Want to Know

- ▪ Are you diplomatic?
- ▪ Are you ready to move or do you like staying in one particular place?
- ▪ Do you like it here? Do you look for the positive?

! Watch Out!

Don't:

- ▪ Show total indifference to this city.
- ▪ Criticize the city, the stress, the lack of nightlife, etc.
- ▪ Infer that you would rather live/work in another city.
- ▪ Infer that you are only looking for work here because you had no other choice.
- ▪ Exaggerate your enthusiasm for the city.
- ▪ Sound too attached to the city.

Don't Say:

- ▪ It suits me fine, as it has an international airport/good commuter train connections.
- ▪ Well, I suppose there is the threat of earthquakes/heat spells/flooding.
- ▪ I don't know this city.

- I would never leave this city for anything!
- I don't like it much.
- I long to go abroad.
- I find the people here are a little unfriendly/superficial/unsophisticated, but the city's nice.

Try This!

Do:

- Associate the town with a professional achievement.
- Try to establish a special contact with the interviewer in order to find out about this new city.
- Give a reasonable show of appreciation for the city.
- Show that you are aware of at least some of the city's qualities/benefits.
- Show that you are sensitive to both its qualities and its drawbacks.

Say:

- I was impressed right away by _____.
- I like this city. I've got roots here.
- I appreciate the warm welcome I've received from people.
- I like it a lot and discover something new every week.
- I feel good here. It's got everything I need.
- I've already looked into the commuter train connections/bike routes/bus or trolley schedules.

BEST ANSWER

It's a great/magnificent city. It has so many things going for it and you can find anything you want. I (would) enjoy living here.

What do think of the weather we're having?

✓ Choose the Best Answer

- ❏ What nasty weather! It makes me depressed.
- ❏ Weather is a relative thing: above the clouds, the sun always shines!
- ❏ I love it when it's nice. I spend all my time skiing/surfing. That's the advantage of being out of work. You can't take advantage of the nice days when you work.
- ❏ The one nice day this week and here I am stuck inside for an interview! I'd rather be outside.
- ❏ You know, I work so much that I don't really notice the weather very much.

? What They Really Want to Know

- ▪ Are you going to elaborate on this subject (which really doesn't interest us) or do you want to talk about the job?
- ▪ How do you answer unexpected questions?
- ▪ Does the weather influence the way you live (where you want to live)?

! Watch Out!

Don't:

- ▪ Attach much importance to this question or spend time on the answer.
- ▪ Be caught off guard by this seemingly non-professional question.
- ▪ Give an answer that is too personal, too detailed, or too long.
- ▪ Make a face, suggesting you find the question trivial.
- ▪ Shrug your shoulders, as if to say, "Who cares!"
- ▪ Underline that it is not in your power to change it anyway.
- ▪ Show that you are indifferent to your surroundings.
- ▪ Ignore the question.
- ▪ React too strongly.

Don't Say:

- ▪ Well, it's always either too hot or too cold here.
- ▪ Well, today I'm in a good mood, so it's a nice day.

- You just have to make do, no matter what the weather.
- I was almost late because of the weather.
- I don't like it when it's too hot/too cold.
- You see, I am like a lizard; I love to soak up the sun, whereas _____.
- I'd rather be somewhere else (on vacation) to enjoy it.
- When you're working, the weather doesn't really matter much.
- When you're out of work, the weather is not really a priority.

Try This!

Do:

- Use the occasion to break the ice with the recruiter/interviewer and establish contact.
- Show that weather is not an element that has much influence on you.
- Answer with a short response.
- Remain positive, regardless of the actual weather.
- See if there's a link between the question and the job's activity. If so, target your reply (landscaping company, ski resort, etc.).
- Refer to a recent news item concerning the weather (a heat/cold spell/flooding)

Say:

- I am still awed by the huge differences in temperature on our globe—up to 150°F.
- I particularly appreciate four distinct seasons.
- I think every kind of weather has its benefits and drawbacks.
- I feel fine in all kinds of weather. It's just a question of adapting.
- So far this year the weather has allowed me to practice my two favorite sports quite frequently.
- Since we can't change the weather, we might as well appreciate the rain when it falls and the sun when it shines.
- Nature needs a change of weather in order to flourish, and so do we.

BEST ANSWER

Weather is a relative thing: above the clouds, the sun always shines!

N° 8

What is your opinion on _____?

✓ Choose the Best Answer

- ❑ Wow, that's a tricky question! Do you want me to tell you that?
- ❑ What a scandal! It's the kind of thing that makes me want to take justice in my own hands.
- ❑ I don't know. That's the kind of subject that doesn't interest me in the slightest. I do think, however, _____. But my opinion won't change anything anyway.
- ❑ I'd rather keep quiet on the subject. I don't always make friends by spouting off my point of view.
- ❑ The information I have on the subject would lead me to believe that _____. But then I may not have all the facts.

? What They Really Want to Know

- How do you express your opinion? Are you cautious?
- Who are you? What do you think?
- Do you keep up with what's going on in the world?

! Watch Out!

Don't:

- Be categorical and act like you know everything there is to know about the subject.
- Make a remark that is totally negative.
- Talk too much.
- Get carried away or too impassioned and spend too much time on the answer.

Don't Say:

- I feel very passionate about this subject, and anyone who thinks differently doesn't understand all the facts.
- I know nothing about the subject.
- The subject doesn't concern me so I have no opinion.

- I'd rather not state my opinion on the subject.
- Why are you asking my opinion on this?

Try This!

Do:

- Try to reply succinctly and get to the next question.
- Be concise and list a fact you are sure of.
- Remain neutral and don't act too emotional/excited.

Say:

- It's such a controversial subject, I find it hard to have a fixed position.
- It's not easy to be objective on such an emotional topic.
- I try to consider both sides of the issue.
- I am aware of the arguments on both sides, but haven't made up my mind yet.
- The "Smith" institute carried out a study on that case which said _____ .

BEST ANSWER

The information I have on the subject would lead me to believe that_____. But then I may not have all the facts.

Would you like a drink?

- ❑ If you're going to have one. I just had coffee but would be happy to join you. Thank you.
- ❑ No thanks. I never drink on the job. In fact, I don't drink at all. It's not good for you.
- ❑ No thanks. It makes me sweat!
- ❑ Sure. That way I'll be able to see if your products match up to your advertisements!
- ❑ I'd love one. With ice and a slice of lemon if possible. That's the way I like it.

? *What They Really Want to Know*

- How are your social skills? Are you convivial?
- Are you thirsty? (It can be as simple as that. Be sensitive to the context.)
- Are you relaxed? At ease?

! *Watch Out!*

Don't:
- Ask for some exotic drink.
- Turn the offer into a joke.
- Forget to add a "thank you," whatever your reply is.
- Overdo a refusal.
- Shake when you take the glass.
- Be indecisive or embarrassed, or say you don't know.

Don't Say:
- I'd rather not right now. I'll have one when the interview is over.
- What have you got in the way of booze?
- I'm dying of thirst!

- I'm addicted to coffee (or any other drink).
- Coffee is a stimulant that clogs up your blood vessels.
- Would you like one yourself?
- Only if you've got some.

Try This!

Do:

- Accept if the interviewer will join you.
- If you accept a drink, make sure to consume it.
- Ask for a familiar drink.
- Show that you appreciate the gesture.
- Offer your thanks.
- Stir your drink discreetly.
- Simply answer the question. There's no point in dwelling on details.

Say:

- Yes, with pleasure!
- Are you having something?
- No, thank you.
- I'd love one. Black coffee would be fine.
- Yes, if you'll join me!

BEST ANSWER

If you're going to have one. I just had coffee but would be happy to join you. Thank you.

2

Self-Evaluation

Q UESTIONS DEALING WITH SELF EVALUATION (self knowledge or self awareness) are asked so an interviewer can get a measure of how well you know yourself and if what you say about yourself is realistic and honest. To be self-aware means you have knowledge of your own individuality. It means knowing what you are good at as well as what you are not so good at. It means having a combination of both humility and confidence (a seeming paradox). No one can do everything well; and no one does nothing well. When faced with questions about how well you know yourself, show that your strong points are the ones needed for the job and that your weaker points are ones you can work to improve or ones that won't impact you profoundly on this particular job.

So, is it enough to say you know something about yourself? Probably not. You will need to also demonstrate how that particular trait or skill or ability has been acted out in your work life. Do you remain consistent in your answers? If you say you are a person who values the opinions of others and then your answers about your interaction with coworkers suggests you forge ahead with little thought for what others may think, the interviewer is going to wonder about you. If you say you are goal oriented and can't give a few examples of goals you have set and reached, they will not believe you are telling the truth. If you are asked what others would say about you and your own self-perception is radically different from theirs, you again cast doubt about how well you do a self-appraisal.

Self-awareness comes with maturity. The longer you work, the more you learn from your experiences and from others how to improve yourself to do your best. Sometimes a person isn't self aware because they haven't thought seriously about their weaknesses and how to improve. Sometimes people know their limitations and don't think they need to do anything about them (the "you either take me as I am or don't take me at all" attitude). There is no penalty for not being perfect (none of us are) but there is a penalty for not looking at yourself realistically and trying to find the situation/job that allows you to do your best.

Self-evaluation questions included here are:

- How long will it take you to contribute to the success of our company?
- How long will it take you to become fully functional?
- Do you think you can realistically handle this job with your handicap/disability?
- How do you judge yourself? What are your best qualities and your biggest limitations?
- How is this job different from the last one you had?
- Is this your dream job? What is it about this job that attracts you? About this kind of work? About our company?
- Don't you think you are a little too old (too young) for this position?
- What do you think of your career path up to now?
- What did you contribute to the top management team?
- What personal characteristics make you think you will be successful at this job?
- How do you judge when you've done a good job?

What the Interviewer Wants to Know About You

By asking questions about self-evaluation, the interviewer is trying to find out:

- Do you have the profile for the job?
- Are you able to evaluate yourself accurately? Can you tell someone else about yourself honestly?
- Do you know yourself? How do you see yourself?
- Are you clear about the duties of this position?
- Do you have concrete evidence to prove that you have successfully performed your duties in the past?
- Would you be on top of the job right away, or will they need to provide training?
- Do you learn quickly? How easily do you adapt?
- Will you need extra training?
- What will you contribute?
- Are you ambitious?
- Do you think in terms of job or results?
- Are you ready to take initiative?
- Do you go the extra mile?
- How do you feel about authority?
- What were your responsibilities?
- Are you really going to be efficient?
- How do other people's judgments affect you? Do you get defensive?
- How do you react when faced with potential criticism and reservations?
- Will you be able to face the problems you will undoubtedly run into in a new job?
- Are you capable of fulfilling the requirements of this position with your disability?

How to Answer

The most important thing about answering questions about your self-awareness is to back up what you say about yourself with concrete examples from your past. Show that you know your strengths and weaknesses, but more importantly show that you know how to look at the big picture of your past and future and keep things in perspective. Rather than use the word "weakness" (which implies there is something "wrong" with you), think of it as "what can I do better" (which implies that you are "working on self improvement"). Framed this way, it won't seem such a show-stopping question to many! We all (yes, every one of us) have areas for personal growth! There's nothing wrong with that, except believing that you are a person who doesn't! Now, that's a weakness!

If asked how long before you can make a meaningful contribution to the company be realistic in your answer. Show that it will take you some time to know the organization well enough to make a major contribution. An honest self-evaluation will tell you that, even if you're a quick study, you will need some time to get the lay of the land. Few interviewers would expect you to say, "From the first day!" If you're asked it this is your dream job, resist the temptation to give a glib answer—if you say that it is before knowing everything about the job it strains your credibility. If you say another job, then you may seem like someone who won't be happy with this job. So, rather than talk of a specific job title (unless you are 100% sure of what that job is) talk about the characteristics of such a "dream" job (one where I can use my favorite skill of _____, one where I can contribute in several important ways, one where I can be part of a team working on projects).

When you talk about your strengths and the contributions you have made in past jobs, talk about them as they relate to the job in question. Don't dwell on a strength if it isn't relative to what you'll be doing next. Talk about what makes you successful—a positive attitude, ability to work under pressure, problem-solving skills, etc.

If you have a limitation of some kind that might cause an interviewer to think you can't do the job, be sure you address it fast and succinctly. It is your job to tell the interviewer how this isn't a problem. Show them that your particular limitation doesn't affect how you can do the job. Talk about solutions, not problems.

How long will it take you to contribute to the success of our company?

✓ Choose the Best Answer

- ❏ Three to five years, if things are easy; over five years if you have major problems.
- ❏ That depends on you and what kind of training you provide to me.
- ❏ Why? I don't see what you're getting at.
- ❏ Not very long, I would think. Between _____ and _____ weeks/months.
- ❏ A certain amount of time. I would think not too long.

? What They Really Want to Know

- Are you ambitious?
- Do you think in terms of job or results?
- Would you be on top of the job right away, or will they need to provide training?

! Watch Out!

Don't:

- Say you need a lot of time to adapt.
- Answer too quickly without knowing enough about the job to make your answer reasonable.
- Make promises you won't be able to keep by suggesting you won't need any time at all to master the job duties.

Don't Say:

- That's a question I need to think about before I can answer you. I guess it depends on how different this job is going to be from my last job.
- I couldn't say, just like that.
- I think I'll need quite some time.
- I am someone who is fast. No time at all.

Do:

- Clarify or probe with another question to make sure you understand clearly what the job entails.
- Use a flexible and reasonable approach in making it clear that you are the person they are seeking to hire.
- Give examples of when you adapted quickly in the past.
- Point out the paragraphs on your list of short-term achievements that highlight how you are a quick study.
- Let your ambition show.

Say:

- Between three and six months to be fully operational and master the job duties.
- What projects are you currently actively involved in?
- Right away, after a short adaptation period. In my last job, I was able to master my duties in only a few weeks/months.
- Very fast if you hire me, and you give me responsibility. I produce results. For example, _____

BEST ANSWER

Not very long, I would think. Between____ and____weeks/months.

How long will it take you to become fully functional?

✓ Choose the Best Answer

- ❑ As soon as it suits you.
- ❑ I'll be fully functional right away. Don't worry.
- ❑ I can be quick or take my time. You tell me what you want.
- ❑ It may take a while. It depends on lots of things, which makes it hard for me to give you a definite answer.
- ❑ As long as it takes for me to get my bearings and be sure I am efficient.

? What They Really Want to Know

- ■ Do you learn quickly? How easily do you adapt?
- ■ Will you need extra training?
- ■ Are you ready to take initiative?

! Watch Out!

Don't:

- ■ Look worried or anxious.
- ■ Mention a precise length of time.
- ■ Request special training.

Don't Say:

- ■ A very short time.
- ■ I need time to get used to a new environment.
- ■ I don't know.
- ■ Faster than you would think.
- ■ Right away.

Do:  →

- Request all available documentation on the position and job tasks.
- Talk about setting up regular evaluation meetings to assess performance when hired.
- Suggest prolonging the trial period by two to four weeks.

Say: 🙶

- I will throw myself fully into this job so I'll be fully functional within your time frame.
- Give me a bit of time to evaluate the situation now that I have more information, and then I'll be glad to answer your question.
- I am a quick learner. In the past it has not taken me long to fully grasp my job and do it well.

BEST ANSWER ✓

As long as it takes for me to get my bearings and be sure I am efficient.

Do you think you can realistically handle this job with your disability?

✓ Choose the Best Answer

- ❑ Is my disability a problem for you?
- ❑ What tasks/operations do you think might cause a problem for me?
- ❑ This question is against the law, but I can assure you that it won't be a problem.
- ❑ I think my disability will help your company's image so that you are perceived to be open and forward thinking.
- ❑ Those of us with disabilities still have the right to work, you know! Your question surprises me, as I had such a good impression of your company.

? What They Really Want to Know

- ■ How do other people's judgments affect you? Do you get defensive?
- ■ Are you capable of fulfilling the requirements of this position with your disability?
- ■ How do you react when faced with potential criticism and reservations about your ability to do the job?

! Watch Out!

Don't:
- ■ Doubt your own competence.
- ■ Talk for too long on the subject of your limitations (if any).
- ■ Dwell on the negative (limiting) aspects of your disability.
- ■ Put yourself in a position of inferiority.
- ■ Justify yourself by making excuses for what you can't do.

Don't Say:
- ■ That's why I have had to change jobs so often.
- ■ I consider this private and I have suffered enough because of it.
- ■ Would that have an effect on my salary?

- I've already had legal problems with employers because of this issue.
- I do not have a disability.
- I refuse to answer this indiscreet (illegal) question.
- I'll need permanent help with ____ .
- I'm not sure if I'll be able to manage this job—what do you think?

Try This!

Do:

- Mention situations in your experience that were positive.
- Illustrate accomplishments you have achieved in spite of your disability.
- Talk about your assets for the position that aren't related to your disability.
- Reply spontaneously and quickly change the subject by asking a question about a job requirement.

Say: 〞

- With my experience in this type of job, I can manage with my disability.
- In a similar situation I was able to ____ .
- I have always been good at managing difficult situations. As an example ____ .
- I can bring my experience and knowledge in the area of ____ .
- I've been living with this disability for a long time and I know how to face several difficulties.
- With minor accommodations, my disability will not be noticeable.

BEST ANSWER ✓

What tasks/operations do you think might cause a problem for me?

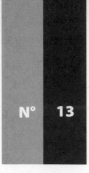

How do you judge yourself? What are your best strengths and your biggest limitations?

✓ Choose the Best Answer

- ❏ I have a hard time evaluating myself. But you can see my work certificates for yourself. They speak for me.
- ❏ I tend to say what I think, which in fact made me bungle my last two negotiations.
- ❏ I manage stress and priorities quite well, and I appreciate efficiency. I have the shortcomings that are inherent in those attributes.
- ❏ I don't have any major shortcomings. As for my qualities, I think I have the ones needed for the job in question.
- ❏ We're the way we are; everyone has shortcomings and positive qualities.

? What They Really Want to Know

- ■ Do you have the profile for the job?
- ■ Are you able to evaluate yourself accurately? Can you tell someone else about yourself honestly?
- ■ Do you know yourself? How do you see yourself?

! Watch Out!

Don't:
- ■ Mention your shortcomings before your strengths.
- ■ Show that you are unable to answer the question because you never thought you would be asked this!
- ■ Drown the interviewer in your qualities or in your shortcomings.
- ■ Let yourself get unnerved by the question.
- ■ Avoid focusing on your weaknesses.
- ■ Answer only part of the questions (you must deal with both strengths and weaknesses).

Don't Say:

- That's very personal. I don't think I can answer it.
- I don't have any faults. I have only good qualities.
- I don't understand what you're getting at.
- I don't know what you expect me to say.
- I'm great at almost everything I undertake. I don't really think I have problems.
- I don't know how to sell myself. Ask my former employers.

Try This!

Do:

- Point out your competencies, talents, or personality traits, and support them with solid facts or proof.
- Start out talking about your good qualities, then address a weakness, but end up with a positive point about yourself.
- Ask what competencies are needed for the job and demonstrate, using concrete examples, that you have them.
- Support each of your personality traits with examples, proof, or accomplishments.
- Identify the most useful qualities and the least serious shortcomings for the job.
- Show how the shortcoming that you chose to mention could be seen positively, depending on the context.

Say:

- I have three qualities: _____, _____, and _____.
- I have a shortcoming, but it doesn't affect my professional life.
- Let me tell you about one of my achievements that I think illustrates my strengths quite well.
- These three strengths, _____, _____, and _____, will be particularly useful in light of the requirements of the position.
- One of my weaknesses used to be _____, but I managed to deal with it by _____ .
- These are the qualities that my former supervisors have recognized: _____ .

BEST ANSWER

I manage stress and priorities quite well, and I appreciate efficiency. I have the shortcomings that are inherent in those attributes.

How is this job different from the last one you had?

✓ Choose the Best Answer

- ❏ In two ways: I would have an opportunity here to involve myself more deeply, and you seem to have more ambitious goals than my last company.
- ❏ That's a difficult question! As far as I'm concerned, a job is a job.
- ❏ I have no idea!
- ❏ Your company is closer to my home.
- ❏ I've been told you pay better.

? What They Really Want to Know

- ■ Details about your last job.
- ■ What do you expect to find with us that you did not find in your last job?
- ■ Will you be able to face the problems you will undoubtedly run into in a new job?

! Watch Out!

Don't:
- ■ Show a total lack of knowledge about this new job/company.
- ■ Suggest that this new job is nothing special to you.
- ■ Show that you feel anxiety about change.

Don't Say:
- ■ This will be so different from what I learned in my old job.
- ■ That depends on your proposal.
- ■ Do you pay an end-of-year bonus?
- ■ If the work demand is too much, I'm afraid I might not be happy with you.
- ■ The work you do here is completely different from what I've been doing.
- ■ If the atmosphere isn't good, I'll leave.
- ■ You're nice.
- ■ You pay better.

Do:

- Underline your wish to evolve in this new job/field.
- Show how the position matches your skills, knowledge, and experience.
- Remind the interviewer of your desire for the position.

Say:

- With you, I believe I will have found a great team that has excellent contact with its clients.
- A detailed list of duties/responsibilities for this job would make it easier for me to answer you.
- The similarities are numerous. For example, _____ .

BEST ANSWER

In two ways: I would have an opportunity here to involve myself more deeply, and you seem to have more ambitious goals than my last company.

Is this your dream job? What is it about this job that attracts you? About this kind of work? About our company?

✓ Choose the Best Answer

- ❏ It's a well-paid job and it's close to my home.
- ❏ I am extremely attracted to your company for the opportunity to put to use all my skills and experience. For example, I would be able to use my _____ .
- ❏ It would look good to list your company on my resume.
- ❏ Everything!
- ❏ A nice atmosphere and excellent working conditions.

? What They Really Want to Know

- ■ Do you really have enthusiasm for the job, or are you willing to take a job that doesn't match your dreams?
- ■ What do you know about us and how do you see yourself integrating here?
- ■ What will you contribute?

! Watch Out!

Don't:
- ■ Be negative or hesitant.
- ■ Over-flatter the company or the recruiter.
- ■ Try to prove that you are the "best match" without supplying proof of what you say.

Don't Say:
- ■ I am so familiar with this job and field of work. I've done it my whole career.
- ■ Yes, just check my resume.
- ■ Your company has a good reputation and your benefits are great.

Do:

- Illustrate your knowledge of the company and the work involved in the job.
- Back up your determination with concrete evidence of your suitability for the job.
- Show your enthusiasm by asking questions that prove your interest and involvement.

Say:

- The job you are offering is right in line with the direction of my chosen career path.
- Yes, this is exactly what I want to do! I like what I do and I do it well.
- Your company is exactly the kind of company I am eager to work for, and I know my skills, abilities, and enthusiasm will be used here.

BEST ANSWER

I am extremely attracted to your company for the opportunity to put to use all my skills and experience. For example, I would be able to use my _____ .

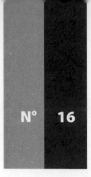

Don't you think you are a little too old (too young) for this position?

✓ Choose the Best Answer

- ❑ That may be true. But what do you expect? Everybody needs a job! That's what I keep hearing on the radio and television.
- ❑ Do you think a younger person could possibly have enough experience?
- ❑ How old do you think I am?
- ❑ Your question is a little unfair.
- ❑ In your opinion, what is the main drawback to hiring a person over 50 (or under 25)?

? What They Really Want to Know

- ▪ Are you going to work well within our hierarchy (regardless of your age)?
- ▪ Do you have self-confidence?
- ▪ **For Younger:** Will your lack of time in the workforce keep you from excelling at this job?
- ▪ **For Older:** Are you going to have problems with your supervisor if he/she is younger than yourself?

! Watch Out!

Don't:

- ▪ Counter-attack or be on the defensive about your age.
- ▪ Question the interviewer's age.
- ▪ Take center stage, in front of younger/older colleagues.
- ▪ Get upset about the question being asked.

Don't Say:

- ▪ It's always the same old thing. You're either too old or too young.
- ▪ No. Why, do you?
- ▪ Maybe, but I have to earn a living.

Try This!

Do: →

- Discuss your experience of having worked with experienced/young/older people in the past.
- Keep your cool.
- Talk about your own experience in terms of measurable achievements.
- Reassure the recruiter/interviewer by citing specific examples of how you fit in with others of different ages.

Say: 🙾

- Value does not depend on the number of years one has worked.
- Yes, I am young. However, let me tell you about a couple of achievements that show that I have the know-how you want.
- Can you tell me just what it is that makes you think I am too old/young?
- An older person can have a stabilizing effect on a young team.
- Here are a couple of examples of a team whose members' average age was 27.

BEST ANSWER

In your opinion, what is the main drawback to hiring a person over 50 (or under 25)?

What do you think of your career path up to now?

✓ Choose the Best Answer

- ❑ Partly good. Mostly I would say not that great.
- ❑ Not too bad.
- ❑ To be perfectly honest, I haven't really made the kind of progress I'd hoped for. I've always done the same thing.
- ❑ I feel proud of myself, because I've moved ahead faster than I expected and my career path is on track to meet my goals.
- ❑ Your question is a little embarrassing. I think I have made some progress, but it's always difficult to judge oneself.

? What They Really Want to Know

- ▪ Are you ambitious? Do you plan ahead or just let things happen to you?
- ▪ How do you see the continuation of your career?
- ▪ What motivates you to work for us?

! Watch Out!

Don't:

- ▪ Show self-satisfaction or a lack of ambition.
- ▪ List in minute detail all the positions you have held.
- ▪ Demonstrate colossal ambition that causes others to feel you will stop at nothing to get what you want.
- ▪ Reveal any frustration, regrets, or bitterness about your past.

Don't Say:

- ▪ Because of a certain colleague, I was just never able to get ahead.
- ▪ I feel stuck, like I haven't evolved at all.
- ▪ I like doing my work without thinking too much about it.
- ▪ I don't really have much personal ambition. I am happy where I am.
- ▪ I want to be promoted very soon.

Try This!

Do:

- Give examples of achievements to demonstrate your abilities.
- Remain objective.
- Demonstrate the proper amount of ambition, which will depend on the position and your experience.

Say:

- I like tackling problems and offering creative solutions when it's possible.
- I thrive on developing my skills and enhancing my knowledge.
- Though I'm not dissatisfied with my career, I really look forward to accepting new challenges.
- I look forward to participating actively in the development of your company.
- Why do you ask this question? Are you thinking of offering me a position involving quite a bit of responsibility?

BEST ANSWER ✓

I feel proud of myself, because I've moved ahead faster than I expected and my career path is on track to meet my goals.

What did you contribute to the top management team?

✓ Choose the Best Answer

- ❏ I was the backbone of the team. I made myself indispensable and I was proud of that accomplishment.
- ❏ I suggested improving three policies/procedures and offered the following ideas: _____ .
- ❏ I carried out orders, and that seemed enough.
- ❏ I just let them work it out. They do it their way. I do it my way.
- ❏ I just did what I was supposed to without ever interfering with top management.

? What They Really Want to Know

- ▪ Are your contributions to top management useful?
- ▪ Do you go the extra mile?
- ▪ What were your responsibilities?

! Watch Out!

Don't:

- ▪ Speak badly of your current/previous top management team.
- ▪ Act as if all the important decisions were made by you.
- ▪ Appear to be domineering and overbearing.
- ▪ Overestimate your previous responsibilities.
- ▪ Suggest that you never offered anything to management.

Don't Say:

- ▪ My ideas seemed useless to them, and they didn't implement any of them.
- ▪ I often disagreed with top management, as they seemed shortsighted to me.
- ▪ I suffered from bad timing. I was never in the right place at the right time to offer suggestions.

- I did not fulfill their expectations. They didn't need my services.
- Nothing.
- We had absolutely no rapport, nor did we even communicate most of the time.

 **Try This!**

Do:

- Produce concrete and quantifiable results that show your contributions.
- Mention a previous contribution that was a determining factor for a decision made by the firm/company.
- Mention a previous achievement or a decision that turned out extremely profitable for the team/company.
- Ask for clarification. Ask what kind of contribution they mean.
- Show your leadership skills using examples.
- Show that you are able to accept a group decision.
- Show your interest in being included in the decision-making team.

Say:

- I offered my experience, my availability, and my enthusiasm to top management.
- On a daily basis, I helped management with the issues they faced.
- I recorded the minutes of all top management meetings.
- I promoted dialogue between different members of the team.
- I was at their beck and call/disposal.
- Our relationship was direct, open and sincere. We solved problems as they arose, one after another.
- We met weekly to measure the impact of my contribution.

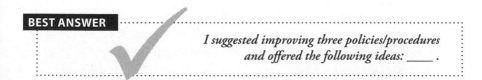

BEST ANSWER

I suggested improving three policies/procedures and offered the following ideas: _____ .

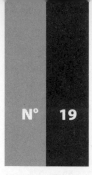

What personal characteristics make you think you will be successful at this job?

✓ Choose the Best Answer

- ❑ I've got the right profile. I'm the one described in your ad. You have nothing to worry about.
- ❑ I've got lots, and you won't have any problems from me.
- ❑ I have gathered a lot of information on this position and the tasks involved. I can already tell you that _____ .
- ❑ I can do everything. I'm a jack-of-all-trades. I may even have too much experience for the job.
- ❑ My former boss pointed all of them out in the letter of recommendation he wrote, which you can read at your convenience.

? What They Really Want to Know

- ▪ Are you familiar with our hierarchy?
- ▪ Are you clear about the duties of this position?
- ▪ Do you know how to get recognition for your experience?

! Watch Out!

Don't:

- ▪ Bluff and say you have the characteristics needed for the job if you don't have them.
- ▪ Give "canned" answers that don't show any real or honest self-evaluation.
- ▪ Remain too modest and do nothing to sell yourself.
- ▪ Express yourself in a pompous or uncompromising way.
- ▪ Find an excuse to hide the fact that you are just not the person for the job.

Don't Say:

- ▪ I've always been good at my other jobs. Why not this one?
- ▪ I've worked in companies more demanding than yours!
- ▪ I don't see any problem. I think I have the characteristics you want.

- Of course I have them; in fact I think I am rather overqualified for this position.
- I'm sure this job suits me.
- Because I was made for this job.

Try This!

Do:

- Show your adaptability, using concrete examples.
- Be very precise in your examples of how you possess the needed qualities.
- Focus on the competencies they need.
- Talk about similar results in other jobs.
- Ask questions to clarify certain tasks (and the inherent qualities needed to do them).
- Present results that are transferable to this position.
- Focus on one of their needs that you can satisfy.

Say:

- I have studied the needs of your position, and my competencies match perfectly. For example, _____ .
- I like taking initiative!
- I check my results against the given objectives.
- My motivation to accept challenges.
- My wish is to be successful, and my results come from that. For example, _____.
- My ambition, my competencies, my availability. In terms of my ambition, _____. In terms of my competencies, _____ . In terms of my availability, _____ .

BEST ANSWER

I have gathered a lot of information on this position and the tasks it involves. I can already tell you that _____.

How do you judge when you've done a good job?

✓ Choose the Best Answer

- ❏ If I feel I have done a good job, I am happy. I also listen to criticism from others.
- ❏ I worked for 20 years in the same firm—I must have done something right!
- ❏ I am always searching for "perfection."
- ❏ When I make up my mind to work, I work hard. I don't work effectively otherwise.
- ❏ I am diligent about measuring my results to make sure I have reached the goals/outcomes I have set for myself and that are expected of me.

? What They Really Want to Know

- Are you really going to be efficient?
- Do you have concrete evidence to prove that you have successfully performed your duties in the past?
- Do you know how to measure your work product?

! Watch Out!

Don't:

- Criticize other people's way of working.
- Act as if you are always the best.
- Show that you don't care what anyone else thinks of your work.
- Show signs that you do not take criticism well.

Don't Say:

- I try to do my best. I'm not good at judging myself.
- I don't pay any attention to comments on the quality of my work.
- I have excellent references.
- My previous employers have recognized my methods and my style.

Do:

- Provide references that will back up what you say about the quality of your work.
- Highlight your achievements that could benefit the company.
- Give examples of your personal investment and motivation for doing a good job.
- Hand over proof of the results you have obtained.

Say:

- I was promoted after I finished that specific project/job.
- I received praise from management many times.
- I received a substantial salary increase.
- I get fully involved in my work and know that I am giving 110% of my effort.

BEST ANSWER

I am diligent about measuring my results to make sure I have reached the goals/outcomes I have set for myself and that are expected of me.

3

Personality, Personal Characteristics, and Style

A N INTERVIEWER NEEDS TO FIND OUT about your personality, personal characteristics, and style. They do this to determine whether you will be a good fit in their company. Personality is often defined as the emotions, thoughts, and behavior patterns that a person has. It is made up of many things, so it's a complex subject and can be quite subjective to judge. When asking questions to elicit information about your personality, an interviewer is trying to find out about your reliability, honesty, aptitude, and social skills, to name just a few characteristics. They want to gain a strong sense of what makes you tick, what interests you, and how you look at the world in general. Questions often deal with personal characteristics such as creativity, perseverance, working style, and definitions of success and happiness.

Interviewers are looking for balanced people who have attained some level of maturity in their personalities. By maturity, we are not talking about age—we are talking about what qualities you value in yourself and others—integrity, loyalty, wisdom, determination in the face of odds, initiative, etc. If you can show how you strive to maintain these qualities, you will impress your interviewer.

Personality, personal characteristics, and style questions included here are:

- How do you define success?
- Are you creative?
- Are you tenacious? Do you persevere?
- Tell me about yourself.
- What is your working style?
- What do you have difficulty coping with? What causes you great distress?
- What experiences have contributed the most to shaping your personality? Talk about your greatest difficulties or greatest joys.
- What are your strengths and your weaknesses?
- Who are you?
- Staying on the same job for too long a time can imply a lack of initiative. What do you think?
- If I were to ask your former boss, what assets and shortcomings would he attribute to you?

What the Interviewer Wants to Know About You

By asking these questions, the interviewer is trying to find out:

- Are you ambitious?
- Do you have a sense of initiative?
- Do you see yourself realistically?
- What are your character traits?
- What are your limitations?
- What are your strengths and your shortcomings?
- Do you really know yourself? Do you know what's important to say about yourself?
- Are you mature?
- What are your professional goals?
- Are you the person we're looking for?

- Have you acquired the new skills you need for this job?
- Do you really fit the job description?
- How do you function in periods of tension?
- What was your reaction to a difficult situation?
- Is it easy to make you lose your efficiency?
- How do you solve problems?
- Can we really depend on you to go the entire distance?
- Are you anti-conformist? Can you think "out of the box"?
- Are you an initiator or a follower?

How to Answer

The good news is that right or wrong doesn't play much into these answers. The concepts involved in these questions are relative—each person has a different take on what they mean. What matters is whether you are honest. It's not a good idea here, however, to dwell on personal issues. Don't tell your life story and all the bad things you've encountered if asked what obstacles you've overcome. Stick to positive examples that show how you face problems and come up with solutions.

When asked about personal characteristics and qualities, be sure that you talk realistically about yourself. Don't give yourself qualities you don't really possess. When you are asked about what makes you tick, there are many ways you could answer—find the qualities that are most important to you and talk about them at this time. If you place a premium on success or creativity, talk about what that word really means to you. Success to one person might be climbing Mount Everest (which would only be helpful to share in an interview if you are applying for a mountain climbing guide job!); to another it might mean working hard to attain significant prosperity; and still to another it might mean doing something good for someone else or for mankind in general. None of these answers are wrong. The only mistake you can make here is not to explain what you mean by your choice. Use examples to illustrate that what you say is true and is a constant theme in your life.

Sometimes when an interviewer is trying to find out about your personality, they will ask questions about what you don't like or what causes problems for you. Think through these answers. It's okay not to like something or have a problem with something, but make sure your answer includes illustrations that explain how you deal with these issues in positive ways. Sometimes questions may seem frivolous, such as "What famous person would you most like to have lunch with, and why?," or "What's your favorite book, and why? Favorite movie, why?"

Your responses to these questions give insight into your personality. It says something quite different about you if you say you'd like to meet Walt Disney, than it does if you say you'd like to meet Caesar Augustus. If you say your favorite book is *War and Peace*, you reveal one thing. If you say your favorite book is *Betty Crocker's Cookbook*, you've said quite a different thing. The important thing to remember is that you must explain your choice. Tell why your answer appealed to you—give the reason for your choice. It's a window into your personality.

Two of the questions people dread fall into this category: "Tell me about yourself" and "Who are you?" They seem so innocent and simple. They are open-ended and leave you with the choice to say anything you want to say, right? No! Think again. What interviewers are asking, without using the words, is, "Tell me what I need to know about your work history, skills, abilities, and traits *so that I can know if I want to hire you.*" This isn't the time to talk about where you were born, where you went to high school, when you got married, how many kids you have, or that you won an award as Best Parent Volunteer at your child's school. Talk only about your professional self here. Talk about how you are the best candidate for the job. Spend about two minutes only—be prepared so you don't drift all over the place. Use an example or two from your background and experience. You can end by asking if there is anything else you can elaborate on so they will know you are a good candidate. They will ask you about the things that captured their interest. Remember, this is your chance to make a strong case for your candidacy—use it wisely!

You can tell your interviewer some personal fact about yourself once rapport is established and the nuts and bolts of the interview are out of the way. It's okay then to show a glimpse into activities that speak to your values in your personal life. Then you can say you trained and ran a marathon last year, or you helped to start a project to provide working clothes to abused women so they could reenter the workforce, or that you read 25 books on the list of the best 100 books ever written. Just don't jump the gun on sharing this kind of information.

How do you define success?

✓ Choose the Best Answer

- ❏ Winning the lottery! Marrying the woman/man of my dreams! Having your job!
- ❏ I don't know how to define it yet.
- ❏ Success is a process called life. It's not one big thing but is made up of lots of little successes that all add up.
- ❏ Sitting in your chair.
- ❏ You represent success itself!

? What They Really Want to Know

- ■ Are you ambitious?
- ■ Tell me about your professional accomplishments.
- ■ What is your professional goal?

! Watch Out!

Don't:

- ■ Be unrealistic in defining success as some "carrot" just outside of your reach.
- ■ Hesitate.
- ■ Underestimate your achievements.
- ■ Talk only about extra-professional things.
- ■ Boast and say you have it all.

Don't Say:

- ■ I lost 10 pounds in a month.
- ■ I don't know.
- ■ I make a success of everything I undertake.
- ■ The company would never have survived without me. I think being needed is success.

Do:

- Pick achievements in line with the future job.
- Give clear examples with measurable results.
- Underline the problems you encountered in a way that enhances your results.

Say:

- In the professional area, personal, or both?
- Thanks to the excellent training my team received, I lowered the turnover rate by 8% in six months, despite serious competition.
- Constantly moving toward the goals I have set for myself.
- A great job, a good family life, and some fun along the way!
- An interesting and rewarding job, like the one I am applying for here.

BEST ANSWER

Success is a process called life. It's not one big thing but is made up of lots of little successes that all add up.

Are you creative?

✓ Choose the Best Answer

- ❑ Even though I'm pretty conventional, I have at times created or improved sales slogans for my company.
- ❑ Yes. Absolutely.
- ❑ Yes. I am creative and I like to make things.
- ❑ Once I put a suggestion in the "idea box." But it wasn't taken into consideration, even though it was good.
- ❑ Yes! Would you like me to show you my latest creation?

? What They Really Want to Know

- ▪ Do you have a sense of initiative?
- ▪ Are you anti-conformist? Can you think "out of the box"?
- ▪ Are you an initiator or a follower?

! Watch Out!

Don't:

- ▪ Put down creative people as being dreamers.
- ▪ Be conventional or show your resistance to change.
- ▪ Exaggerate your creative side.
- ▪ Show that you're always critical and have a better idea than anyone else.

Don't Say:

- ▪ Yes and no.
- ▪ Of course. It's no problem for me.
- ▪ Not really. It scares me a little.

Try This!

Do: →

- Back up your positive answer with an example.
- Show you understand limits and don't reach for the moon.
- Suggest a new idea for the firm.
- Be realistic and reasonable, but very positive.
- Bring a portfolio so you can show a tangible example of how you are creative.

Say: 🔢

- I am constantly reading about new technologies, and that often gives me ideas for improving my projects.
- Yes, I like to look at problems and find solutions that no one else has thought of yet. For example, _____ .
- Can I show you one of my creations? It involves _____ .
- What are your latest creations?

BEST ANSWER

Yes! Would you like me to show you my latest creation?

Are you tenacious? Do you persevere?

✓ Choose the Best Answer

- ❏ I can't see that as an asset. I like to go with the flow.
- ❏ It's no problem for me!
- ❏ As a bulldog!
- ❏ Perseverance is one of the personality traits that I cultivate the most—with enthusiasm.
- ❏ Sometimes you just have to wait, and with a little luck the right moment will surface. If that's what you call persevering, I am.

? What They Really Want to Know

- How do you function in periods of tension?
- What was your reaction to a difficult situation?
- Can we really depend on you to go the entire distance?

! Watch Out!

Don't:

- Be pretentious or overly enthusiastic and act like you never give up on anything.
- Lie and say this is a characteristic of yours if it is not.
- Remain silent or hesitate, as if you don't understand what they are asking.

Don't Say:

- Well, um, yeah . . . sort of.
- I don't know. I've never been tested.
- I prefer simple and predictable situations.

Do: →

- Give a couple of professional or personal examples that show how you persevered in the face of a difficult situation.
- Ask questions if you would like them to be more specific in their intent with this question.
- Show that you are dynamic and committed, by using an example from your life.

Say: 🙿

- For me it's a basic rule, although I am not rigid about these things. It's just if I start something I like to see it through to completion.
- I am very thorough and like to finish what I start before going on to something else.
- Here is a non-professional example: _____ .

BEST ANSWER

Perseverance is one of the personality traits that I cultivate the most—with enthusiasm.

Tell me about yourself!

✓ Choose the Best Answer

- ❑ I was born on _____.
- ❑ I am without a doubt the person you're looking for. I think I have all the talents you need.
- ❑ You want to know what I have done?
- ❑ Thanks, but that would take too much time. Let's talk about something else!
- ❑ My real strength is my attention to detail. I am proud of my ability to follow through and meet deadlines. If I commit to doing something, I make sure it gets done well and on time.

? What They Really Want to Know

- ▪ Do you really fit the job description?
- ▪ Tell me about your assets and vulnerabilities.
- ▪ Do you really know yourself? Do you know what's important to say about yourself?

! Watch Out!

Don't:
- ▪ Be arrogant or aggressive.
- ▪ Hesitate to reframe the question.
- ▪ Give only negative information about yourself.
- ▪ Talk about your private life.
- ▪ Talk more than five minutes.
- ▪ Go off on tangents you had no intention of sharing with the recruiter because you are nervous.

Don't Say:
- ▪ It's hard to talk about one's self. I don't know.
- ▪ I don't like talking about myself. I'm not sure what you want me to say.
- ▪ I hate talking about myself because I'm shy.
- ▪ I have just got to be the person you need!

- I'm just like everybody else.
- I'm going to tell you about an experience that left a big impression on me: my trip to Katmandu in 1998.
- Everything's on my resume. Should I tell you about my last job?
- I was born in New York City in 1954 and I have four children who are all grown now.

Try This!

Do: →

- Describe your assets that correspond with the job.
- Ask the recruiter/interviewer what he/she particularly wants to know, or reframe the question if you are not sure what information to give him/her.
- Be precise, factual, and quantify your accomplishments.
- Give a brief answer (not over two minutes) and go on to something else by asking a question.
- Stick to qualities about yourself that correspond to the job.
- Tell them the most important thing about why you think you should get the job.

Say: 〞

- Professionally speaking, my best experience was _____ .
- In the job you are offering, three things correspond to _____ .
- Would you like me to go over my entire career or give you details on my last job?
- I had a job like this two years ago. Here's what we did.
- I am a resourceful person. Here are a couple of examples that illustrate that.
- I'll tell you about an experience that left its mark: the launch of (a product), which generated a 10% increase in revenue for my former employers.
- My career path goes in three directions, all of which are relevant to your area of activity.
- Here are three things I've accomplished during my career so far, that are probably needed in the job you are offering.
- Something I did that I'm particularly proud of was to start a volunteer project.

BEST ANSWER

My real strength is my attention to detail. I am proud of my ability to follow through and meet deadlines. If I commit to doing something, I make sure it gets done well and on time.

What is your working style?

✓ Choose the Best Answer

- ❏ Dynamic, innovative, and intuitive.
- ❏ Being available, listening to others, suggesting ways to get the job done.
- ❏ I've got my own style, which works for me.
- ❏ I think I've got what it takes to be a manager. I don't like being managed. I'd rather do the managing.
- ❏ What exactly do you mean by "working style"?

? What They Really Want to Know

- How do you solve problems?
- Are you more solitary or do you like being part of a group? Are you open-minded?
- Are you willing to accept overtime and/or work on the weekend?

! Watch Out!

Don't:

- Refer to limiting or negative elements from past jobs that you thought held you back.
- Bring up failures at work that have never been resolved.
- Show that you are capable of being stubborn and not willing to work as part of a team.
- Suggest that you don't know what your style is, or that you have never given this thought.
- Take extreme/radical positions.

Don't Say:

- I like things done right away.
- I hate waiting and doing the same thing over and over.

- I haven't found out enough about your company.
- I'm not the communicator type.

Try This!

Do:

- Be straightforward and frank, and list two or three elements that describe how you work best.
- Show that you know how to keep your head above the crowd, and get ahead, in a particular situation. Use examples.
- Mention the achievements you are proud of where your working style helped smooth the road.

Say:

- I listen, I analyze, and then I act.
- I appreciate all styles of communication, as long as they are being used properly.
- I ask for the opinion of my colleagues before every important decision.
- I take time to explain things to others so everyone is on the same page.
- I submit my goals, and then we discuss them as a team so that everyone is involved.

BEST ANSWER

Being available, listening to others, suggesting ways to get the job done.

What do you have difficulty coping with?
What causes you great distress?

✓ Choose the Best Answer

- ❑ I am fairly patient, though inefficiency can drive me crazy!
- ❑ In general, I'm pretty strong, but of course it depends. At my last job there was some harassment, which is why I left.
- ❑ I don't fall apart easily. But, to be perfectly honest, it can happen.
- ❑ Repeated job interviews can undo me!
- ❑ A chief/boss who gets on my nerves and never lets me get my work done.

? What They Really Want to Know

- ■ Have you ever committed a professional mistake?
- ■ How do you react to work overload?
- ■ Is it easy to make you lose your emotional balance?

! Watch Out!

Don't:
- ■ Give a negative example.
- ■ Be too explicit in the details of what distresses you.
- ■ Avoid answering in effect by saying nothing distresses you.
- ■ Blush and lose your composure.
- ■ Appear to be offended by the question.

Don't Say:
- ■ It's the stress that caused me to leave my last job.
- ■ This very kind of situation—job interviews!
- ■ I could never accept a job that involves too much stress.
- ■ I don't know what stress is.
- ■ I only work well under stress. It doesn't scare me.
- ■ When we were overcome by the situation, for example, when _____ .

Do:

- Give a couple of precise examples of your prioritizing skills.
- Reassure the interviewer by answering what bothers you and how you overcome it or compensate for it.
- Maintain your confidence knowing there is something that's hard for everyone to cope with.
- Show that you know how to handle stress and poor behavior from others.

Say:

- I did a course on stress management, which helped me a great deal.
- I try to anticipate the risks that might occur from my decisions so I'm not surprised.
- I try to plan my decisions and to anticipate the stress.
- I don't suffer fools easily, but luckily my co-workers have been bright people who are willing to always go the extra mile.
- I try to categorize the problems so as to avoid undertaking everything at the same time.
- I take a deep breath, which allows me to control the build-up of stress.
- I'm human, it happens, but I know how to deal with it. For example, _____ .
- Could I ask you to make your question more precise?
- If I'm feeling swamped, I talk to my supervisor.

BEST ANSWER

I am fairly patient, though inefficiency can drive me crazy!

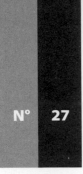

N° 27 — What experiences have contributed the most to shaping your personality? Talk about your greatest difficulties or greatest joys.

✓ Choose the Best Answer

- ❑ I've been in financial difficulty for a long time now. I've had some very hard times in the last couple of months.
- ❑ Several complicated personal relationships that I had to deal with had a big influence on my personality.
- ❑ My greatest joys have been my family and my employers' recognition of my work. Those things that have been difficult have taught me important lessons.
- ❑ Being without work is the biggest and most depressing problem.
- ❑ Here are my three greatest difficulties: _____ . As for my joys _____ .

? What They Really Want to Know

- ▪ Are you happy with yourself? Can you overcome diversity?
- ▪ Do you have a "big picture" outlook?
- ▪ Are you well balanced/mature/dependable? What kinds of things have shaped you?

! Watch Out!

Don't:
- ▪ Get too familiar, talk too much, and lose control.
- ▪ Go into too much detail.
- ▪ Be too sensitive or emotional.
- ▪ Become too philosophical and not answer with specifics from your life.
- ▪ End on a negative note.

Don't Say:
- ▪ I can only remember some recent problems that were pretty heavy and did not provide any new insight.
- ▪ We live in a world of individuals. I educated myself alone.

- The world resents us and is full of injustice. That has shaped me.
- The difficulties we have to endure are often caused by others.
- I find it difficult to get along with my in-laws! I think that makes me appreciate my job more.

 Try This!

Do:

- Tell about a moment of extreme happiness, and a difficulty that you overcame.
- Give a couple of examples related to the job in question.
- Limit your bad experience to one or two examples.
- Link one or two experiences to demonstrate your motivation/determination and how you overcome roadblocks or obstacles placed in your path.

Say:

- Working with my colleagues gave me the opportunity to also work on improving my listening skills and managing conflicts.
- I took a training workshop to learn how to do one of the most unpleasant things a manager has to do: make the decision to fire someone.
- When I became a mother/father for the first time!
- The hardest thing for me was to unite my need for independence with the need to work as a team.
- I suppose the things that shape us most are the things that we find most difficult. Overcoming adversity with the knowledge that we can survive it allows us to tap into strengths we may not know we had. For myself, I experienced _____ .

BEST ANSWER

My greatest joys have been my family and my employers' recognition of my work. Those things that have been difficult have taught me important lessons.

What are your strengths and your weaknesses?

✓ Choose the Best Answer

- ❑ I was waiting for that one! It's an excellent question. I know exactly what I want to say.
- ❑ I have made a success out of everything I have undertaken. I like success and I have ambition. I'm also a hard worker.
- ❑ I get tired after 18 hours of work non-stop! [laughter]
- ❑ My strength is all my extraordinary experience.
- ❑ My strong points are punctuality, a sense of innately knowing what's important, and my good nature. My weak point: I am a perfectionist; I take time to do things well.

? What They Really Want to Know

- ▪ Do you see yourself realistically?
- ▪ What are your character traits?
- ▪ What are your limitations?

! Watch Out!

Don't:

- ▪ Mention your faults or weaknesses without saying something about how you deal with them.
- ▪ Act as if you have never thought about this question before.
- ▪ Tell your life story.

Don't Say:

- ▪ While I am punctual, when others are late I get really upset!
- ▪ I don't have any faults.
- ▪ How about you?
- ▪ I have relationship problems in my personal life.
- ▪ I am the best.

Do: →

- Answer briefly and carry on with a question.
- Transform your weaknesses by showing what you do to overcome them.
- Describe a project that was doomed for failure, but which you managed to carry out successfully.
- List at least three strengths and one weakness honestly. Move to another topic immediately after answering.

Say: 🙶

- As soon as I recognize a weakness, I work on it and always manage to overcome it. Maybe that's one of my strengths!
- My strengths are _____ and a weakness is _____, but I _____ .
- Let me show you a project where I was really able to invest myself.

BEST ANSWER

My strong points are punctuality, a sense of innately knowing what's important, and my good nature. My weak point: I am a perfectionist; I take time to do things well.

Who are you?

✓ Choose the Best Answer

- ❑ I am "me."
- ❑ I'm the son of _____ .
- ❑ I think I am someone who can make a contribution to your firm by _____ .
- ❑ I'm your man/woman!
- ❑ Someone who is looking to find himself, and, if you hire me, I'll be able to do just that.

? What They Really Want to Know

- How do you see yourself?
- Are you the person we're looking for?
- What are your qualities and your shortcomings?

! Watch Out!

Don't:
- Start off talking about your weaknesses.
- Give the impression you can't answer.
- Give trivial information [name, address, etc.].
- Act like you have never thought about this question.
- Lie or give misrepresentations.
- Give too much importance to the negative aspects of your personality.
- Spend too much time thinking about what you're going to say.
- Laugh nervously.
- Be intimidated.
- Feel embarrassed.

Don't Say:
- That's too personal.
- I'm a person who likes people.

- I can't just list my qualities.
- I am a person who wants to work for you.
- I'm married. I have one child.
- Good question. Got any more of those?

Try This!

Do:

- See this question as an opportunity to tell the interviewer why you are the person for the job.
- Talk about a good experience that is relevant in some way to the job in question.
- Start introducing yourself by talking about your qualities.
- Act cheerful and delighted with the question.
- Act natural and show self-confidence.
- Talk about qualities that are relevant to the job. Include some information about your interpersonal skills.
- Demonstrate that you fit the job description.
- Offer carefully thought-out answers.
- Turn your weak points into strong points and use the question as a way to bring forth information that you might not otherwise get a chance to tell.
- Show yourself as being open.

Say:

- What would you like to know about me?
- I have curiosity, empathy, and serenity. I like to _____ .
- I'm an energetic and enthusiastic person.
- My qualities are _____, and my weakness is _____ .
- I am a person who could fit in at your organization because I possess _____ and _____ and _____ .

BEST ANSWER

I think I am someone who can make a contribution to your firm by _____ .

Staying on the same job for too long a time can imply a lack of initiative. What do you think?

✓ Choose the Best Answer

- ❑ Oh, that. I entirely agree with you. And it can get so boring!
- ❑ I constantly strive to try to bring new ideas and new ways of doing things to the job. For example, _____ .
- ❑ It really depends on how interested you are in the work. But it's more or less true that after 12 to 18 months the job will probably not be so interesting anymore.
- ❑ I have no idea on the subject.
- ❑ It could mean that, but it could just mean you really like your job.

? What They Really Want to Know

- ■ Have you acquired the new techniques you need for this job?
- ■ How long did you stay in the same position?
- ■ How did you evolve/develop in the past?

! Watch Out!

Don't:
- ■ Show a lack of ambition and initiative.
- ■ Avoid showing interest in getting another job.
- ■ Show that routine is fine with you.
- ■ Act overly interested in mobility.
- ■ Rely on your past achievements to show how well you do at your job.

Don't Say:
- ■ It depends.
- ■ When I get bored, I move on.
- ■ I should have had some training if I wanted to get ahead.
- ■ I was very good in that job.
- ■ My salary was good so I stayed.

- Don't worry. I know how to keep a job interesting.
- Why change if the job is okay?

Try This!

Do:

- Describe what growth/development was necessary for keeping the job interesting.
- Point out how the salary progressed in line with the development of the required skills.
- Show how the job evolved and how you were personally invested in the job responsibilities.
- Show that you were able to advance in the past by taking new and different responsibilities.

Say:

- It's thanks to the great variety of experiences I had in this job that I can apply for a job with you today.
- There are three things that I think allowed me to excel: _____ and _____ and _____.
- I chose this work because I love it. And it still suits me today. I particularly like _____.
- I am stable and ambitious, a combination I hope you will find interesting!
- I'm always ready to learn new things. I am interested in advancing my skills in the area of _____ .
- The guiding light to my career path is _____ .

BEST ANSWER

I constantly strive to try to bring new ideas and new ways of doing things to the job. For example, _____ .

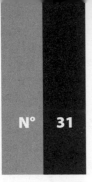

If I were to ask your former boss, what assets and shortcomings would he attribute to you?

✓ Choose the Best Answer

- ❏ The last time we met together, he complimented me on the quality of my work. We also talked about what could be improved. Many of my ideas were implemented.
- ❏ I don't think talking to my former boss would be a good idea.
- ❏ She couldn't say much, as she never really worked with me.
- ❏ He would tell you how exceptional our relationship was. As for any short-comings, I would be curious to know what he might say. I think he would be quite positive.
- ❏ I think she would mention the same qualities that I already mentioned.

? What They Really Want to Know

- How do others see you?
- Do you see yourself as others see you?
- What are your qualities and your shortcomings?

! Watch Out!

Don't:
- Mention any shortcomings first.
- Avoid the subject by not answering the full question.
- Show a considerable difference between your last boss's analysis and your own.
- Underestimate yourself and think that your last boss thought only badly of you.

Don't Say:
- He didn't give me credit for my talents.
- He never liked me.
- She didn't know me well enough to give you much useful information.

- He probably doesn't even remember me.
- She thought I was terrific!

 Try This!

Do:

- Point out any former weaknesses and how you dealt with them so they are no longer weaknesses.
- Focus on your positive qualities, without sounding pompous.
- Avoid going into your weaknesses at length.
- Refrain from talking about a weakness for too long.

Say:

- I think he would say I grew tremendously while in his department.
- I saw him by chance the other day, and he said to me how much he appreciated my work.
- I told her I was meeting with you. She said she would be delighted to speak to you about me.
- I think he would give you quite positive feedback. We were pretty complementary.
- She told me that she appreciated my willingness to go the extra mile; she also thought I would benefit from a continuing education class to strengthen my skills.

BEST ANSWER

The last time we met together, he complimented me on the quality of my work. We also talked about what could be improved. Many of my ideas were implemented.

4

Competencies and Skills

$\mathbf{Q}$ UESTIONS ABOUT YOUR COMPETENCIES AND SKILLS are important for an interviewer to ask. They often set the stage for the interviewer to know if your candidacy is a viable one and if they should spend more time with you. They are not usually as specific as questions that deal with your past professional experience (to find out if you have the skills needed), but are asked to probe into areas of more general themes, like leadership and responsibility. They often deal more with traits and personal abilities than they do with specific job skill issues.

Questions asked about responsibility and leadership (if the job is a "growth track" position within a company), your preferred skills (usually asked in the context of the skills needed for the job), your facility for and knowledge of other languages, your ability to contribute to the company, and how you would behave in certain situations (like when you weren't able to meet an objective or were criticized) help the interviewer get a measure of the level of maturity and sophistication you possess and if you can handle stress and unexpected outcomes. They are often looking to see how you behaved in past situations.

Competencies and skills questions included here are:

- Do you like responsibility? What are your major responsibilities?
- In what way did your last (or present) job prepare you to assume greater responsibility?
- In what situation have you used this competency or skill?
- Describe a time when your work was criticized.
- Describe a time when you were not able to obtain your objective.
- Describe a situation in which you felt you proved your competency in the area of _____ .
- Talk to me about a responsibility (in your last job) that you would like to take on again.
- Do you speak any foreign languages? At what level? Have you ever lived in any countries where the language you studied is spoken?
- What makes you think you can contribute to our company's development/growth?
- What more can you offer us than other candidates?
- What was the outcome of your last evaluation?
- What skills and experience make you think you would be good at this job?
- Your evaluation in your last job was only average. Can you explain that?

What the Interviewer Wants to Know About You

By asking questions about your competencies and certain skills, the interviewer is trying to find out:

- Have you had complete responsibility for any projects/people/budgets/material?
- Do you consider yourself ready to assume responsibility?
- Do you understand what is involved by taking more responsibility?
- Do others judge you well?

- Are you a leader?
- Can you make difficult decisions?
- Do you like taking risks, and are you good at it?
- How well have you mastered the skill of _____?
- Do you know how to analyze/evaluate your previous achievements?
- What talents/skills/knowledge do you possess?
- Can you take criticism? If not, do you get angry?
- Are you quick to react strongly when something doesn't go in your favor?
- Are you good at making use of criticism?
- How do you handle situations of failure?
- Do you recognize your limits? Do you recognize your weaknesses?
- Do you persevere even in the face of failure?
- Have you been in contact with cultures and environments other than your own?
- Are you able to understand mail, reports, and directives coming from our home office abroad?
- What efforts have you made toward identifying and understanding our needs?
- Do you really understand the job's key criteria?
- Do you fully understand the job requirements?
- Do you have a "value added" quality that might have escaped me?
- Do you see yourself as special?
- Are you the candidate I should pick?
- Are you sure you know yourself? Can you sell yourself?

How to Answer

It is best to answer questions about leadership and responsibility by giving examples from your past work experience where you have demonstrated your ability in these areas. Know how to describe your leadership style so the interviewer can judge if it is congruent with the culture of the organization. If you have not had a lot of leadership experience, show that you understand what makes a good leader—an ability to bring out the best in others and create solutions to unexpected situations. Show by example how you have taken measurable risks when needed. Be sure you know the kind of responsibility you want to take on—show how you like to take on extra tasks by giving an example of when you sought out extra responsibility in the past. Talk about your understanding of time management, especially when you are under pressure. It takes confidence in yourself to make decisions and take on bigger projects. You must show through your answers that you are a person who possesses these traits. Leaders and those who are willing take on more responsibility are people who deal in solutions and don't get bogged down in problems. That is what the interviewer wants to know.

You will have to talk about how you react when you run into problems. No interviewer can reasonably expect that you have never faced problems or criticism. They are not so much interested in the problems you faced but the ways you dealt with them. That should be the focus of your answers when asked about difficulties in the workplace.

Be sure you sell yourself. If you know foreign languages, talk about your fluency level. Show that you understand the needs of the company and how you can meet those needs. This is the time to show that you possess the traits they are looking for. Answer with confidence, while maintaining eye contact. If you do this, you will make a strong case about how you are special and the person they should hire for the job.

Do you like responsibility? What are your major responsibilities?

✓ Choose the Best Answer

❑ I've always been successful in my profession. Don't worry about a thing. I make things work and I know how to use my power.

❑ I used to have a boss who managed his entire company by himself and didn't allow any of us to take much responsibility.

❑ I started at the bottom of the ladder, and in three years was named head of a team of 10 people with a budget of $1 million.

❑ I'm a very responsible person, believe me.

❑ Major responsibilities mean major worries! I've sometimes been torn between _____ .

? What They Really Want to Know

■ Have you had complete responsibility for any projects/people/budgets/material?

■ Are you a leader?

■ Can you make difficult decisions?

! Watch Out!

Don't:

■ Give the impression that you have never accepted any real responsibility or are incapable of assuming any.

■ Be vague or try to avoid the subject.

■ Exaggerate your real responsibilities from past jobs.

■ Show any signs of nervousness.

■ Run your hands through your hair.

■ Look up the ceiling or down at your hands.

■ Remain tongue-tied for a long time or just stare at the recruiter/interviewer.

Don't Say:

- I've never really had any major responsibilities.
- I think I am a responsible person.
- I can do anything; just put me to the task.
- Oh! I'm not quite sure what to say.

Try This!

Do:

- List responsibilities you have assumed, in order of importance.
- Briefly describe your career path.
- Relax your face when you smile.
- Show your self-assurance with a pause (before replying) and then say, "I was responsible for _____ ."
- Prove your motivation with precise questions.

Say:

- As sales manager, I reduced the stocking charges by 15%, by implementing a new system for handling returns.
- I have three children, all of whom have graduated from college!
- Submitting the accounts on the 28th of each month was a priority that I had complete responsibility for.

BEST ANSWER

I started at the bottom of the ladder, and in three years was named head of a team of 10 people with a budget of $1 million.

In what way did your last (or present) job prepare you to assume greater responsibility?

✓ Choose the Best Answer

- ❑ I've always wanted to have more responsibility. I'll adapt to this new situation very fast.
- ❑ In my last job, I developed three valuable skills that allow me to assume more responsibility now: working autonomously, prioritizing, and decision making.
- ❑ I wasn't used to my full capacity. That's why I decided to change jobs—to have more responsibility.
- ❑ I'm looking for a job with real responsibilities, for I think that too often I have had jobs where I just followed orders.
- ❑ I don't feel I am quite ready for a job with more responsibility.

? What They Really Want to Know

- ■ Do you like taking risks, and are you good at it?
- ■ Do you consider yourself ready to assume responsibility?
- ■ Do you understand what is involved by taking more responsibility? Are you ambitious enough to want to do that?

! Watch Out!

Don't:

- ■ Look at your resume for responsibilities you have had and then recite them from the paper.
- ■ Complain that previous bosses have never had enough confidence in you to give you responsibility.
- ■ Show your fear that you don't measure up to the job for which you are interviewing.

Don't Say:

- ■ I quit because I was never given any substantial responsibility. I want more.
- ■ I have never had any responsibilities. I was just a subordinate, not a chief.

- I do not like to take risks.
- I don't like to take responsibility. It only leads to trouble.

 Try This!

Do:

- Describe how you assumed risks inherent in a diversification of products.
- Give a concrete and positive example of a responsibility that you managed well.
- Illustrate your career progression.

Say:

- I started out in the company as team manager and I've had two promotions in four years. With each promotion, I was given more responsibility.
- I took care of invoices and the budget. Due to our results, I was promoted to head of the department.
- I oversaw the daily opening and closing of two stores as well as the training of four apprentices who all came through with flying colors.
- Within one year I was assigned the task of reorganizing the data processing unit with over 500 employees.

BEST ANSWER

In my last job, I developed three valuable skills that allow me to assume more responsibility now: working autonomously, prioritizing, and decision making.

In what situation have you used this competency or skill?

✓ Choose the Best Answer

- ❑ I've never really used it professionally. I can tell you when I used it in my leisure time.
- ❑ I'd say I have more of a theoretical approach to this skill.
- ❑ Not often, as my boss didn't give me much opportunity to do it.
- ❑ You can contact my supervisor, who could fill you in on that better than I.
- ❑ That's a skill I use professionally as well as in my personal life. For example, ____ .

? What They Really Want to Know

- ▪ Do you like and have you used this skill?
- ▪ Did the tasks in your last job require this skill?
- ▪ How well have you mastered this skill?

! Watch Out!

Don't:

- ▪ Refer to some minor piece of work instead of a real task or duty.
- ▪ Give unnecessary details that might be badly interpreted.
- ▪ Merely enumerate several situations without substantiating them with details of the particulars.
- ▪ Find yourself without examples to illustrate your point.
- ▪ Freely give names of people who can give you credit or are willing to serve as a reference.
- ▪ Bring up an example from your distant past.
- ▪ Mention a personal situation.
- ▪ Forget to elaborate on the situation in which you used the skill.

Don't Say:

- ▪ That skill is not the one I've developed the best.

- That skill can easily be replaced by others, like ____ .
- I don't often use that skill, and if I run into a situation that requires it, I let someone else take over.
- I don't remember. It's been such a long time!
- I'm not sure of myself when I need to use this skill.
- Professionally, I've never needed this skill, but I've used it in my family.
- You can contact my reference, who will tell you more about me.

Try This!

Do:

- Use an example that corresponds to the needs of the firm.
- Highlight your professional activities with your achievements.
- Bring out the positive aspects of the current situation and your results.
- Put together a portfolio that you can use to illustrate how you have used the skill in question.

Say:

- This skill is one of my strong points. For example, ____ .
- I find this skill extremely interesting and would jump at the opportunity to further develop it.
- I use this skill on a regular basis. For example, ____ . Can you tell me if it would be applicable to this job?
- I'm glad you asked, because I just recently had the opportunity to use it at work. Let me tell you about it.
- I realize the position I'm interested in requires this skill, and I'd like you to know that I applied it daily with my boss, Mr. X at XYZ. For example, ____ .

BEST ANSWER

That's a skill I use professionally as well as in my personal life. For example, ____ .

Describe a time when your work was criticized.

✓ Choose the Best Answer

- ❏ That's happened to me a lot. Not because my work was basically bad, but at XYZ it was just how they treated everybody.
- ❏ It would take me too long to tell you!
- ❏ No one has ever criticized my work. If they did, they'd hear from me.
- ❏ When I'm in a group, I or, rather, some of my ideas, may get criticized. But it's always good to be challenged and use the feedback you get to improve yourself. For example, once I worked on a project at _____. I was told _____.
- ❏ No one dares criticize my work! I'm indispensable!

? What They Really Want to Know

- ▪ Can you take criticism? If not, do you get angry?
- ▪ Are you quick to react strongly when something doesn't go in your favor?
- ▪ Are you good at making use of criticism?

! Watch Out!

Don't:

- ▪ Overly dramatize things and act like others have persecuted you unfairly.
- ▪ Explain by going into too much detail.
- ▪ Get irritated, impolite, or rigid.
- ▪ Act like you have never needed help to improve your work.

Don't Say:

- ▪ I've never done anything wrong.
- ▪ I don't remember.
- ▪ Once and we ended up going to court. I won.
- ▪ Many times. It happens.

Do:

- Put into context any situation you describe.
- Describe the final results you obtained after being criticized.
- Tell of the lesson you learned from the criticism.
- Show how you progressed and haven't made the same mistake again.
- Use examples to illustrate your answer.

Say:

- There were several concerns my boss had when we worked on a project for the marketing team. He outlined them to me and I could see how I could improve. I then instigated the following behaviors to show how I had learned: _____.
- Teamwork is inevitably going to be criticized. Yet, it works when everyone is tuned into improvement. One time when I worked on _____, I needed to change the way I _____ .
- I appreciate honest feedback. Once my co-worker mentioned a way to make our department more productive that I had not thought of, and I listened and integrated her suggestions into our system.
- Certain remarks are justified and helpful. I have certainly used them to correct things that needed correcting, which has allowed me to finish projects on time. For example, _____ .

BEST ANSWER

When I'm working in a group, I or, rather, some of my ideas may get criticized. But it's always good to be challenged and use the feedback you get to improve yourself. For example, once when I worked on a project at _____ , I was told _____ .

Describe a time when you were not able to obtain your objective.

✓ Choose the Best Answer

- ☐ My colleagues did their own thing, and I didn't have their support. I am demanding and efficient.
- ☐ When I was asked to carry out tasks that were not included in the terms and conditions of my job.
- ☐ One day, when two senior colleagues caused the team to communicate badly, we failed to meet our goal.
- ☐ Once, it was for failing to respect delivery deadlines, following an evening out with too much partying. It's the kind of thing that leaves its mark and I certainly won't repeat again.
- ☐ We experienced a rather delicate/difficult situation when _____. Despite the team's efforts, we were not able to meet our deadline because the resources necessary did not arrive in time. Eventually, we did manage to finish the project, but we were behind schedule by several weeks.

? What They Really Want to Know

- How do you handle situations of failure?
- Do you recognize your limits?
- Do you persevere even in the face of failure?

! Watch Out!

Don't:

- Describe a serious failure that might scare the recruiter/interviewer into thinking you are not able to handle the job you are interviewing for.
- Insist that if you didn't reach your objectives, it was clearly someone else's fault.
- Try to minimize the significance of the failure.
- Pretend you never fail.

Don't Say:

- It wasn't my fault. It was because _____.
- I just dropped the ball. It only happened that once.
- I've never failed to reach my goals.

Try This!

Do: →

- Choose a situation that is not too recent.
- Mention an experience or goal that couldn't be reached, not because of any incompetence on your part but because of the general problems that happen in any company.
- Explain how you managed to deal with the failure.
- Maintain a positive attitude.
- Emphasize what you were able to learn from the situation.
- Bring up an insignificant situation so it is clear that you do not let big things get away from you.
- Look at the situation in a positive light by emphasizing the skills it allowed you to acquire.

Say: 🙶

- This happened twice to me: The first time _____.
- When I saw that it was going to be too risky to go ahead and the goal could not be achieved in time, I narrowed it down to a reasonable and manageable goal. For example, once when I _____ .
- If the goal seems impossible to reach, I suggest a team effort. That way it is more likely to be reached. I do this by _____ .

BEST ANSWER

We experienced a rather delicate/difficult situation when _____ . Despite the team's efforts, we were not able to meet our deadline because the necessary resources did not arrive in time. Eventually, we did manage to finish the project, but we were behind schedule by several weeks.

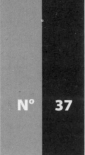

N° 37

Describe a situation in which you felt you proved your competency in the area of _____ .

✓ Choose the Best Answer

- ❏ In my last job I had to _____ (give an example of something you accomplished that required the skill in question).
- ❏ Just offhand, I can't think of a situation. But I specialize in _____.
- ❏ I can't really think of an example to illustrate that strength. But I think I've got what you are looking for.
- ❏ Why don't we have a look at my resume?
- ❏ Fifteen years ago, I _____.

? What They Really Want to Know

- ▪ Are your achievements in sync with your personality?
- ▪ Do you think you are the person for the job?
- ▪ Do you know how to analyze/evaluate your previous achievements?

! Watch Out!

Don't:
- ▪ Give a vague example or one that has nothing to do with the desired quality for the job.
- ▪ Be too demonstrative or go into too much detail over a conflict you were involved in.
- ▪ Lose perspective about your actual contribution by allowing your ego to take over.
- ▪ Speak in generalities, which have no substance.

Don't Say:
- ▪ I can't think of any examples to share with you.
- ▪ I am competent in all areas when I really like something.
- ▪ I always worked alone, and followed my boss's orders.

Do:

- Describe a specific professional accomplishment, explaining the outcome.
- Look for an example that coincides with the firm's image.
- Elaborate on one or two competencies or skills that strengthen your case for the job.

Say:

- Of course. When I was in charge of _____ , I trained a team of nine people.
- In your sector I have _____ .
- I found this quality indispensable in my last job when _____ .
- This skill has been absolutely invaluable in my previous experience. For example, _____
- Would you prefer a professional or personal example?

BEST ANSWER

In my last job I had to _____ (give an example of something you accomplished that required the skill in question).

Talk to me about a responsibility (in your last job) that you would like to take on again.

✓ Choose the Best Answer

- ❑ I liked being the person who got to order lunch.
- ❑ During my last job, I also assumed the role of mediator. I would like the opportunity to do that for you.
- ❑ I'd like to keep on doing what I've always done.
- ❑ I've had lots of responsibilities, so it's hard to choose just one. My jobs have all been different and the responsibilities have been different.
- ❑ I've never had any real responsibility, but I would like to.

? What They Really Want to Know

- ▪ Have you assumed responsibility?
- ▪ What do you really like to do?
- ▪ Are you really motivated for this position?

! Watch Out!

Don't:

- ▪ Make up an answer and name something you have not done before.
- ▪ Talk about something inconsequential.
- ▪ Talk too long.
- ▪ Suggest that you don't like responsibility or have never had any.
- ▪ Fail to name a specific responsibility you like.

Don't Say:

- ▪ I had too many responsibilities in my last job. I want something more defined in my next job so I know exactly what to expect.
- ▪ I'm looking for a job without too much responsibility.
- ▪ Heap them on. I love responsibility.
- ▪ These are my three weak points: _____.

Try This!

Do: →

- Briefly describe a situation you experienced which illustrates that you have the right profile for the job.
- Explain that you enjoy assuming responsibility and name the one or two that you most want to have in the job.
- Speak with enthusiasm and use specific examples.
- Describe yourself as someone who values responsibility, and name the ones you most like.

Say: 🗦🗦

- I loved the challenges of _____. I particularly like to _____ .
- I fully assumed the responsibility of _____ .
- I always make a point of assuming my responsibilities. I most enjoy the role of _____ .
- One of my current/previous responsibilities that I would like to assume with you is _____ .

BEST ANSWER ✓

During my last job, I also assumed the role of mediator. I would like the opportunity to do that for you.

Do you speak any foreign languages? At what level? Have you ever lived in any countries where the language you studied is spoken?

✓ Choose the Best Answer

- ❑ I studied German and English at school but haven't had much opportunity to use them.
- ❑ I have lived in various countries and speak several languages.
- ❑ Languages are not my strong point, but I'll study one if I have to.
- ❑ I speak _____ and _____ fluently and I've just started studying _____. I like keeping up on the languages I have mastered. I lived in _____ for one year during my junior year of college.
- ❑ I am a polyglot, so I am highly competent.

? What They Really Want to Know

- ■ Have you been in contact with cultures and environments other than your own?
- ■ Are you able to understand mail, reports, and directives coming from our home office abroad?
- ■ Could we send you on a mission abroad? Could we put you in contact with our foreign clients?

! Watch Out!

Don't:

- ■ Bluff on your level of fluency—they may begin to speak to you in the language immediately.
- ■ Depend on a certificate to prove your competence.
- ■ Be vague about your willingness to brush up on or learn a language.
- ■ Limit evaluating your language acquisition skills to reading, speaking, writing, or rating them fair, good, or excellent.

Don't Say:

- ■ No problem. I speak three languages.
- ■ I got a certificate/degree in _____ 10 years ago.

- I have spent a lot of time abroad.
- I understand _____ but don't speak it.
- I can understand a normal conversation.
- I get along pretty well in _____ although I never formally studied it.

Try This!

Do: →

- Question your interviewer about the usefulness/relevancy of this language in this job.
- Provide concrete examples and/or illustrations of your fluency in this language.
- Mention that you are willing to attend a crash course to improve your level of fluency.
- Answer this question in the language mentioned.

Say: „

- I trained my own staff in _____.
- I have had advanced training in _____.
- I translated the entire pamphlet of staff rules into _____ and _____.
- I have worked in _____
- I lived in _____ and worked there where we dealt with contracts with three nationalities.
- I went to study in _____ .
- I've been working for the last six years with clients from four different countries.
- My spouse is from _____, and we speak both _____ and _____ at home.

BEST ANSWER ✓

I speak _____ and _____ fluently and I've just started studying _____. I like keeping up on the languages I have mastered. I lived in _____ for one year during my junior year of college.

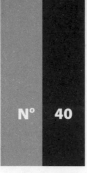
What makes you think you can contribute to our company's development/growth?

✓ Choose the Best Answer

- ❑ With all my years of experience in various firms, I have become extremely versatile and dynamic.
- ❑ I don't know, I've never asked myself that question. It would seem to me that you are in a better position to say how I might be useful to you. My resume's right there.
- ❑ I am good at running things, and staff members respect me.
- ❑ I'm as good as they get in my area!
- ❑ I have the skills and know-how you need. I can bring _____ and _____ to the job. I have the energy, enthusiasm, and drive that will bring results.

? What They Really Want to Know

- ▪ What efforts have you made toward identifying and understanding our needs?
- ▪ What talents/skills/knowledge do you possess?
- ▪ How do you see the needs of our organization? Can you meet them?

! Watch Out!

Don't:
- ▪ Degrade the organization you are interested in with over-simplified or obvious solutions.
- ▪ Point out their problems.
- ▪ Underestimate the company you are negotiating with by being flippant.
- ▪ Overestimate your own competence and suggest you can do it all.
- ▪ Show you are not a person who takes initiative.
- ▪ Talk in generalities.

Don't Say:
- ▪ Thanks to my versatility, I was able to _____.

- Since I just finished my studies, I am not sure exactly what I can bring to the company. What I need at this point is a chance to get some on-the-job training.
- Your goals are my goals.
- You're the boss and you're the one who doles out the work. What do you think I could do for you?
- In view of the predicament you've been in for the past year, I think my skills and knowledge of the market will help you see the light at the end of the tunnel.

 Try This!

Do: →

- Show your knowledge of the position/firm/field of work. Use very specific examples of what you can bring to the company.
- Specify your knowledge/learning and entice the interviewer with two or three possible goals you could meet for the company.
- Give a couple of examples that prove your motivation/determination/interest.
- Remember you are offering your services, not begging to be hired.

Say: 99

- I have done some research on the geographical area in which you wish to expand your services and I see a trend toward _____ .
- According to your growth/development plan, I could bring _____ .
- You are good at _____ and I am good at _____ . Therefore, together we could _____ .
- You indicated that you were going to develop a new product. Now, it just happens that last year I developed the flagship product for my company.

BEST ANSWER

✓ *I have the skills and know-how you need. I can bring _____ and _____ to the job. I have the energy, enthusiasm, and drive that will bring results.*

What more can you offer us than other candidates?

✓ Choose the Best Answer

- ❏ Since I haven't met the other candidates, it's hard to say.
- ❏ My profile is right on target with the selection criteria.
- ❏ I have the profile required for the job and I sincerely wish to work for you. I have the unique experience of _____ . You can count on my enthusiasm and determination.
- ❏ You have my resume. You have met with me twice. I have told you everything about myself. By now, you must know what I can offer you!
- ❏ Besides fitting the profile, I possess an additional skill of great benefit for your company.

? What They Really Want to Know

- ■ Do you really understand the job's key criteria?
- ■ Do you have a "value-added" quality that might have escaped me? Do you see yourself as special?
- ■ Are you really determined, or are you just flirting with different employers?

! Watch Out!

Don't:

- ■ Neglect to highlight a strong point that could be particularly useful for the job.
- ■ Say that you cannot answer the question because you don't know who the other candidates are.
- ■ Compare yourself with other candidates you know.
- ■ Miss your opportunity to stress why you are special.

Don't Say:

- ■ But I don't know the other candidates.
- ■ I don't know. What are you looking for now?

- I am the best. You can't go wrong with me.
- I am bringing you other skills not listed in your job profile, but useful nevertheless.

Try This!

Do:

- Develop one of your strong points showing how you saved your (current/previous) employer money (or how the employer benefited from your skill).
- Use this question to highlight a strong point that you would bring to the firm (and use a supporting achievement).
- Personalize your candidacy by drawing from personal activities or life experience.

Say:

- Besides the skills we've talked about already, I'd say my positive character and optimism.
- I match all the criteria you are looking for and am especially interested in the tasks of _____ for which I bring the necessary skills.
- My past successful experience at _____ where I managed to _____ .

BEST ANSWER

I have the profile required for the job and I sincerely wish to work for you. I have the unique experience of _____ . You can count on my enthusiasm and determination.

What was the outcome of your last evaluation?

✓ Choose the Best Answer

- ❏ That's confidential.
- ❏ I don't know. They never told me.
- ❏ Very good! My strongest point was _____.
- ❏ Pretty good, average output. But the person evaluating me was _____.
- ❏ It was fine. Do you want to talk to my last boss?

? What They Really Want to Know

- ■ Do you know what you're worth?
- ■ Do others judge you well?
- ■ Is there something we should be on the lookout for if we hire you?

! Watch Out!

Don't:
- ■ Argue your case if the evaluation wasn't good.
- ■ Focus on your weak points.
- ■ Make excuses or blame someone else for a bad evaluation.
- ■ Get lost in details and talk too long.
- ■ Boast about how great you are.

Don't Say:
- ■ Anyway, these evaluations don't mean a thing; they're just to keep the managers busy.
- ■ I've never been evaluated. We didn't do that at my last company.
- ■ I wasn't there long enough to get one.
- ■ I've only had bad ones because of jealousy.
- ■ I am bound by professional secrecy not to talk about it.
- ■ Everything was just great. I got a raise.

Do: →

- Keep a low profile and mention one point where you excelled.
- Describe your contribution to your present/previous employer.
- Say how your last boss perceived you.
- Be concise.
- Present hard facts and numbers as evidence of your contribution.
- Underline your strong points as they were outlined in the evaluation.
- Use a statement that was written by someone else about you to show your strong points.

Say: "

- Good, and this, among others, is one of the positive points about my career.
- Good, and it was a great opportunity to get some constructive feedback. I realized I could strengthen my skill in _____.
- Good. I reached my goals, and it turned out to be a nice exchange with my boss.
- Excellent. I managed to reach all the goals I had set, including _____ and _____ .
- Good, and here are the three outcomes: _____.
- Very good. My boss said about me, "_____."

BEST ANSWER

Very good! My strongest point was _____ .

What skills and experience make you think you would be good at this job?

✓ Choose the Best Answer

- ❑ In a similar job, I always reached the goals set for me. My experience in ____ will allow me to master this area very quickly.
- ❑ It's up to you to tell me. We have spent over 40 minutes together. You must have an opinion.
- ❑ I really don't know. We never know what the future will bring.
- ❑ I'm not sure I'll be good, but I'll give it a try. When there's a will there's a way!
- ❑ Well, I'm good with people and I like sales.

? What They Really Want to Know

- ■ Do you fully understand the job requirements?
- ■ Are you the candidate I should pick?
- ■ Are you sure you know yourself? Can you sell yourself?

! Watch Out!

Don't:

- ■ Be too specific if you aren't completely sure what the job requires.
- ■ Ignore tasks that are critical for the position.
- ■ Mention characteristics or skills that are not pertinent.

Don't Say:

- ■ I don't like to brag. I can do the job, trust me!
- ■ I can't tell you yet. I need to know more first.
- ■ What will I have to do? You can see from my resume what I have done in the past.
- ■ I'm a quick learner. I will catch on here very fast.

Do: →

- Point out talents and experience that are relevant to the requirements of the job.
- Highlight tasks you have managed well and which are similar to those required by the job you are interviewing for.
- Show that you did your homework on the job requirements, the recruitment procedure, the company, and the field of work—before the interview.

Say: 🙻

- I am good at the kind of work this job involves. As head of _____ , I managed to _____.
- The training I have recently received has given me the tools I need and will allow me to meet this challenge with confidence.
- My experience in a similar job at _____ and my skill in _____ will be an asset to this job.

BEST ANSWER

✓

In a similar job, I always reached the goals set for me. My experience in _____ will allow me to master this area very quickly.

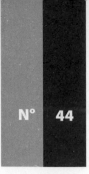

Your evaluation in your last job was only average. Can you explain that?

✓ Choose the Best Answer

- ❑ I'd like to know, too. My boss never explained why. Yet I managed to do everything I set out to do. I think there was some kind of jealousy involved.
- ❑ I was in the midst of a difficult family situation at the time, and this indeed affected my productivity. The situation is now perfectly under control.
- ❑ My boss was too strict!
- ❑ My boss and I didn't always see eye to eye.
- ❑ I didn't think it was average. Everything seemed okay to me.

? What They Really Want to Know

- ■ Do you recognize your weaknesses?
- ■ What problems might have been going on at the time?
- ■ Do you involve yourself wholeheartedly in your work?

! Watch Out!

Don't:
- ■ Criticize your former boss and blame a bad/average review on him/her.
- ■ Suggest that you don't know what happened.
- ■ Defend yourself too forcefully.

Don't Say:
- ■ I was often sick.
- ■ The work didn't really interest me.
- ■ I didn't get along with my boss.
- ■ I'd rather not talk about it.
- ■ Yes, it wasn't great. I'll do better here.

 **Try This!**

Do: →

- Be precise about the circumstances of the evaluation and explain briefly without going into petty details.
- Talk about the strong points of the last job, in terms of skills and qualities.
- Turn the setback into a learning experience. Explain why it happened and why it won't happen again.

Say: 🗲

- I went through a bad spell following a death in the family. Everything's all right now.
- We've had a reduction in personnel, and I have often had to work under pressure with long hours and I became exhausted.
- What is it you would like to know? I am not certain what part of my evaluation you are referring to.

BEST ANSWER ✓

I was in the midst of a difficult family situation at the time, and this indeed affected my productivity. The situation is now perfectly under control.

5

Problem Solving and Decision Making

I T'S HARD FOR AN INTERVIEWER to make an accurate evaluation of a candidate without finding out about their problem-solving and decision-making skills. Since practically every job has its share of problems, interviewers need to get a sense of a candidate's reaction to, and strategy for, solving them. Decisions have to be made, and sometimes on a daily basis. If candidates can't talk about how they handle problems and how they make decisions to solve those problems, an interviewer won't have the information they need in order to decide whom to hire.

Problem solving involves critical and strategic thinking. Problems have to be defined and then solved. Not everyone approaches problem solving in the same way. Some people prefer to break into totally new ground—"going where no one has gone before"—these people thrive on new, sometimes ambiguous situations and challenges, and they seek out opportunities to problem solve. Other people prefer to improve on existing ideas, products, processes, or services, adding a new twist here, changing one dimension there, to make them better or expand their uses in new directions. These people like to organize, synthesize, refine, and enhance existing ideas and things, and in doing so they develop and shape them into a more complete, functional, or useful form or result. And, of course, there are those whose tendency is to avoid problems at all costs and just pretend they don't exist.

Just as people solve problems differently, people's decision-making strategies are different. Some people prefer to make quick decisions, relying on the information they have and trusting themselves to make the right decision. Others prefer to weigh all alternatives, taking time to measure every dimension of a problem. Some decide which of a number of variables to change, while others weigh the pros and cons of making any decision. Still others will look at a decision by considering all the different perspectives (emotional, intuitive, creative, or negative viewpoints). Others challenge underlying assumptions or use the trial-and-error method.

No method is always right or always wrong. Some are more effective in certain situations and under certain conditions. What is important for an interviewer to know is how your reasoning, methods, and strategies were used to solve problems and make decisions in specific instances.

Problem-solving and decision-making questions included here are:

- How would you go about making a decision not covered in our procedures manual?
- Tell me about a situation in which you had to make a very difficult or painful decision.
- Tell me about a situation where you had to work under pressure/ against the clock.
- Describe a complex situation/problem that you had to deal with.
- Let's say we have a problem with _____. How might you go about solving it?
- Tell me about an unpopular decision you had to make.
- In your opinion, what is the most difficult thing about being a manager?
- What kinds of things do you find hard to do? Why?
- What are the most difficult decisions you have had to make?

What the Interviewer Wants to Know About You

By asking questions about problem solving and decision making, the interviewer is trying to find out:

- What problems have you come up against? How were you able to deal with them?
- How do you go about solving a complex problem?
- How do you react to the unexpected?
- Can you make decisions quickly and come up with workable solutions for solving problems?
- Can you make hard decisions in the face of opposition?
- What decision-making process do you use to make tough choices?
- What kinds of situations require more time to decide or make you indecisive?
- What is your technique/strategy for making an important decision?
- Can you resolve conflicts between other people?
- Do you know how to assert yourself? Can you manage difficult people?
- Are you ready to fire someone?
- Will you be able to manage delicate situations/tasks we are going to ask of you?
- Do you know how to take initiative when it's appropriate?
- How well do you work under stress?
- Do you ask for help when you need it?

How to Answer

Questions about problem solving and decision making must be answered using examples from your past experience. You cannot simply say, "I know how to solve problems," or "I know how to make decisions," as an answer. You must show how you solve problems and what kind of problems you have faced in the past. You must show how you make decisions and why you have chosen the option you've chosen. Many of the questions in this section are formed in the behavioral style of interviewing (See Chapter 19, *Behavioral Interviewing*), where the interviewer will ask for an example of a time you faced a problem or had to make a decision. Write out examples to use, before the interview, so you will be prepared for these kinds of questions. Concentrate your answers on how your solved your problem rather than on the actual problem. Show what kind of techniques you use to resolve issues. Since many problems in the workplace have to do with other people, talk about how you have managed conflicts in the past. Show that you understand that strategic thinking is a process of learning and applying that learning to situations you face. If you are asked how you might solve a problem in the future, show how you will arrive at the answer based on how you have behaved in the past.

When you talk about decision making, show that you understand that, in order to make any decision, options must be reviewed and considered. Sometimes making a decision comes down to choosing from only two alternatives; many times it is much more involved than that. It can seem that making a decision is easy, and many times it is (should we go to the movie tonight or not?), but in our work life decisions can have huge consequences and influence everything that comes after the decision is made. So, many times making a decision is a complex action with substantial ramifications to a company or organization. Making a decision means moving between the alternatives of the characteristics we want our choice to fulfill and the possibilities we can choose among. The available alternatives influence the criteria we apply to them, and the criteria we establish influence the alternatives we will consider. Don't treat questions about problem solving or decision making as simple; these two processes involve highly sophisticated thinking.

Life is full of problems and obstacles—anyone who says different is selling something! Meeting problems head on and not letting them get the best of you is the real challenge. Show how your courage, commitment, and drive have allowed you to become the person you are today. Problem solved!

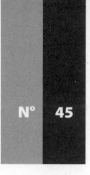

How would you go about making a decision not covered in our procedures manual?

✓ Choose the Best Answer

- ❏ I make up my mind and take action.
- ❏ I give it a lot of thought and, if I'm inspired, I will take initiative.
- ❏ I submit a proposal to my boss to create a new procedure so work can move forward quickly.
- ❏ I follow my instinct. I am rarely wrong.
- ❏ If it's not included in my list of duties, I don't do it. That's a good basic principle. Otherwise, nobody knows what's going on.

? What They Really Want to Know

- ▪ Do you accept hierarchy and not try to take over?
- ▪ Do you respect procedures?
- ▪ Do you know how to take initiative when it's appropriate?

! Watch Out!

Don't:

- ▪ Go beyond your duties without talking to your boss.
- ▪ Delegate the decision to a third person.
- ▪ Say you do this kind of thing all the time.
- ▪ Present the hierarchy with a "fait accompli."
- ▪ Show that it's not a problem for you.

Don't say:

- ▪ You have to go where the opportunities lie.
- ▪ You shouldn't let yourself get locked into procedures. If you do, nothing ever gets done.
- ▪ I like to improvise as I go along.
- ▪ I love to take initiative, so I have no problem acting when there is work to be done.

- I have to protect my professional free will and my creativity.
- I don't see why I shouldn't have decision-making powers.
- I don't think you should be too bureaucratic. It slows things down too much.
- Freedom of speech is a fundamental right. I say what I think should be done.

 Try This!

Do: →

- Describe how you weigh the risks carefully.
- Avoid taking a stand on hierarchical matters.
- Ask questions to verify what your role should be.
- Show that you take the time to phone your immediate boss and talk with him/her.
- Underline how you present alternatives.
- Give an example of how you have pointed out problems and offered solutions in the past.
- Use an example to show how you find out everything you can about a specific situation before taking any kind of action.

Say: 🙾

- Would my job description allow me to act on a problem of this nature?
- It has happened, after having met with my colleagues and managers I have acted.
- I have an analytical mind that helps me respond to this kind of situation (cite an example).
- I would defer such decisions to my boss.
- I would play for time to get my proposals approved.
- I understand the need for standard procedures; nevertheless, I would suggest ways we could evolve and plan for this kind of contingency in the future.
- I take the risk of informing the people involved.
- I would suggest integrating this point into our standard procedures manual.
- I would hope to talk it over with my colleagues and managers.

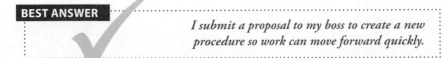

BEST ANSWER

I submit a proposal to my boss to create a new procedure so work can move forward quickly.

Tell me about a situation in which you had to make a very difficult or painful decision.

✓ Choose the Best Answer

- ☐ I once had to fire a colleague who was also a friend. I did it and then helped her with her job search process as best I could.
- ☐ I'd rather not talk about it, unless you insist. It's quite personal.
- ☐ Every time my boss was gone. Which means quite often.
- ☐ 15 years ago! I had to _____.
- ☐ I have a hard time remembering. I tend to get these things out of my mind as fast as possible.

? What They Really Want to Know

- How well do you manage painful tasks? Can you make hard decisions?
- How do you react in a stressful situation?
- What is the most painful thing you have ever had to do in your career?

! Watch Out!

Don't:
- Talk about personal or private affairs.
- Go into detail about your past.
- Play the victim and act like you resent having to do difficult things.
- Talk badly about your colleagues.
- Give the impression you don't want to take responsibility for a hard decision.

Don't say:
- I'm not good at making difficult decisions.
- I never took any initiative.
- No, I left all decisions up to top management.

Do:

- Ask for clarification if you need it.
- Describe how you handled this decision, and what your goal was.
- Always give positive examples that are related to work; this is not the time for personal stories.
- Underline how this decision provided a valuable learning opportunity.

Say:

- At the time of my transfer, I was given only one hour to find a competent person to replace me.
- I have always managed to make difficult decisions, but they do require serious reflection.
- Life is full of surprises! To avoid getting stuck, I just face up to them.

BEST ANSWER ✓

I once had to fire a colleague who was also a friend. I did it and then helped her with her job search process as best I could.

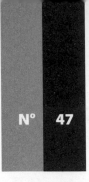

Tell me about a situation where you had to work under pressure/against the clock.

✓ Choose the Best Answer

- ❏ I can't take stress. It makes me botch things up. About a year ago it got so bad I had a nervous breakdown.
- ❏ I set my priorities and arrange my personal agenda so that I have more time in the evening or on the weekend to finish what I've been asked to do. As an example, I was once asked to finish a project of great importance to my boss within a very tight time frame.
- ❏ I like to do one thing after another in order so I don't get confused.
- ❏ I've never had to work under pressure.
- ❏ When I have a lot to do, I ask for help. Everything always turns out fine.

? What They Really Want to Know

- ▪ How well do you work under stress?
- ▪ Do you ask for help when you need it?
- ▪ Are you good at delegating?

! Watch Out!

Don't:

- ▪ Forget to cite an example from your past of how you work under pressure.
- ▪ Admit that you don't know how to delegate so you aren't good at time-sensitive projects.
- ▪ Say that you don't like to ask for help so you do everything yourself.
- ▪ Show that you get aggressive when you are stressed.
- ▪ Reveal that you left your last job because you couldn't take the stress.
- ▪ Suggest that you have never had to work under pressure.

Don't Say:

- ▪ I just need time to get my work done. If I am not rushed, I don't make mistakes.

- I am totally immune to stress. It is a part of everyday life.
- I tend to get sick during the stressful periods.
- Stress? Never heard of it!
- When stressed, I tend to screw up.
- Any kind of stress makes me lose my cool.
- I can't think of any time that happened.

Try This!

Do:

- Show you are aware that stress exists in any firm and that you can handle it.
- Explain how you go about delegating. Cite an example of how you have done this in the past.
- Show that stress is not something that bothers you but, instead, stimulates you. Give an example.
- Point out how, in a stressful situation, you look for solutions to alleviate the stress. Use an example from your past to show how you do this.
- Prove that you know how to set priorities. Use an example to demonstrate this.

Say:

- I have learned how to delegate and trust my team. In my last job, I had to _____ .
- I am used to setting priorities and handling stress. I do this by _____ .
- I actually find a little stress can be quite stimulating. For example, _____ .
- Stress stimulates my creativity by forcing me to _____ .
- It all depends on the cause of the pressure: does it come from an inadvertent lack of organization or from a chronic habit? When I am up against the clock, I like to _____ .

BEST ANSWER

I set my priorities and arrange my personal agenda so that I have more time in the evening or on the weekend to finish what I've been asked to do. As an example, I was once asked to finish a project of great importance to my boss within a very tight time frame.

Describe a complex situation/problem that you had to deal with.

✓ Choose the Best Answer

❑ Fortunately there's always been someone above me for this kind of situation.

❑ I've never really run up against this kind of problem. Thank heavens!

❑ I am constantly confronted with complex problems. I know how to deal with them.

❑ I'm a hard worker. Nothing scares me. When a decision is needed, I make it and carry on with my work.

❑ In my last job, I had to manage a project on my own that came up very quickly and had to be done in three days. To do it, I re-organized my commitments.

? What They Really Want to Know

▪ How do you go about solving a complex problem?

▪ What are you most proud of?

▪ What initiatives have you taken? Have you taken risks?

! Watch Out!

Don't:

▪ Mention a minor problem that has an obvious solution.

▪ Criticize your supervisors for not doing their job (causing the problem).

▪ Give the idea that you often encounter problems in your job.

▪ Show signs of exhaustion or appear to be dumfounded by the question.

▪ Answer in a way that suggests you do not know how or like to take risks.

Don't Say:

▪ I would have to refer to my file before I could answer that. I don't want to get the details wrong.

▪ I can't think of one in particular. I work hard at everything I do.

▪ I leave those kinds of problems to my supervisor.

- What do you mean by complex problem? Aren't all problems complex in the 21st century?
- Once I had to deal with an irate customer who yelled at me.

 Try This!

- Give examples from your professional experience that include specific details and the outcome(s).
- Mention a challenge you dealt with (alone or as part of a team), as well as the final resolution.
- Highlight your answer with real workplace example(s) from your past.

Say: 🙶

- In my professional life, I have had to solve _____ .
- I had to insure the follow-up of the decisions made during our weekly meetings. I did this thanks to a communication system I developed which _____ .
- The complexity of a problem was always directly proportional to the number of people involved in the project, so I used to meet with my department/team members in small groups so we could be more productive. For example, _____ .
- I was given a free hand to reorganize the service we provided and I did that by _____ .
- In order of importance, I would mention these three examples: _____ .

BEST ANSWER

✓ *In my last job, I had to manage a project on my own that came up very quickly and had to be done in three days. To do it, I _____ .*

Let's say we have a problem with_____. How might you go about solving it?

✓ Choose the Best Answer

- ❑ I don't like to get worked up over nothing, so I would ask around to see what should be done.
- ❑ I don't get mixed up in other people's business. That's a management principle that I always respect. So if the problem didn't concern me personally, I would steer clear of it.
- ❑ I would call a meeting of the parties involved and lay out the problem. After discussion, I believe enough information would be on the table to find the solution or some compromise that would solve the dilemma.
- ❑ I adhere to the wait-and-see policy. It always works. Some idea always comes out of it eventually.
- ❑ Some solution is certainly out there. I'm sure I would find it if given enough time.

? What They Really Want to Know

- ▪ How do you react to the unexpected?
- ▪ Can you make decisions quickly and come up with workable solutions for solving problems?
- ▪ What are your main character traits and your work style?

! Watch Out!

Don't:
- ▪ Ask for time to think about it.
- ▪ Say that without the necessary personnel and resources, you cannot resolve anything.
- ▪ Give an example of a past conflict where the problem wasn't solved by you.
- ▪ Express your regret that you don't know how to solve the problem he/she mentioned.

Don't Say:

- Just throw him out!
- I just don't know in this case. May I think about it?
- I have a hard time standing up for my ideas and convincing others to support them.
- I would call my boss and ask him/her.
- I would probably feel unsure about how to fix the problem since I would be new to the job, so I would ask a co-worker.

 Try This!

Do: →

- Think about the problem mentioned for a moment and suggest solutions and/or backup measures to avoid the worst.
- Suggest that you would ask the appropriate people to come fix the problem.
- If the problem they mention is of a technical nature, suggest the proper procedure or action to fix it.
- Offer two or three possible strategies that would address the problem.
- Be decisive in your response.

Say: 🗩

- It all depends on my role and duties in the firm.
- I would listen, observe, analyze, set goals, and then take action! For this problem that you mention, I would _____ .
- If the problem proved to be major, I would create a task force to study it and make recommendations on how we could move forward.
- I look for the reason the problem has occurred, and in that way I can find a quick solution. For example, you mentioned _____ .
- If that were part of my job description, I would take the appropriate steps, such as _____ .

BEST ANSWER

I would call a meeting of the parties involved and lay out the problem. After discussion, I believe enough information would be on the table to find the solution or some compromise that would solve the dilemma.

Tell me about an unpopular decision you had to make.

✓ Choose the Best Answer

- ❑ That's sort of the story of my life. I make them all the time.
- ❑ I had to put my mother in a nursing home.
- ❑ I did have to do that once but would rather not talk about it. It's personal and it is indiscreet to talk about it.
- ❑ Due to restructuring, I had to fire a colleague whom everyone, including myself, liked and appreciated.
- ❑ I've never made a decision that was unpopular.

? What They Really Want to Know

- ▪ Can you make hard decisions in the face of opposition?
- ▪ Are you ready to fire someone?
- ▪ What decision-making process do you use to make tough choices?

! Watch Out!

Don't:
- ▪ Go into too much detail.
- ▪ Blame the decision on others and not take responsibility for yourself.
- ▪ Use a personal example.

Don't Say:
- ▪ Deciding to come here for this interview today!
- ▪ I had to deal with a lot of family problems without much help.
- ▪ I hate taking orders, so I go my own way.
- ▪ I categorically refuse to make unpopular decisions.

Do:

- Give an example and explain how you dealt with the situation.
- Be concise. Tell what you learned.
- Show your ability to balance firmness and compassion.

Say:

- With good communication, even an unpopular decision will be accepted. (Give an example).
- I have never had to make an unpopular decision, as I believe in talking things over before it reaches this point.
- I always try to use a little psychology. For example, _____.
- I take manageable steps in figuring out the problem and the best solution and then I act.
- I look for positive outcomes, which can generally diffuse a tough situation.

BEST ANSWER

Due to restructuring, I had to fire a colleague whom everyone, including myself, liked and appreciated.

In your opinion, what is the most difficult thing about being a manager?

✓ Choose the Best Answer

- ❑ Reaching precise goals.
- ❑ Managing petty staff problems.
- ❑ Having irregular hours.
- ❑ Continually working under pressure and against the clock. Especially if one has to depend on inexperienced people to carry out the work.
- ❑ Having to lay off staff members. I have had to do that, and this is how I went about it: _____.

? What They Really Want to Know

- ■ Can you resolve conflicts between other people?
- ■ What problems have you come up against? How were you able to deal with them?
- ■ Do you know how to assert yourself? Can you manage difficult people?

! Watch Out!

Don't:

- ■ Admit that there were/are a lot of problems at your last/current job.
- ■ Mention a problem without offering a possible/positive solution.
- ■ Suggest that you treat people unjustly or neglect to give them recognition.
- ■ Take sides so that some people feel slighted.
- ■ Pretend that everything is fine and nothing is difficult about being a manager.

Don't Say:

- ■ Almost everything is difficult.
- ■ I don't envy managers. I've never been one but see how hard it is.
- ■ I haven't always done the right thing in these kinds of situations.
- ■ Managing people is always difficult because no one is ever honest about their feelings.

Do:

- Mention three major problems and how they can be handled.
- Give concrete examples you have experienced and what the outcomes were.
- Show that you treat everyone fairly.
- Give an example of how you trust your staff.
- Put enthusiasm into problem solving. Mention how you go about solving a problem.

Say:

- It's difficult for a manager when they have to make unpopular decisions. But I have found that open and honest communication about what is going to happen can lessen the pain for those involved.
- It is never easy to fire someone. It takes diplomacy and compassion.
- I find being a manager means working alone a great deal of the time, as it is not easy to confide in everyone what strategies and plans are necessary all the time.

BEST ANSWER

Having to lay off staff members. I have had to do that, and this is how I went about it: _____.

What kinds of things do you find hard to do? Why?

✓ Choose the Best Answer

- ❏ Being on time for appointments. It must be the south-of-the-border in me. I tend to think that business can always wait.
- ❏ I hate administrative stuff. It bores me to death to have to fill out paperwork and file. I am much better at making decisions.
- ❏ I find it very hard to work with people who are lazy. I resent that they are not willing to carry their part of the work and expect others to pick up their slack. Here is how I managed to deal with a situation like that once: _____.
- ❏ Getting up in the morning. I'm not a morning person.
- ❏ Nothing. I'm pretty good at doing most everything.

? What They Really Want to Know

- ▪ Are you aware of your limits?
- ▪ What are your weak points?
- ▪ Will you be able to manage delicate situations/tasks we ask of you?

! Watch Out!

Don't:
- ▪ Act defensive like it is a fault if you find something hard to do.
- ▪ Mention the wrong qualities.
- ▪ Give too many examples. One or two are enough.
- ▪ List your shortcomings or what you don't know how to do.

Don't Say:
- ▪ I don't know what to tell you.
- ▪ I find it hard to _____ . In fact, I have never been able to face it.
- ▪ Why are you asking me this question?
- ▪ Nothing is difficult when you have time to prepare for it.

Do: →

- Use an example that has nothing to do with the job description.
- Describe how you have managed difficult things before. Use a concrete example. Show why you found the situation problematic.
- Take some time to think about this one in advance. Everyone finds something difficult. Frame your answer to show how you dealt with the problem.
- Choose some difficulty/problem in your extra-professional activities.

Say: 🗝

- For me a difficulty is a challenge! Let me tell you about the last time I had to deal with a delicate situation: _____.
- Problems are challenges and I love a good challenge. I once had to _____ .
- The most recent example I can give you is _____ .
- According to the job description, I don't see any major problems for me.
- I'll just mention a couple of things I find difficult to do and how I have so far managed to deal with them: _____ .
- Everyone finds some things more difficult to do than others. For myself, I have found it hard to do _____, and this is what I have done to handle it: _____ .

BEST ANSWER ···

✓ *I find it very hard to work with people who are lazy. I resent that they are not willing to carry their part of the work and expect others to pick up their slack. Here is how I managed to deal with a situation like that once: _____ .*

What are the most difficult decisions you have had to make?

✓ Choose the Best Answer

- ❏ As I don't like conflict, I avoid making decisions that involve others.
- ❏ Decisions with obvious economic implications.
- ❏ All of them and none of them. Decisions are always difficult to make, and they always cause me a certain amount of stress. But I can make them when I have to.
- ❏ The only way I can give you a valid answer is if you tell me what decision-making responsibilities the position requires and then I can correlate my answer to the specific concerns you might have.
- ❏ I was once asked to fire someone. I handled that by _____ .

? What They Really Want to Know

- What kinds of situations require more time to decide or make you indecisive?
- Are you willing to risk making a difficult decision?
- What is your technique/strategy for making an important decision?

! Watch Out!

Don't:

- Admit that you have never really had to make a decision of any consequence.
- Give example after example with the hope it will prove your sincerity.
- Offer examples that make you look egocentric or too ambitious.
- Use an example where the negative consequences of the action might be checked.
- Indicate that decision making in general is difficult for you.
- Give the impression that you avoid making decisions.
- Suggest that you avoided responsibility under the pretext that the job did not require any responsibility for making difficult decisions.

Don't Say:

- Ever since I was a child, everyone has made decisions for me. First it was my mother, and now my wife.

- I have no problem making decisions, whatever they may be.
- I've never really been asked to make decisions in my past jobs.
- I don't think making a decision is particularly difficult.
- My boss made all the important decisions.
- It's difficult when I have to reprimand a subordinate/colleague.
- Any decision deserves consideration.

Try This!

Do:

- Give examples of decisions you have made, and show that you considered the consequences. Show the resolution of the problem.
- Explain your decision-making process using an example.
- Explain that you know how to gather opinions of the people around you and use them to help make decisions.
- List the people who have benefited from important decisions you have made.
- Mention the functions of colleagues who have benefited from your decisions.
- Show that you know how to make a decision when you must. Give an example.
- Ask the interviewer about the degree of decision making the job involves.
- Bring up a few situations in which the decision produced a quantifiable outcome.

Say:

- Generally, major decisions are made in agreement with all those who are involved.
- It's hard to have to incriminate or decide to get rid of a colleague. For example, _____ .
- I ask for others' opinions, without letting them decide for me, and then I make the final decision when I have all the facts. As an example, my team _____ .
- I am particularly careful about gathering all the information possible before making difficult decisions. For example, _____ .
- When a decision is hard to make, I take the time to think deeply about all the ramifications of it. I can cite this as an example: when I had to _____ .
- For example, decisions concerning collaboration among colleagues need to be taken seriously with respect to the firm's policy.

BEST ANSWER

The only way I can give you a valid answer is if you tell me what decision-making responsibilities the position requires and then I can correlate my answer to the specific concerns you might have.

6

Education and Learning

I T IS IMPORTANT FOR EMPLOYERS to find out what, if any, kind of formal
education or training a candidate might have. If a job calls for a very specific
kind of degree or training, the interviewer will need to ask questions about that
to make certain the candidate comes with the necessary credentials in hand.

But what's generally even more important than the degree(s) a person might
hold is their interest in trying to improve as a lifelong goal. So, what most
interviewers are probing for when they ask about your education or training
is to find out how you best learn and what you are interested in learning, if
anything. A candidate who shows a lifelong pattern of continuously striving
to learn new things and keep current with world events and new trends and
technologies is going to be more impressive than the candidate who complains
they don't have time for any outside learning.

Interviewers want to know how what you have studied/learned is directly
related to the job in question. They will want to know the value of your educational efforts to see if you are prepared with the needed knowledge to do the
job right. It's helpful for an interviewer to know that they don't have to start
you off at the beginning—that you can hit the ground running. However, not
having a specific degree or training program under your belt will not always

hold you back from getting a job you want if you can demonstrate how you have picked up the knowledge you need to do the job well in less traditional ways. Not having a degree is not the problem in many cases; it's not having taken steps to get what you need in other ways that shows the interviewer who you really are.

A candidate should be able to articulate their preferred learning style. If you are a person who learns best by doing, say so. If you learn best by reading and digesting information, say so. If you learn best by attending lectures and classes, say so. There is no real right or wrong answer to this kind of query as long as you demonstrate that you are committed to improving yourself.

Education and learning questions included here are:

- I see you have done a course on _____. What did you think of it?
- Do you participate in any type of continuing education/learning?
- Why did you choose the institute/school/college you attended?
- What have you learned during these last 12 months?
- What did you learn during your studies that will be useful in this job?
- What did you most enjoy studying?
- What kind of learner are you?
- What is your educational background?
- How do you learn best?
- What kind of continuing education/learning courses have you found particularly useful in the past three years?
- How do your studies relate to this job? What is the link?

What the Interviewer Wants to Know About You

By asking questions about your education/training, the interviewer is trying to find out:

- Do you like learning and self-improvement?
- Are you open to continuing learning opportunities?

- Do you like to improve yourself / brush up on your skills?
- Are you interested in continuing education and learning? Are you dying to learn new things?
- Are you conscientious about keeping up on new techniques/methods/products in your field?
- Do you like to challenge your ideas?
- Are you curious-minded? Do you like to keep learning?
- Are you open to training?
- In what way is your background useful for us?
- What have you learned in theory that you can put into practice?
- Is your knowledge up to date?
- Is your education/experience/training relevant to this job?
- Have you specialized in any specific areas?
- Can you learn things you don't like?
- Are you visual or auditory?
- Do you read directions or do you jump right in?
- Do you respond best to lectures/books, or do you learn best by doing?
- Did you make a commitment to go to college or another postsecondary institution?

How to Answer

Before attending an interview, be sure to make a list of all the degrees and educational credentials you have, and include training courses you have taken. Write down the dates, subjects covered, and one or two of the major things you learned. Study this list so you will be able to easily answer any questions asked about your educational background. Make sure you can link how your studies relate to the job. Use examples of how you are able to translate theory into practical use, especially in the context of the job. If you received special training for skills needed in this job, be sure to point them out.

Talk about the value of learning/continuing education as a lifelong goal. Show that you are a person with curiosity about life and the world around you. Talk about the things you really like to learn and how this passion translates into action in your life. Talk about your learning style. Demonstrate with examples how you have learned something in the past.

Questions about your education aren't just about a degree (although it never hurts to demonstrate that you have the perseverance needed to get a degree). They are about your basic philosophy of life and your commitment to self-improvement.

I see you have done a course on____ . What did you think of it?

✓ Choose the Best Answer

- ❑ It was fine.
- ❑ I did it just to keep busy. I didn't learn much.
- ❑ It was a course my former boss signed me up for. He thought it might help, but I can't say it did much for me.
- ❑ The course was very useful to me for doing tables and monthly statistics. I'll be able to create a new presentation on the results of ____ .
- ❑ It was all right, but I haven't finished the training yet. It's partly my fault, but the objectives were not very clear.

? What They Really Want to Know

- ◢ Have you specialized in any specific areas?
- ■ Are you open to training and continuing education?
- ■ Will we be able to use your skills?

! Watch Out!

Don't:

- ■ Criticize the content, the trainer, or the participants.
- ■ Describe the course as a fill-in activity with no benefit for the next job.
- ■ Develop your answer saying the course was boring.
- ■ Admit that you didn't get much out of the course.
- ■ Remain tongue-tied or claim not to know if you benefited from it.
- ■ Forget to present achievements that demonstrate the course's worth.
- ■ Point out that the level of the course did not correspond with your needs.
- ■ Talk about the course as an obligation or a constraint.
- ■ Stress the negative aspects of the course.

Don't Say:

- ■ This course did not offer me what I was expecting.
- ■ It was not really useful.
- ■ I did it just to do it.

- I didn't get much out of it. I was already familiar with the subject.
- The course content was not very interesting.
- The teachers were not very competent.
- I was enrolled in that course, but I still don't understand why I needed it.
- It was okay. The unemployment office paid for the courses.
- All employees had to do those courses.

Try This!

Do: →

- Have strong arguments for how and why you chose this type of course.
- Find out if there are any courses related to the new position.
- Be enthusiastic. Smile.
- Point out the links between the course and the position.
- Highlight any new responsibilities you assumed because you took the course.
- Show how you could use what you learned in the course in the new job.
- Present the course as a reward and a privilege.
- Prove, using concrete evidence, the positive aspects of your background experience/education/training.

Say: 🙶

- It offered me a great deal on both the professional and personal level.
- Those very useful courses will benefit you as well as me.
- I appreciated the training. Do you have a continuing education program?
- The subject matter was basic but it offered a new way to look at old concepts.
- I use what I learned in the course on a regular basis. For example, ____ .
- I see these courses as relevant to the position you are offering. What do you think?
- The learning from these courses has allowed me to ____.
- After these courses I was promoted to a supervisory position.
- I was selected to do these courses. There were three of us invited to undergo the training in this area.
- Am I the only candidate with this specialty?

BEST ANSWER

The course was very useful to me for doing tables and monthly statistics. I'll be able to create a new presentation on the results of ____ .

Do you participate in any type of continuing education/learning?

✓ Choose the Best Answer

- ☐ Due to my lack of education/training, I did a training course in _____.
- ☐ My education/training covers the job's requirements by far.
- ☐ I didn't have time to complete my education, as I had to work, and I don't have time to take courses now.
- ☐ My experience and basic knowledge are sufficient. I don't need any more courses.
- ☐ I'm a self-learner and spend my free time learning something new. It's what I like to do. Right now I am studying _____ .

? What They Really Want to Know

- ■ Are you conscientious about keeping up on new techniques/methods/products in your field?
- ■ Do you ever challenge your own beliefs or question yourself? Are you interested in personal development and professional development?
- ■ Are you committed to lifelong learning?

! Watch Out!

Don't:

- ■ Draw attention to any of your degrees/certificates that might put off the interviewer.
- ■ Put too much importance on certificates, rather than on the skills, experience, and knowledge that allowed you to get those certificates.
- ■ Go on and on about courses or training that is not useful or necessary for the job in question.
- ■ Suggest that you don't do any form of continuing learning/education.

Don't Say:

- ■ I completed my studies when I was 22. I've been working ever since.
- ■ I was a good student and still keep collecting degrees/certificates.

- I have never done any continuous learning or night courses. I just don't have time.
- I think I am competent for the job since I have a degree from the University of _____.
- Yes. I am always going to personal development seminars.

Try This!

Do:

- Back up your degrees or certificates with concrete experience from your courses, or as a result of training you received. Show how it applies to the job in question.
- List any training directly useful for the job. Tell what you learned that can be applied.
- Show that you have managed to keep yourself up to date and ahead of the game.
- Mention how you try to better yourself by learning new things.

Say:

- Thanks to an intensive course on _____, I was able to manage a team of 15 people and we met our goals on time.
- My boss gave me the green light for my continuous learning plan which included _____.
- I have laid out a five-year self-learning plan for myself. It includes ____ .
- The course in ____ allowed me to see how I fit in and how to become more effective at my work.

BEST ANSWER ✓

I'm a self-learner and spend my free time learning something new. It's what I like to do. Right now I am studying ____ .

Why did you choose the institute/school/college you attended?

✓ Choose the Best Answer

- ❏ I didn't choose it. My career counselor did.
- ❏ I went where my friends went. Besides, I live right nearby. And, above all, it meant I could get out of the house and have my independence.
- ❏ I didn't know what to do, so I followed my parents' advice. After all, they're the ones who were paying. And then it was the least costly and, above all, the only one where I was accepted.
- ❏ I choose it because of the excellent teachers/professors and its reputation in the subjects I wanted to study.
- ❏ They told us it was the most reputable school, but I didn't think it was particularly special.

? What They Really Want to Know

- ▪ Do you like learning and self-improvement?
- ▪ Are you ready to get yourself up to date?
- ▪ Do you make decisions based on your own criteria or that of others?

! Watch Out!

Don't:

- ▪ Give the impression you made a haphazard/impulsive choice.
- ▪ Indicate that it made little difference to you what school you attended.
- ▪ Suggest your choice was forced by others and out of your control.
- ▪ State that you did not pay for any of your education.

Don't Say:

- ▪ It's the only school that accepted me.
- ▪ It was the least expensive.
- ▪ I had no choice. I had to get out of the house.

- The atmosphere was better than in other schools.
- The other schools I looked at had bad reputations.
- The hours were cool. Not too early!
- Dad decided it was the best school for me.
- It was close to me and I liked their football team.

Try This!

Do:

- Talk about the quality of the teachers and the teaching.
- Demonstrate that you chose it because the level of teaching was known to be extremely high.
- Highlight the diversity of the different courses you took.
- Highlight the cultural attractions of the (geographical) area and the professional competence of the institution.

Say:

- It's the only school that specializes in this field.
- It is an excellent school that opens doors to the world of industry.
- This school allowed me to major in _____ , as well as to do a MA in the same field.
- I made my choice after sitting in on some open courses in several colleges/universities and comparing the instructors, information given, textbooks, and so forth.
- I chose this institution because of several specific attractions in addition to its program. These included _____ .
- The exchange program with _____ University was one of the advantages I was able to benefit from by attending.

BEST ANSWER

I chose it because of the excellent teachers/professors and its reputation in the subjects I wanted to study.

What have you learned during these last 12 months?

✓ Choose the Best Answer

- ❏ After working for this firm for eight years, there was little left for me to learn in my position.
- ❏ During these last 12 months I have improved my knowledge of_____. I did a course on_____, which will benefit your company by _____ .
- ❏ A lot.
- ❏ I have learned how to fill up my days, as it's been a year since my last job.
- ❏ Not much. Nothing in particular that stands out.

? What They Really Want to Know

- Do you like to challenge your ideas?
- Are you curious-minded? Do you like to keep learning?
- How are you at managing your personal development?

! Watch Out!

Don't:

- Criticize new things.
- Fail to make eye contact with the interviewer.
- Give the impression that there is no skill you need to improve on or area of interest that appeals to you.
- Act surprised and answer that you haven't had time because you are unemployed.
- Suggest that learning only takes place in a school setting and is not something that you are involved in all the time.

Don't Say:

- I haven't had a chance to use what I learned.
- I haven't learned anything in particular.
- I haven't done anything. I'm unemployed.

- I haven't given it any thought.
- I didn't take any classes this past year so I haven't learned much.

Try This!

Do:

- Describe what you have accomplished in concrete terms.
- Underline the aspects of what you've done/learned the last year that are pertinent to the job.
- Show articles/evaluations of any extra-professional accomplishments.
- Point out the positive aspects of having time to learn new things.
- Show how learning is an activity that never ceases.
- Talk about how the Internet has allowed you to study something new in your spare time.

Say:

- I have taken a great interest in the top 100 nonprofit organizations in our state and have visited the websites of all of them to read their mission statements. I am particularly impressed by _____ .
- I took an evening course on writing and have produced two papers.
  May I show you one?
- I have enrolled in a new exercise program that combines yoga principles, martial arts, and aerobic training so I can keep in shape. I have also learned through this course the value of combining different disciplines in one program. This can be applied to the job by _____ .

BEST ANSWER

During these last 12 months I have improved my knowledge of _____ . I did a course on _____ , which will benefit your company by _____ .

What did you learn during your studies that will be useful in this job?

✓ Choose the Best Answer

- ❑ Many things.
- ❑ I don't understand your question. Could you reword it or else let me know what it has to do with me getting this job?
- ❑ Besides the subjects themselves, three main things: how to deal with stress, how to organize, and how to work on a team.
- ❑ Very little, as I studied music.
- ❑ Nothing at all.

? What They Really Want to Know

- ▪ In what way is your background useful for us?
- ▪ What have you learned in theory that you can put into practice?
- ▪ Which of your qualities and talents would be useful for this job?

! Watch Out!

Don't:
- ▪ Doubt yourself by thinking that what you have learned in school/courses won't be useful in your job.
- ▪ Focus on your studies to the detriment of your experience.
- ▪ Flatter yourself by saying you went to an Ivy League school or talk about multiple degrees.
- ▪ Get lost in details and go on too long.

Don't Say:
- ▪ I've forgotten everything I learned in college.
- ▪ I don't have any background in this area.
- ▪ I don't know; probably not much since my degree was in another field.
- ▪ I know my education is lacking. I didn't attend college.

- School is useless. I think on-the-job experience tells the real truth about someone's abilities.
- My background has nothing to do with the position.
- My studies are not related to your area of activity.
- I have two master's degrees in ___ and ___, and I think they qualify me for this job.

Try This!

Do: →

- Describe your education and apprenticeship path. Include information on internships if applicable.
- Give pertinent information that matches the job's criteria.
- Show the link between your theoretical learning and practice in the real world.
- Indicate a common denominator between the two areas (studies and work).
- Talk about courses/studies that can be specifically useful in this job.

Say: 🙿

- I learned to be very systematic by taking _____ .
- I now have the knowledge and the know-how necessary for this job. For example, my studies of _____ .
- My studies prepared me for this job.
- My experience corresponds to the post offered by _____ .

BEST ANSWER

Besides the subjects themselves, three main things: how to deal with stress, how to organize, and how to work on a team.

What did you most enjoy studying?

✓ *Choose the Best Answer*

❏ All the subjects interested me. I always like those that help me grow professionally by teaching me new concepts and new ways of looking at problems to find solutions. I particularly like _____ .

❏ It's not possible to be an expert in everything, and I most enjoy learning on television. I like the Discovery Channel.

❏ It depends on the teacher, but I've preferred working to studying ever since I was a kid.

❏ I'm a sort of generalist and pretty much like all subjects.

❏ A little bit of everything, but I really don't remember.

? *What They Really Want to Know*

■ Do you have a passion?

■ Are you open to continuing education opportunities?

■ Can you learn things you don't like or aren't interested in?

! *Watch Out!*

Don't:

■ Advertise your lack of general culture.

■ Be vague, hesitant, or noncommittal about what you like to study.

■ Emphasize your difficulties rather than your successes.

■ Avoid the question by giving too general an answer.

■ Let your lack of interest for new subjects show.

■ Show a certain weariness or little enthusiasm about your studies.

■ Bring up the school name rather than what you have learned.

■ Talk about your scholastic failures.

■ Belittle yourself if you have no higher education.

Don't Say:

■ I was a real dunce at school!

■ It's been too long ago for me to remember what left an impression on me.

- I changed directions all the time without ever finding my calling.
- I liked studying everything.
- Speaking of studying, I hope you don't require too much continuing education. I don't appreciate some young kid telling me what I need to study.
- My teachers were incompetent, so I never really developed a love of studying.
- I never liked studying.

Try This!

Do: →

- Bring up tangible results from your course of study.
- Use examples of how you have applied techniques you learned as a student.
- Show that you had a facility for learning and a desire to keep at it.
- Describe your studies as a period that allowed you to stretch yourself beyond your limits.
- Mention your thesis or any publications you've written.
- Show how you ended up doing well in a subject you found difficult and what made the difference for you.

Say: ⟩⟩

- Every day I study new things—in my work as well as in my leisure activities.
- Studying has provided me with useful knowledge and know-how for a lifetime.
- I always liked learning, and this kept me interested in continuing education.
- I learned how to structure my work in order to get results.
- Learning about life is never over, and each day brings us new experiences and new knowledge if we are open to take it in.
- The ideal job allows you to learn new things while you are working.
- I still enjoy learning that allows me to build up my knowledge. For example, I recently took a course on ____ .
- I like to study human behavior. I see the parallels between job fulfillment and successful family relationships, and feel that striving to find the right job offers much more than just a paycheck.

BEST ANSWER

All the subjects interested me. I always like those that help me grow professionally by teaching me new concepts and new ways of looking at problems to find solutions. I particularly liked ____ .

What kind of learner are you?

✓ *Choose the Best Answer*

- ❏ I understand quickly as long as the person explains clearly what he wants.
- ❏ I have no idea!
- ❏ I am more or less visual and practical. I like to learn.
- ❏ When I don't know what to do, I call a friend or colleague.
- ❏ Don't worry. I'm fast. Everything comes easily to me.

? *What They Really Want to Know*

- ▪ Do you like to improve yourself or brush up on your skills?
- ▪ Are you visual or auditory?
- ▪ Do you read directions or do you jump right in?

! *Watch Out!*

Don't:

- ▪ Shrug your shoulders, as if to say, "I don't know."
- ▪ Boast that you can learn anything.
- ▪ Say that you learn best by watching others, or suggest that others dictate how you learn.
- ▪ Underestimate the importance of your answer.

Don't Say:

- ▪ It depends on the circumstances, but I'm good at memorizing.
- ▪ I don't like learning if it takes too long. I'm all for "fast learning."
- ▪ I've got my own method that works for me. I'd rather not talk about it. It's hard to explain.

Do:

- Give an example of something you learned quickly and explain how you did it.
- List the practical applications of what you have learned in theory.
- Say that you look for all possible solutions that could be considered and that you consult your boss.
- Be ready to show documents or other proof that you have brought with you about where you have learned different things.

Say:

- When someone shows me how to do something new, I always take notes.
- When someone shows me how to do something new, I always check right away to see if I can do it and can do it right.
- I am both auditory and visual, so I have better recall than most people.
- Perseverance and repetition. This is how I learn so it stays with me.

BEST ANSWER

I am more or less visual and practical. I like to learn.

What is your educational background?

✓ Choose the Best Answer

- ❑ I have done lots of training courses, but none directly related to this job.
- ❑ I went into the field my father wanted me to. I've never worked in it, though, because I don't like that kind of work. Besides, I have to admit, my studies were always on and off.
- ❑ Continuing education/training has not been that important to me. I'd rather work.
- ❑ In addition to my basic college education in _____ , I have done several specific courses in relation to my various jobs. Last year I studied _____ .
- ❑ I have a good educational background with a degree in _____ .

? What They Really Want to Know

- ▪ Do you make education a priority in your life?
- ▪ Are you interested in continuing education and learning? Are you dying to learn new things?
- ▪ Did you take time to go to college?

! Watch Out!

Don't:

- ▪ Identify only the training that corresponds to the job description.
- ▪ List all the courses you intend to do in the next five years.
- ▪ Show off your diplomas as if that were enough.
- ▪ Remain tongue-tied, especially if you didn't attend college.
- ▪ Rate yourself merely on experience.
- ▪ Apologize if you didn't go to college.

Don't Say:

- ▪ I've always worked a lot and haven't had much time to take courses or undergo training.

- I spent a long time studying, and that should suffice to prove I'd be good at this job.
- I've learned everything on the job.
- My resume tells the story. I have several degrees.

Try This!

Do:

- Look ahead by asking if they provide/encourage training.
- Outline very briefly the schools you attended and the subject of your degrees.
- Give some positive feedback from your last course.
- Let it be known that you have diversified your skills by acquiring new tools through learning.
- Show that your personal growth is compatible with professional demands.
- Show how you have compensated for learning if you didn't attend college.

Say:

- I am open to continuous learning. I would like to take a course on _____ .
- My night courses are compatible with my work. I am studying _____ .
- I read all kinds of things so that I am always learning. Last week I read an article on _____ .
- I attended the University of _____ and got my degree in _____. Since that time I have also attended classes/courses in _____ .
- I learn from newspapers and magazines, networking, friends, and finding out what's new. I use the Internet as a tool to help me research areas of interest.

BEST ANSWER

In addition to my basic college education in _____ , I have done several specific courses in relation to my various jobs. Last year I studied _____ .

How do you learn best?

✓ Choose the Best Answer

- ❏ I learned everything I know at school. Now I think I have finished learning.
- ❏ I do what I'm told. And I learn what I'm asked to learn.
- ❏ I've never really thought about it. But I always figure things out.
- ❏ I'm paid to carry out orders, not to learn.
- ❏ I always do things in three steps: I think about it, I do it, and then I see how I could do it better. That's how I learn.

? What They Really Want to Know

- ▪ Are you autonomous? Ambitious?
- ▪ What kind of a learner are you? Do you respond best to lectures/books, or do you learn best by doing?
- ▪ Do you know how to question what you learn, to see the greater applications?

! Watch Out!

Don't:

- ▪ List all your diplomas.
- ▪ Explain that it depends on what you need to learn.
- ▪ Give the impression that you don't have any learning style.
- ▪ Say that you never liked school.
- ▪ Brag that you are a quick study and don't need help from others to learn.

Don't Say:

- ▪ If we look at my results, my methods work well.
- ▪ I used to follow my professors' instructions/advice to the letter.
- ▪ I would study at every opportunity.
- ▪ I read novels all the time.

Do: →

- Give examples that bring out positive elements of your personality [team spirit, initiative, etc.].
- Explain how your results prove the effectiveness of your learning style.
- Show that you are a self-learner, with specific examples of areas of study you have undertaken for yourself (not because it was required of you).

Say: „

- I adopted a very professional time frame for my studies.
- I developed several different learning techniques. I learn best by _____ in this circumstance, and best by _____ in that circumstance.
- I observe, I listen, I read, and then I put into practice what I've learned. That's what works for me.
- I always planned my schedule so that I could concentrate on my studies as much as on my work. I like to read everything I can find about a subject.
- My learning technique involves creativity, logic, and memorization.
- I like to read manuals and then attempt to do the work. I find if I have clear instructions, I can do most things.

BEST ANSWER ✓

I always do things in three steps: I think about it, I do it, and then I see how I could do it better. That's how I learn.

What kind of continuing education/learning courses have you found particularly useful in the past three years?

✓ Choose the Best Answer

- ❑ None. I haven't done any training lately.
- ❑ I learn things on the job.
- ❑ I don't think training can replace practice.
- ❑ A training course on _____ , and what I got out of it was _____ , which will benefit you by _____ .
- ❑ Training has not been one of my priorities during these last three years. I've been too busy with my family.

? What They Really Want to Know

- ▪ Do you believe in continuous learning? Do you make it a priority to advance your knowledge base?
- ▪ Are you ambitious?
- ▪ Is your knowledge up to date?

! Watch Out!

Don't:
- ▪ Ask what kind of training they finance.
- ▪ Carry on with examples of courses you have not appreciated.
- ▪ Give the impression you don't need any more training.
- ▪ Let it be known that you haven't done any courses/had any training since your college years.
- ▪ Show that you are reticent to do any ongoing training.
- ▪ Refuse any training offered to you.
- ▪ Try to prove that ongoing training doesn't serve any purpose.

Don't Say:
- ▪ I had to take a course in _____ .
- ▪ I've never undergone training, but hope to have the opportunity in this job.

- I have not undergone any training. I pursued serious academic studies, which should certainly be enough.
- I don't like taking courses at night, because I am so tired from the day.

Try This!

Do:

- Mention two or three courses that you appreciated and why.
- Show that you keep up professionally through the Internet or specialty journals/magazines.
- Demonstrate one of your accomplishments (by briefly using a foreign language, for example).
- Point out that you have undergone training in relation to your job/area of work, and state the most important thing you learned from the training.
- Take a few certificates for the courses mentioned out of your briefcase/portfolio to show them.

Say:

- I am very determined to get ahead in my field. This is why I did these courses.
- Adapting to continuous learning is like adapting to professional work. It takes commitment and a real desire to want to do better for yourself and others.
- My courses in communication taught me how to approach people, which has resulted in a whole network of acquaintances.

BEST ANSWER

A training course on _____, and what I got out of it was_____, which will benefit you by _____ .

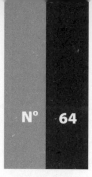
How do your studies relate to this job? What is the link?

✓ Choose the Best Answer

- ❑ My strong points for this job are the experience I have acquired as well as recent refresher courses I have completed.
- ❑ It's not easy to say, as I don't yet know exactly what the job entails.
- ❑ I am totally prepared, I hope. I never want to go back to school.
- ❑ It's true, there's not much of a link. But the job really attracts me.
- ❑ Perfectly, as I got my degree in a subject that corresponds exactly with the line of work the job entails.

? What They Really Want to Know

- ■ Is your education/experience/training relevant to this job?
- ■ Are you the person for the job?
- ■ Do you know how to marry what you have learned with what you do?

! Watch Out!

Don't:

- ■ Try to impress the interviewer with all your degrees. Don't mention too many degrees.
- ■ Criticize the subjects taught at your school/college/classes.
- ■ Imagine that the recruiter is more qualified than you or has more degrees.
- ■ Misunderstand the requirements of the job and talk about studies that do not relate.
- ■ Talk about other things that have nothing to do with the job.
- ■ Apologize if you do not have a degree.

Don't Say:

- ■ I have no knowledge in this area.
- ■ I never went to school as I had to begin working immediately.
- ■ I can't see any connection.

- I don't know.
- My studies have nothing to with this job, as I got my degree in _____.

Do:

- Talk about the know-how you will bring to the firm.
- Look for links or bridges between your studies and the job requirements.
- Express your wish for orientation to help you get the hang of things and be productive as soon as possible.
- Take advantage of the occasion to suggest completing or complementing your qualifications with in-house training.
- Propose a new training course that could be offered in-house.
- Make it clear that the courses you have taken were in line with this kind of work.

Say:

- It's thanks to my studies and my professional experience that I would be able to assume the responsibilities of this position.
- I like studying, but I like putting what I have learned into practice even more!
- I enjoyed studying this subject and that is precisely why I wanted to meet you.
- My studies in this area were only a springboard for the job you are offering.
- My studies have provided me with a solid basis for adapting to your field of work. For example, _____ .

BEST ANSWER ✓

> *My strong points for this job are the experience I have acquired, as well as recent refresher courses I have completed.*

7

Work Habits

I NTERVIEWERS MUST GET A SENSE of the work habits/style of candidates they talk with to know if they possess the required behaviors that are needed to execute the tasks of the position and to discern if they will fit into the company. These questions often deal with issues of change in the work environment or job requirements, stress, how you seek help when you need it, what you have learned from past jobs, how you deal with routine or repetitive work, and how you interact with people and within a team, particularly as it relates to leadership issues, such as ability to lead, inspire others, delegate, and supervise.

Work habits questions included here are:

- Did you ever change the nature and/or requirements of your job? How did you go about it?
- How good are you at planning when you are heavily involved in a major project/long-term assignment?
- Describe a situation where your team became demoralized. What was your role?

- What have you learned from your previous jobs?
- Describe a time when you had to make a quick and intuitive decision.
- Describe a situation where you needed an outside opinion. How did you go about getting it?
- Describe a time when you had to excel as a leader.
- Describe a time when you succeeded in inspiring team spirit.
- Do you think you have a potential for leadership?
- Would you rather delegate or constantly supervise?
- How do you feel when you are asked to do a routine job?
- How good are you at taking authority? Have you ever been in command of a group of people?

What the Interviewer Wants to Know About You

By asking questions about your work habits, the interviewer is trying to find out:

- Do you know what makes a good leader?
- Are you a leader, a mediator, or a go-between?
- Can you handle delicate situations and inspire others?
- Do you think you have leadership potential?
- Are you a "control freak"? Do you like to maintain control at all times?
- Are you willing to delegate?
- Do you know how to delegate?
- How sure of yourself are you? Do you trust others to do their jobs?
- Can you lead others without being overbearing or ineffective?
- Have you ever led a team?
- Do you know how to enrich your job?
- Are you good at getting your ideas across?

- Do you know how to recognize your competencies?
- Do you have an analytical mind that works fast?
- How well do you handle responsibility and stress?
- How do you react to adversity?
- Are you good at handling difficult situations at work and in your life in general?
- Can you make important/quick/unpopular decisions?
- Are you organized and systematic?
- Are you good at analysis, criticism, or self-evaluation?
- Are you good at pulling up your bootstraps / motivating yourself again?
- Are you able to learn from your mistakes?

How to Answer

The key to answering many of the questions about work habits will require that you furnish examples from your past. Write down examples ahead of your interview so you will be sure to have a few on hand to validate your responses. Show how you resolved any difficulties and successfully handled problematical situations and individuals.

If you are asked about stress or pressure, show by example how you successfully deal with pressure. Talk about what you do to relieve stress, including exercising, relaxing with a good book, socializing with friends, or turning stress into productive energy by creating something new.

Talk about what distinguishes you from others who can do the same tasks that you can. Do you have better work habits than the others, do you show up earlier, stay later, work more thoroughly, work faster, maintain higher standards, go the extra mile? Talk about your qualities to show how you will not only fit in but also contribute in positive ways.

When asked what you learned from previous jobs, be sure you have at least three to five areas you would like to cover. Keep your sentences short but give enough information so your interviewer will understand what you valued most from your past experience. What you choose to talk about when you answer a question like this reveals much about your values and your interests. Choose wisely so that what you describe matches the job you are interested in getting.

Questions dealing with leadership will require that you demonstrate you have leadership skills and abilities and know how to motivate others. It is especially important here to use examples of how you have assisted others in their personal development to achieve common goals and how your ideas create solutions to complicated and unexpected situations when exceptional leadership skills are called for. Show that you understand that respect for each member of the team is vital to success, and talk about what you do to make team members feel important. Use examples to back up what you say. Talk about your leadership style so the interviewer will know if it is congruent with the culture of the organization. Leadership demands maturity if it is to be reasonable and fair. Show that you realize that you cannot change others' behavior, but you can change your reaction to their behavior and, in doing so, become a person who can influence, motivate, and enable others to contribute to the success of the organization. Show that you understand that the best leaders have vision, encourage people to think for themselves, do their research, don't ask of others what they are unwilling to do themselves, value excellence, take care of those around them, remain humble, and have integrity. If you can get these points across to your interviewer, you will lead the competition!

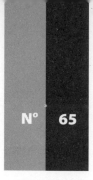

Did you ever change the nature and/or requirements of your job? How did you go about it?

✓ Choose the Best Answer

- ❑ It's never been necessary, as everything has always been well established.
- ❑ I'm not a complainer. I do what I'm told. I like order and expect the same from others.
- ❑ In agreement with my boss, I presented a project to modify the requirements of my job, and we managed to _____ .
- ❑ My chief was fairly authoritative, which left no room for autonomy. But I certainly would have changed a few things.
- ❑ Never. I knew what my job entailed before I was hired, and I didn't change anything.

? What They Really Want to Know

- ▪ Do you know how to enrich your job?
- ▪ Are you good at getting your ideas across?
- ▪ Do you know how to recognize your competencies?

! Watch Out!

Don't:

- ▪ Say you have never tried to modify your job's requirements.
- ▪ Give the impression that you never propose anything new.
- ▪ Indicate that you are rigid in your thinking and unwilling to change.
- ▪ Show that you have been incapable of implementing your ideas.
- ▪ Point out that you have never reached a job's limits.

Don't Say:

- ▪ I've tried, but with no success.
- ▪ I've never seen any reason to. I liked the things the way they were.
- ▪ I've never dared to try.
- ▪ I've never had the opportunity to suggest new ways to do things.

- No. I've never seen any need.
- We were not allowed.
- I was the boss. I could do what I wanted.

Try This!

Do:

- Show how you improved your day-to-day work at your last job.
- Say how you were able to make your job more interesting and more useful.
- Explain how you managed to grow professionally. Use a concrete example to justify what you say.
- Talk about some ideas you managed to get across and how the changes affected your job.
- Prove that your competencies/skills were useful for the firm.

Say:

- Thanks to my skills in the area of _____ , I managed to submit a project for improvement to my boss.
- I like the feeling of growing with the firm. For example, _____ .
- I like sharing ideas and making things happen. Among other things, I _____ .
- The job and I have developed together. I suggested we change _____ .
- Yes, I think it's necessary to develop/grow by _____ .

BEST ANSWER

In agreement with my boss, I presented a project to modify the requirements of my job, and we managed to _____ .

How good are you at planning when you are heavily involved in a major project / long-term assignmnent?

✓ Choose the Best Answer

- ❏ I wait until the last minute to get going. I work well under stress. To launch a project all you really need to do is decide what needs to be done and who will do it.
- ❏ I establish an agenda, list the tasks, identify the necessary resources, and spread out the work among the team members. For example, ____.
- ❏ I have to admit that I am not very good at planning and organizing.
- ❏ I've never been in charge of a project, or of planning. I'm good at getting things done, though. However, if I were in charge of a project, here's what I would do: ____.
- ❏ My weak point is delegating. I usually end up trying to do everything myself.

? What They Really Want to Know

- ■ How well do you handle responsibility and stress?
- ■ Do you know how to delegate?
- ■ Are you organized and systematic?

! Watch Out!

Don't:

- ■ Give a haphazard answer that shows no experience with this kind of task.
- ■ Show that you cannot keep to a timetable.
- ■ Neglect using an example to support your answer.
- ■ Go into too much detail about your personal procedures.

Don't Say:

- ■ I rely on instinct and improvising.
- ■ I am comfortable with my disorganized organization. Only I know what's going on, but the job gets done.

- I'd rather be told what to do.
- I just take things step by step. What else can a person do?

Try This!

Do:

- Give one or two examples of your projects and how you accomplished them.
- Structure your reply carefully.
- Highlight the results of a project(s) in terms of timing, budget, and objectives.
- Show that you know how to delegate efficiently and that you believe in team-work.
- Ask about the kind of projects you will be asked to develop.

Say:

- I am very systematic and structured. These qualities served me well in developing this kind of project. (Give example.)
- I appreciate clear objectives which allow me organize my work efficiently.
- I function by analysis, planning, and management. In my last project _____ .
- I respect deadlines and organize myself accordingly.

BEST ANSWER

I establish an agenda, list the tasks, identify the necessary resources, and spread out the work among the team members. For example, _____.

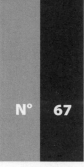

Describe a situation where your team became demoralized. What was your role?

✓ Choose the Best Answer

- ❑ This often happened during end-of-the year bonuses. I used to tell them, "*C'est la vie.*"
- ❑ You really have to crack down when there's a crisis. I know from experience.
- ❑ I am very supportive and always go with the majority.
- ❑ You've stumped me there. That's never happened.
- ❑ I called the team together to talk. We ended up adjusting our goals and starting over on a new basis.

? What They Really Want to Know

- ▪ Are you good at analysis, criticism, or self-evaluation?
- ▪ Are you a leader, a mediator, or a go-between?
- ▪ Are you good at pulling up your bootstraps / motivating yourself again?

! Watch Out!

Don't:
- ▪ Blame others for any failures.
- ▪ Speak in terms of glib or trite solutions, which don't really work in the real world.
- ▪ Sidestep the question by suggesting this has never happened to you.
- ▪ Attribute all kinds of merit to yourself.
- ▪ Take a long time to set the stage (justifying why the incident happened).

Don't Say:
- ▪ It happens occasionally.
- ▪ It's always the same people who screw up a team's efforts, making it ineffective.

- I keep plugging on. I don't really use a specific strategy.
- I can't stand complainers on my team.

Try This!

Do:

- Analyze your role and show that you understand the importance of strong/ flexible leadership.
- Make it clear that your goal was to end up in a stronger position, to come up with solutions.
- Explain what you did to bounce back, using examples.
- End your story on a positive note.
- Speak in terms of "we" and "us" and "the team." Avoid "I" and "me."
- Keep your focus on the solutions you found and not on the problems.

Say:

- I analyze my team's behavior, and then I take action. For example, when _____ occurred, we _____.
- I make sure the team fully understands the firm's vision and we readjust our priorities/goals/expectations.
- I believe in a regular exchange of ideas with my team.
- I always show recognition for the teamwork.

BEST ANSWER

I called the team together to talk. We ended up adjusting our goals and starting over on a new basis.

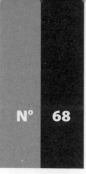

What have you learned from your previous jobs?

✓ *Choose the Best Answer*

- ❏ Lots of things, but unfortunately nothing useful for the job in question.
- ❏ Not much lately. I know my job backwards and forwards.
- ❏ That in spite of situations that are sometimes complicated to manage, there is always something to be learned and a way to grow personally. For example, I have learned how to _____ , and have acquired the skill of _____.
- ❏ Nothing very useful for you, as I am making a radical change in my career.
- ❏ That in most cases it's the women/men/foreigners/young people who are difficult to manage.

? *What They Really Want to Know*

- ▪ Do you like learning?
- ▪ Have you done an assessment of your career choices?
- ▪ Are you able to learn from your mistakes?

! *Watch Out!*

Don't:
- ▪ Run down your previous jobs.
- ▪ Give examples that show a lack of respect for your colleagues.
- ▪ Enumerate the kinds of knowledge/skills you have transmitted to others.
- ▪ Suggest that work does not form one's personality.
- ▪ Dwell on skills that would be counter-productive for this particular job.
- ▪ Talk about a failure that you've never been able to get over.

Don't Say:
- ▪ I need to learn to write in French!
- ▪ Self-assurance.
- ▪ Well, I know an employer fires you when they no longer need you.
- ▪ I left with an excellent image of myself. I have always performed well.

Do:

- Give yourself credit for keeping your work tools/resources up to date.
- Expand the responsibilities for each position.
- Give positive examples of accomplishments.
- List the skills you have acquired and those you are presently working on.
- Assess the development of your professional skills.
- Point out the links between your different professional experiences and if you can apply it to this job.

Say:

- How to manage complex planning where necessary.
- How to work autonomously and set priorities. For example, _____.
- I do not waste time on unimportant/irrelevant tasks. I have learned how to prioritize the importance of tasks and make sure they are done efficiently and quickly. For example, _____.

BEST ANSWER

That in spite of situations that are sometimes complicated to manage, there is always something to be learned and a way to grow personally. For example, I have learned how to _____, and have acquired the skill of _____.

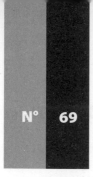
Describe a time when you had to make a quick and intuitive decision.

✓ Choose the Best Answer

- ❏ Here is a situation in which I had no choice but to act intuitively: (give brief description). It turned out all right, but it was risky.
- ❏ I am not one who makes sudden decisions. It's always good to give it some thought.
- ❏ It doesn't work to decide like that. I don't think it's a good idea to make decisions quickly. It usually turns out bad.
- ❏ I have to all the time. All my decision making is intuitive.
- ❏ I quit my last job just like that, with no dwelling on it.

? What They Really Want to Know

- ▪ Do you have an analytical mind that works fast?
- ▪ How do you react under stress?
- ▪ Do you have confidence in yourself and your decisions/choices?

! Watch Out!

Don't:
- ▪ Praise intuition as the way you always operate.
- ▪ Hesitate in your reply [suggests bad decision-making skills].
- ▪ Resist quick decisions as unreliable.

Don't Say:
- ▪ I'm not good at situations that need quick decisions.
- ▪ I don't know of any time when I had to do this.
- ▪ When certain colleagues were fired, I had to make quick adjustments.

Do:

- Describe situations where your decisions proved helpful and you emerged with flying colors.
- Give examples where you played a role in the success of a project.
- Show that you are competent at decision making.
- Prove that you can react calmly without necessarily waiting for formal orders.

Say:

- I had to stop a certain machine when it started malfunctioning, and improvise a new solution within one hour.
- During a major exposition, I had to replace a colleague at the last minute, and I had to quickly decide how to handle our presentation.
- I saved a fellow boatman once, who had fallen in the water in the middle of winter and couldn't swim.
- We had three proposals out to vendors at the same time, and I had to decide quickly which one to go with.

BEST ANSWER

Here is a situation in which I had no choice but to act intuitively: (give brief description). It turned out all right, but it was risky.

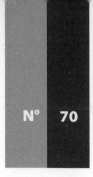

Describe a situation where you needed an outside opinion. How did you go about getting it?

✓ Choose the Best Answer

☐ It's always tricky since people can be so evasive.

☐ I've never been in such a situation.

☐ In general, I ask a competitor. They're good for that kind of thing.

☐ When we realized we did not have the required skills internally, we found ourselves a consultant who was able to pass on to us the know-how we were lacking. I asked three people in the business whom they would recommend and went with their suggestion.

☐ It's rare that I ask for an outside opinion. I read a lot and trust my own knowledge and experience.

? What They Really Want to Know

■ Have you got team spirit?

■ Are you autonomous in your work, yet keep your ears and eyes open?

■ Are you good at/do you like taking initiative to solve problems?

! Watch Out!

Don't:

■ Admit that you chose the wrong consultant.

■ Say you couldn't find anyone capable of helping you.

■ Ignore the usefulness of asking for outside help.

■ Admit that you don't know how to use your network for help.

Don't Say:

■ I've always needed help from others, so I know how to ask for it.

■ I don't know anyone in a position to advise us.

■ I don't need outside help.

Try This!

Do: →

- Illustrate the usefulness of asking for assistance.
- Talk about the concrete results of such an action.
- Describe how you came up with a solution, giving examples.
- Show you know the process of getting what you need.

Say:

- I belong to a club of specialists. It's easy to find someone competent.
- Easy! I contacted three businessmen I admire and conferred with them about the best way to get an outside opinion.
- An outside point of view is always welcome. I have established a core group of people over the years I can call on to help me.

BEST ANSWER

✓ *When we realized we did not have the required skills internally, we found ourselves a consultant who was able to pass on to us the know-how we were lacking. I asked three people in the business whom they would recommend and went with their suggestion.*

Describe a time when you had to excel as a leader.

- ❏ I make my team members get going. This generally works because they respect me and are somewhat afraid of me.
- ❏ I have had to replace my boss on several occasions. The team spirit has remained high and we accomplish a lot because I _____ .
- ❏ I haven't had enough experience doing teamwork to give you a valid answer. I think it's better to keep quiet when you don't know something.
- ❏ I've never been asked to be a leader.
- ❏ I once caught a mistake made by a new colleague.

? What They Really Want to Know

- ▪ Do you know what makes a good leader?
- ▪ Can you lead others without being overbearing or ineffective?
- ▪ Are you good at handling difficult situations at work and in your life in general?

! Watch Out!

Don't:

- ▪ Lie or invent a situation where you were supposedly a leader.
- ▪ Avoid answering the question by saying you have never had to lead anything.
- ▪ Describe an atypical situation that doesn't reflect reality or the kind of situations you would run across in a work environment.

Don't Say:

- ▪ This kind of responsibility requires a big effort on my part.
- ▪ I've always tried to do my best, but _____.
- ▪ I've never had the chance to be a leader.

- I don't think I was very good at being a leader because no one brought their work in on time.

Try This!

Do:

- Give an example of leadership from your personal experience.
- Describe a past situation that resembles the firm's present situation.
- Demonstrate your leadership skills.
- If you haven't had much experience as a leader, let them know you understand what qualities and characteristics are needed to be a leader.

Say:

- In the context of my last job, I reorganized my service by _____ and was able to lead my group to accomplish _____ .
- Thanks to my team management skills, I was able to deal with the following situation: _____ .
- When my company went through its last reorganization, I was suddenly thrust into the role of leader in my department and needed to manage five important projects at once. The way I organized my team was to _____, which allowed us to accomplish _____ .
- While I've not been able to be in a leadership role much in my career yet, I believe a good leader has to help set direction, build commitment, and align his/her team with a larger mission of the company.

BEST ANSWER

I have had to replace my boss on several occasions. The team spirit has remained high and we accomplish a lot because I _____ .

Describe a time when you succeeded in inspiring team spirit.

✓ Choose the Best Answer

- ❏ Unfortunately, it was often every man for himself. So, it took time and I would often end up just taking over.
- ❏ I would constantly put pressure on my team.
- ❏ I used to let the team discuss the subject and then I would make the decision.
- ❏ Since I get along with everyone, I've never had a problem with team spirit.
- ❏ Once when we had to decide ____, I asked the team to take part in the decision-making process. It worked.

? What They Really Want to Know

- ▪ Have you ever led a team?
- ▪ How do you react to adversity?
- ▪ Prove to me you are a leader.

! Watch Out!

Don't:
- ▪ Exaggerate your role in making a team strong.
- ▪ Hesitate, waver, and act like you don't know how to inspire others.
- ▪ Boast that you are a great leader.

Don't Say:
- ▪ It's hard to create team spirit.
- ▪ That's a challenge I have not been faced with yet.
- ▪ To be perfectly honest, I'd rather work alone.

Do:

- Give a positive, concrete answer and outline an example of a time you and your team worked on some kind of project.
- Show that you know how to encourage your co-workers.
- Speak with enthusiasm and use a story to illustrate your point.
- Use an example that indicates that you are dynamic and enterprising.

Say:

- In my professional life, I have had to lead many teams. One example that comes to mind is when I had to ____ .
- I managed a team of 10 people and we ended up ____ .
- The involvement of my entire team allowed us to reach our goal.

BEST ANSWER

Once when we had to decide ____, I asked the team to take part in the decision-making process. It worked.

Do you think you have a potential for leadership?

✓ Choose the Best Answer

- ❑ It's up to you to say!
- ❑ If I didn't become head of the department, it would be a disaster for my family.
- ❑ Trust me. I'm a born manager. Just put me to the test.
- ❑ As head of the _____ department at _____ , I managed a team of five, which allowed me to _____ .
- ❑ No. I've never had to lead people. It does tempt me, but my success will depend on the context and colleagues involved.

? What They Really Want to Know

- ▪ Can you handle delicate situations and inspire others?
- ▪ Do you think you have leadership qualities?
- ▪ Can you make important/quick/unpopular decisions?

! Watch Out!

Don't:
- ▪ Give details without being aware of the job's responsibilities.
- ▪ Show too much ambition.
- ▪ Appear nervous or irritated.
- ▪ Pretend to be the future Bill Gates of this industry.
- ▪ Underestimate yourself.
- ▪ Be unaware of what makes a good leader.

Don't Say:
- ▪ Of course. Haven't I already demonstrated that?
- ▪ I don't like risky situations.
- ▪ I'd rather have clear instructions and just carry them out.
- ▪ Administration is not my strong point.

- Let me tell you about responsibility _____
- I think I have the potential, but so far I haven't really been able to prove it on the job.

 Try This!

Do:

- Keep a positive attitude and show you understand what makes a good leader.
- Mention accomplishments that demonstrate your track record.
- Show your understanding of the profile and duties of the job in terms of its leadership aspects.
- Use an example that demonstrates your ability to lead others.

Say:

- In the context of my previous job, I was put in charge of _____ .
- In my previous job at _____ , I demonstrated my competence on numerous occasions by _____ .
- I accept responsibility. I've been managing the _____ department for several years and have accomplished these three major initiatives: _____ , _____ , and _____ .
- Team management is something I am truly interested in. It motivates me a great deal.

BEST ANSWER

As head of the _____ department at _____ , I managed a team of five, which allowed me to _____ .

Would you rather delegate or constantly supervise?

✓ Choose the Best Answer

❑ I am comfortable with either action. What counts for me is that my role is clear. I can easily adapt to your management style. By the way, what exactly is it?

❑ I do delegate when I need to lighten my workload. That I like, but being in control is not my thing.

❑ Delegating is not my strong point. That's why I'm more comfortable when I'm in control of everything.

❑ Sometimes you have to do both. I will undoubtedly have to supervise my colleagues' training and follow-up before I dare delegate any tasks. On the other hand, if their work is not satisfactory, I'll have to supervise constantly.

❑ Neither one nor the other. I am totally autonomous.

? What They Really Want to Know

▪ Are you a "control freak"? Do you like to maintain control at all times?

▪ Are you willing, and do you know how, to delegate?

▪ How sure of yourself are you? Do you trust others to do their jobs?

! Watch Out!

Don't:

▪ Act autocratically by not trusting anyone else.

▪ Express your belief that only you can really do the job.

▪ Reveal any difficulty in managing a team.

▪ Reveal a lack of confidence in others.

▪ Think your skills are the only ones that are important.

Don't Say:

▪ There are just some people you can't trust. You have to check on them for everything.

- I like to delegate tasks I don't relish doing.
- I've never needed/had the chance to delegate.
- No one does a job like I do.
- If you want something done right, do it yourself.

Try This!

Do:

- Show that you are fully equipped with effective delegation tools.
- Give some examples of effective delegation.
- Explain that you like to delegate and follow up. Give an example.

Say:

- When working with a team, I consider it my responsibility to always value my colleagues' input and expertise as well as to constantly motivate them.
- It's not only necessary to know how to delegate, but also how to follow up once you have delegated tasks.
- In both cases, it's the personal contact that I particularly appreciate.
- I think if you want results, you have to delegate and oversee at the right time, with skill.
- Confidence allows for delegation, but it does not exclude oversight.

BEST ANSWER

✓ *I am comfortable with either action. What counts for me is that my role is clear. I can easily adapt to your management style. By the way, what exactly is it?*

How do you feel when you are asked to do a routine job?

✓ Choose the Best Answer

- ❏ The job has to be done.
- ❏ I feel discouraged and humiliated, especially when it's really boring.
- ❏ I really don't like it.
- ❏ Sometimes I'm delighted to have routine work to do. If this work must be done, it can also be seen as a moment of rest. I believe in doing what is needed to get the job done right.
- ❏ I find it questionable and think that at my skill level I should be used to do things that are going to make the company money.

? What They Really Want to Know

- ▪ Will you accept everything you will be asked to do?
- ▪ Are you going to want to change everything?
- ▪ Do you consider your own interests more important than the firm's?

! Watch Out!

Don't:

- ▪ Announce your distaste for routine work.
- ▪ Show too much enthusiasm and say you love it.
- ▪ Rely on your level of education/training to make you exempt from routine tasks.

Don't Say:

- ▪ With my level of experience and my career path, I shouldn't be asked to do routine tasks.
- ▪ I hate routine tasks.
- ▪ I pass them on to my assistants.
- ▪ I find routine jobs degrading.

Do:  →

- Stress that all jobs require a certain amount of routine work. Emphasize your professional attitude.
- Show that you understand the importance of all tasks.
- Speak in terms of daily management and not routine and repetition.

Say: 🙼

- Every job involves certain routine tasks that have to be managed.
- Can you tell me a little bit about the work we're talking about?
- Probably the same way you feel. It's not usually the best part of the job, but it's work that needs to be done with care and attention.
- I like to do my work with pride, whatever the task.

BEST ANSWER ✓

> *Sometimes I'm delighted to have routine work to do. If this work must be done, it can also be seen as a moment of rest. I believe in doing what is needed to get the job done right.*

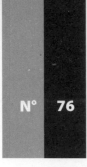

How good are you at taking authority? Have you ever been in command of a group of people?

✓ Choose the Best Answer

❑ It's not easy for me to impose myself. I'm too sensitive to others. If I have to, I will. But I can honestly say it's not my favorite thing.

❑ I should do a course on that. As a matter of fact, I have had a few problems, but they weren't serious. Don't worry.

❑ I don't know. I've always worked alone.

❑ When I am in command, I know how to make myself respected.

❑ I was in charge of a team of eight people. We finished several projects to everyone's satisfaction.

? What They Really Want to Know

- What did you add to the team?
- What are your strong/weak points in this area?
- Are you a leader or a follower?

! Watch Out!

Don't:

- Give an example with inappropriate accomplishments.
- Explain a failure, in detail.
- Make it clear that you do not want to be a leader.
- Show that you have never taken on the role of manager.
- Lay out your vulnerabilities without underlining your corresponding assets.
- Waver on whether you are a good leader or not.
- Act like the "perfect boss."

Don't Say:

- I don't like responsibility.
- I don't think I have the capacity to manage people.

- I'm a loner, not a leader.
- The only time I was in charge of a team, it went well.
- I am absolutely capable of being a leader.

 Try This!

Do:

- Give a couple of references or examples of when you took command and the results you got.
- Show you are comfortable in a leadership role.
- Insist on your competence in, and enthusiasm for, leading individuals and teams by substantiating what you say with real examples.
- Prepare three paragraphs to illustrate your leadership skills.

Say:

- I have done several management courses, which have allowed me to prove myself in this area. For example, _____ .
- My management style is participative, as is yours, from what I have seen.
- I have studied your firm's strategy and find my aspirations are in line with yours.
- My previous employer recognized my talent for leading and put me in charge of 10 people after only six months of service.
- Yes, I am good at it. I supervised several people and was always appreciated at my last job.
- Yes, at my last position I was placed in command of a team of 20 people to complete a project on _____ .

BEST ANSWER

I was in charge of a team of eight people. We finished several projects to everyone's satisfaction.

8

Likes and Preferences

AN INTERVIEWER ASKS QUESTIONS about the likes/preferences of a candidate to see if they can get a better insight into the person. These questions aren't so much about whether or not you can do the job, but who you really are. It's important for an interviewer to find out if you are qualified for a job, but equally (and maybe more so) important is the question of who the candidate really is—what makes him/her tick. They want to know, bottom line, are you the kind of person they want to hire? Will you fit in here? Questions about a candidate's likes and preferences open a window into the deepest part of a person's wants and needs.

These questions can deal with a gamut of issues, from your willingness to work overtime or travel, your preferred skills and tasks, your hobbies and outside interests, what you liked and didn't like about your previous jobs. Each answer will give the interviewer a bit more insight into you.

Likes and preferences questions included here are:

- Would you like to have my job?
- Describe the best job you ever had.
- Describe a key mission or independent assignment you recently carried out which you really enjoyed?
- Are you ready to travel or possibly move? Are you willing to travel frequently?
- Can you work overtime, and work early/late/weekends?
- Do you prefer working for a man or a woman?
- What do you like doing when you are not working?
- What kinds of work activities really interest you, really excite you?
- What kind of things did you dislike about your last job?
- What are your interests or hobbies? How do you spend your vacations?

What the Interviewer Wants to Know About You

By asking questions about your likes and preferences, the interviewer is trying to find out:

- What are your ambitions in our firm?
- Are you ready to commit to a long-term involvement with our company?
- Are you ready to give us your best and place our needs first?
- Will you be available for us? Are you reluctant to work overtime because your personal life is so full?
- How autonomous are you? What do you consider "key"?
- What inspires you the most?
- What are your real talents? Do you know what you are best at doing?
- Does your personality match the job?

- Do you get involved in your work?
- Are you responsible and do you accept some tasks you don't like?
- Are you ready to relocate on a regular basis?
- Are you flexible in terms of family life?
- Are you adaptable? Can you work with everybody?
- Are you good-natured? How do you react when faced with difficulty?
- How do you choose your colleagues/collaborators?
- Do you have derogatory attitudes about the opposite/same sex?
- How do you re-energize yourself?
- Are you more physical, or more intellectual?
- Are you attracted to cultural/club/sports events?
- Do you respect the need to "recharge your batteries"?

How to Answer

The good news about being asked questions about your likes and preferences is that these questions are easy to answer! You know what you like (if you don't, sit down right now and make a list of the things you like with respect to your skills, job tasks, hobbies, overtime, travel, etc.). There are no real right or wrong answers here as long as you are honest and stay positive. As you get ready for your interviews and talking about your preferences, be sure you can answer why you like (or dislike) something. It's not sufficient to say, "I like sports." You must follow up a statement like this with the reason you like sports. "I like sports because it shows what a group of people working together toward a goal can accomplish." Or, "I like sports because participating in these kind of activities gives me a needed outlet for my physical conditioning, which recharges my batteries after a long day at work." Or, "I like sports, particularly baseball, because it's a sport that is subtle. You have to really watch the game closely to see the strategy of the coaches. There are so many nuances in the game." Don't answer these questions without saying why. Train yourself to hear the "why" even if the interviewer doesn't ask it. Always make your answers a two-part sentence. "I like ____ , because ____ ." This is one of the few times where it's good (and even essential) to say a bit more than has been asked, because, without explaining the real reasons for your preferences, you won't be telling the interviewer what they need to know to hire you.

When you talk about your preferences, you will be more at ease in most cases—you know there isn't only one way to answer. It would be a mistake, however, to let your guard down so much that you forget these answers are being judged carefully. They are very revealing to an interviewer. They let the interviewer discern important information about you. If you think your hobbies and interests outside of work don't say something about you, you are wrong. If you talk about the things you loved in your previous jobs, and the skills you most like using, and they have very little or nothing to do with the job you are interviewing for, or aren't the skills most needed, the interviewer will notice it! If you start talking about your family and their needs and demands on you, the interviewer may perceive a red flag.

It's important that you do an honest appraisal of your preferences, particularly when it comes to overtime, weekend work, travel, and even your willingness to move. Do not say you can work overtime on weekdays if you know you have to pick up your children at daycare at 5:15 every day. Do not say you can work weekends when you know that your other commitments prevent this. Do not say you will travel (extensively) when you know family obligations make this impossible. You can show by your answers how you will be able to get around these obstacles so that you can accomplish what is needed to do the job. Just don't say you can do something when you know the cost is too great. It is the same as a lie and may come back to haunt you later on if you are given the job.

Think carefully about the issue of relocation—it is a biggie! If you know that you are so entrenched in your life where you live now that moving is not possible, you will have to be honest about it. Think about whether you can take a job that may ask this of you. It will not be fair to anyone if you say, "Oh, that's not a problem," thinking it will never come up. It may be an important criterion for the employer and one on which a big part of their decision to hire is based. Be honest here. If moving is part of the package and you know it's going to jeopardize your family's happiness, it's better to find a job that doesn't ask this of you. In the long run, it will be the better course.

Would you like to have my job?

❑ I don't really know. But just offhand I'd say I probably don't have the skills necessary for it.

❑ No, not in any way. I think it involves too much responsibility.

❑ Absolutely. Right now! When are you quitting?

❑ I find your firm very attractive. If there are opportunities for developing my career over time, I'd love to one day sit in your chair!

❑ In your kind of job you need to have qualifications I don't have. Nevertheless, if you want to train me and give me your salary, I'm ready and willing!

? **What They Really Want to Know**

- Are you quick at repartee?
- Do you have a career plan or professional goals?
- What are your ambitions in our firm?

! **Watch Out!**

Don't:

- Nod your agreement with a knowing smile.
- Give the impression that you're only there for that job, with no real interest in the job for which you are applying.
- Act blasé and ambivalent about having some ambition.
- Act overly ambitious and make them think you will try to get their job too quickly.

Don't Say:

- No, I really wouldn't. I'm sure it's difficult at times.
- Yes, I would indeed.
- Your job doesn't really attract me, but the salary certainly does.

Do:

- Have a positive attitude without seeming overly opportunistic.
- Ask why they want to know if you want their job.
- Show your ambition in the context of the prospective job, but avoid showing impatience to climb the career ladder.

Say:

- I could imagine having a job like yours in the future.
- It is indeed interesting, but the job we're talking about today is what especially interests me.
- What jobs involving responsibility are likely to become available here in the next year?

BEST ANSWER

I find your firm very attractive. If there are opportunities for developing my career over time, I'd love to one day sit in your chair!

Describe the best job you ever had.

✓ Choose the Best Answer

- ☐ Difficult to say. How about you?
- ☐ I've had so many!
- ☐ I've never had a really interesting job.
- ☐ The last job I had was ideal! I'll have a hard time finding another one like it. But maybe you can offer me an even better one.
- ☐ Each job I've had has provided valuable experience. These three are particularly significant: ____, ____, ____ .

? What They Really Want to Know

- ▪ Are you aware of your strengths and weaknesses?
- ▪ What kind of environment do you like and function best in?
- ▪ Do you know how to use and transfer your talents?

! Watch Out!

Don't:

- ▪ Criticize your former jobs or bosses.
- ▪ Describe a job that is just the opposite from the one being offered.
- ▪ Say that you have never experienced a job you liked.
- ▪ Talk about relationship problems or about the firm/organization unless it is positive.
- ▪ Talk about unrealistic work/jobs you wanted but didn't get.
- ▪ Say you loved every job you ever had.

Don't Say:

- ▪ It would be hard to find a job as good as my last one.
- ▪ My bosses were my buddies.
- ▪ We could talk about this for a long time.
- ▪ Every job has its pros and cons.

- Great pay. Not too much work.
- This job is going to be the best. I can tell.

Try This!

Do:

- Bring the conversation around to the subject of a successful project that illustrates what you like about working or about your past jobs.
- Communicate in a positive mode.
- Describe a job that you particularly enjoyed and tell why you enjoyed it.
- Be sincere about what you liked in your former jobs. Don't lie because you think it will be impressive to get this job.
- Furnish proof of personal and team successes by giving examples.
- Talk about development and learning and what your favorite jobs offered you.
- Point out that you are used to having responsibilities that correspond with your competencies.
- Talk about your skills and marry their results to the job in question.

Say:

- It was a particularly prosperous market and _____.
- Each job allowed me to develop new competencies.
- My colleagues were not only nice but efficient.
- The contributions I made to my last job are still in use today.
- My boss allowed me to grow and is the one who put me on the road to success.
- The further ahead I get, the more my responsibilities flourish.

BEST ANSWER ✓

Each job I've had has provided valuable experience. These three are particularly significant: _____, _____, _____.

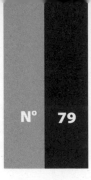

Describe a key mission or independent assignment you recently carried out which you really enjoyed.

✓ Choose the Best Answer

- ❏ That is a difficult question, but it's a good question!
- ❏ In my last job I led a project that ____ with ____ and resulted in ____ .
- ❏ I had a supervisor who gave orders and hovered over me. I couldn't work independently.
- ❏ I haven't done anything recently.
- ❏ What kind of mission?

? What They Really Want to Know

- ▪ Have you managed several successful professional projects?
- ▪ Are you good at analyzing what you have experienced after some time has passed?
- ▪ How autonomous are you? What do you consider "key"?

! Watch Out!

Don't:
- ▪ Admit dependence on others to the exclusion of being able to work independently.
- ▪ Reveal that you have led projects that failed.
- ▪ Give the impression that you're not good at taking initiative.
- ▪ Minimize your contributions by under-valuing them.
- ▪ Find yourself with no examples to talk about.

Don't Say:
- ▪ I've never managed a project.
- ▪ I wouldn't say that I led a key project, but I did reorganize the supply closet.
- ▪ I've never really worked autonomously because my bosses never let me.
- ▪ Managing a real important project would make me too nervous.

Do: →

- Show the usefulness of a project you managed and how you did it.
- Explain the effects your contribution had on the smooth running of the company.
- Describe a project that might be interesting for the recruiter's/interviewer's firm.
- Use tangible methods and results in your answer so they can see how and what you accomplished.

Say: 🙶

- I contributed to the smooth running of _____ by completing a project that consisted of _____ .
- I took the initiative to submit a project on _____ to my boss.
- My project was successful. I took the initiative to reorganize _____ .
- A project that I managed efficiently was _____.

BEST ANSWER

In my last job I led a project that _____ with _____ and resulted in _____.

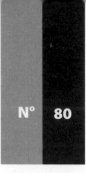

Are you ready to travel or possibly move?
Are you willing to travel frequently?

✓ **Choose the Best Answer**

- ❏ I consider that as one of the advantages of this kind of work.
- ❏ I'm used to having lunch with my kids. I'm a good parent.
- ❏ I hope to travel First Class!
- ❏ I don't like flying. It makes me sick.
- ❏ I don't mind, as long as it's not more than 10 or 15 miles away.

? **What They Really Want to Know**

- ▪ Are you ready to move on a regular basis?
- ▪ Are you ready to commit to a long-term involvement with our company?
- ▪ Are you flexible in terms of family life?

! **Watch Out!**

Don't:
- ▪ Announce that you change jobs every year.
- ▪ Say that you just bought a house that is very important to you.
- ▪ Suggest that you wouldn't consider moving your entire family or making your children change schools.
- ▪ Indicate that you left your last job because you had to travel too much.
- ▪ Admit that you don't like traveling.

Don't Say:
- ▪ I won't be here in two or three years anyway!
- ▪ I have to go home at noon every day.
- ▪ I haven't got a car.
- ▪ I can't have my children change schools.
- ▪ I don't want to waste time traveling.
- ▪ I just moved into my new place and don't intend on moving again soon.

Try This!

Do: →

- Get more information on the kind of the traveling you would have to do: how much, how often, how far.
- Give examples of situations that illustrate your flexibility as far as travel is concerned.
- Show that the travel aspect of the job is attractive to you.
- State that it's fine with you.
- Prove, with examples, that you have always been flexible.

Say:

- I've always figured out something when travel has been needed for my job.
- I like moving around for my work. That's what I'm looking for.
- I'll do everything to adjust to the needs of the company within reason.
- Moving around doesn't bother me. In fact, that's what I like.

BEST ANSWER

I consider that as one of the advantages of this kind of work.

Can you work overtime, and work early/late/weekends?

✓ Choose the Best Answer

- ❑ It depends. I have a very active sports schedule, which could create a conflict. We'll have to be careful.
- ❑ When it is necessary I can always manage to be available.
- ❑ I've got a family life, which I place above all else.
- ❑ I'll have to speak to my family about it first.
- ❑ Of course, whenever you need me! Daytime, nighttime, weekends, vacations. I live to work!

? What They Really Want to Know

- ▪ Are you ready to give us your best and place our needs first?
- ▪ How willing will you be to get the work done?
- ▪ Do you get involved in your work?

! Watch Out!

Don't:

- ▪ Give the impression you are ready to accept anything they ask no matter what the cost in the rest of your life.
- ▪ Show that you are pretty rigid about your hours.
- ▪ Act like there are no limits to what can be asked of you.
- ▪ Neglect to talk about how overtime is structured/compensated.
- ▪ Refuse to have any discussion about this topic.

Don't Say:

- ▪ I only work overtime if it's paid.
- ▪ I intend to keep my private life the most important thing in my priorities.
- ▪ I want to be able to leave every day at 5. I cannot stay later.
- ▪ No, I will not do overtime. You're not that kind of company!
- ▪ Yes, I'm ready for whatever you ask of me.

Do:

- Ask about the reasons for the possibly excessive workload.
- Find out if it is a temporary situation.
- Establish some limits but show your willingness to help when you can.
- Stay open to a discussion of what can be reasonably expected of you.
- Find out how overtime is compensated.

Say:

- Of course, I've always accepted reasonable overtime.
- Perhaps we could work out a way to avoid overtime.
- How are these hours compensated?
- I am happy to carry a full share of the work. Would some of this extra work be the kind that would lend itself to working from home?
- It would depend on the proportion. In theory, I would say 'yes' now and find ways so that I don't compromise either my job or my family.
- Yes, of course, as long as it doesn't become the rule.

BEST ANSWER ✓

When it is necessary I can always manage to be available.

Do you prefer working for a man or a woman?

✓ Choose the Best Answer

❑ It doesn't matter. But, in general, I prefer working with men/women.
❑ The last time I worked for a man/woman it was trouble.
❑ I just love being the only woman in a men's universe (or vice versa).
❑ I'd rather be under the authority of a man/woman.
❑ I don't have a preference. It's their competencies that count.

? What They Really Want to Know

▪ Are you adaptable? Can you work with everybody?
▪ How do you choose your colleagues/collaborators?
▪ Do you have prejudiced attitudes about the opposite/same sex?

! Watch Out!

Don't:
▪ Compare statistics on the efficiency of the two sexes.
▪ Describe problems you have had with former colleagues and employers of either gender.
▪ Show a distinct preference for one gender or the other.
▪ Give examples where you have worked with only one or the other.
▪ Get into a political debate about the merits of either gender.

Don't Say:
▪ Do you have a preference about the gender of your colleagues?
▪ How about you?
▪ A woman's place is at home.
▪ Forewarned is forearmed.
▪ Men don't understand me.

Do:

- Say you do not have a preference and that you get along with men as well as with women.
- Show you are conscious of the consequences such preferences can have.
- Sincerely act surprised to be asked this question and respond, "Heavens, I am happy either way!
- Reword the question to see why the interviewer is trying to find out if you have a preference. Say, "Is there some reason it would be a problem to have a man/woman boss here?"
- Refuse to take sides and name a preference.
- Show how you have successfully worked with both genders over your career.

Say:

- I am interested in the duties of my job and trust that my boss would be likewise.
- I've never had a negative experience with one or the other.
- My preference would be for the most efficient people.
- I function just as well with both. I have worked for both men and women with equally good results.

BEST ANSWER

I don't have a preference.
It's their competencies that count.

What do you like doing when you are not working?

✓ Choose the Best Answer

- ❏ I like reading the tabloids and *People* magazine. They're good for a change of subject.
- ❏ I don't see what this question has to do with the job.
- ❏ I like doing nothing in particular.
- ❏ I love sports and cultural activities. They refuel my energies and allow me to stand up under pressure at work.
- ❏ Watching TV.

? What They Really Want to Know

- ■ How do you re-energize yourself?
- ■ Are you more physical, or more intellectual?
- ■ Will you be available for us? Are you reluctant to work extra because your personal life is so full?

! Watch Out!

Don't:

- ■ Give too much importance to leisure activities; focus on the job.
- ■ Suggest that you work in order to pay for your leisure activities.
- ■ Talk too much about your private life.
- ■ Show that you spend more time at another activity than at your work.
- ■ Talk about extreme or reckless sports.
- ■ Go into too much detail about your passion.

Don't Say:

- ■ I love to go shopping.
- ■ I devote a lot of my time to religion/politics.
- ■ I compete in extreme sports.
- ■ I don't do anything outside work.
- ■ I go out to nightclubs a lot.

Do:

- Show that leisure is complementary to work.
- Demonstrate your energy by the things you do outside of work.
- Say that you appreciate things other than work, and list a few.
- Explain how your leisure activities have contributed to your overall development.
- Illustrate the fact that you like the outdoors.
- Show that you know how to keep busy and manage your time.
- Highlight the fact that you are active.
- Suggest an activity that would be a plus in your new work.

Say:

- I teach _____.
- I take care of my family by _____.
- I work in my garden, cook, read, and putter around.
- I sail, because I like being up against the elements
- I play chess and take part in tournaments.
- I am active. I take part in   and _____.

BEST ANSWER

I love sports and cultural activities. They refuel my energies and allow me to stand up under pressure at work.

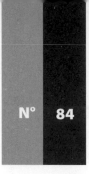

What kinds of work activities really interest you, really excite you?

✓ Choose the Best Answer

- ❑ I get more turned on by my hobbies than work!
- ❑ In my job . . . um . . . all kinds of things.
- ❑ Work that gives me a chance to use my full potential. When I was working at _____ , I loved doing _____ .
- ❑ Describe the tasks the job involves and I'll tell you. How can I answer you otherwise?
- ❑ Not the work of a subordinate. I prefer to lead.

? What They Really Want to Know

- ▪ What inspires you the most?
- ▪ What are your real talents? Do you know what you are best at doing?
- ▪ Does your personality match the job?

! Watch Out!

Don't:
- ▪ Talk about work you don't like to do.
- ▪ Mention tasks that are not relevant to the job.
- ▪ Describe your preferences only in connection with your hobbies.

Don't Say:
- ▪ That's a difficult question because I like everything.
- ▪ The kind of work that lets me earn the most.
- ▪ Not much, really. I'm very demanding and expect a lot of others and myself.
- ▪ Not much, when I really think about it.
- ▪ I hate anything repetitive.

Do: →

- Give an example related to one of the tasks relevant to the job.
- Show that even small tasks can bring satisfaction if they are done with heart.
- Focus on three to five tasks.

Say: 🗲

- Being able to bring new blood and/or a long-term vision to this company by doing _____ .
- I'm interested in many things. For example, _____ .
- Databases, programming _____ .
- Fresh challenges! I love to look problems in a new way and to find innovative solutions.
- I like to continue ongoing projects, predict potential problems, and anticipate future tasks.

BEST ANSWER ✓

Work that gives me a chance to use my full potential. When I was working at _____, I loved doing _____.

What kind of things did you dislike about your last job?

✓ Choose the Best Answer

- ❏ I can't see anything and I don't ask myself that kind of question. A job is a job, with all its pleasures and difficulties.
- ❏ The challenges I faced compensated for any negative elements. My least favorite thing was _____, but it helped me to _____.
- ❏ Repetition and not being able to move up the ladder. I like things to move, and life there was a little too calm.
- ❏ There were never any surprises.
- ❏ Taking orders and being supervised by someone I don't like.

? What They Really Want to Know

- ■ Are you good-natured? How do you react when faced with difficulties?
- ■ Are you responsible and do you accept some tasks you don't like?
- ■ What are your preferences? What is your motivation?

! Watch Out!

Don't:
- ■ Make a long list of dysfunctions from your last job.
- ■ Criticize the last firm, supervisor, or your former colleagues.
- ■ Give an example of a particular task you will have to perform in the new job.
- ■ List only the negative points and nothing positive.
- ■ Complain about your job's lack of social advantages.

Don't Say:
- ■ That's not really important. I'm sure I'll like everything here.
- ■ I never understood what they expected of me.

- I didn't earn enough. My salary was not in line with my level of responsibility.
- I had trouble learning how to ____ and no one would help me.
- The overtime at the end of every month.
- Nothing!
- Everything was badly organized and it was not in my power to change their structure.
- The people there were so mean and unfriendly.

 *Try This!*

Do:

- Mention points that cannot have a negative impact on the job in question.
- Think of something, at least one thing, to show that you have likes and dislikes.
- Stress your mobility/flexibility.
- Talk about what you brought to the team that advanced the priorities of the department/company even if you didn't particularly like the task.
- Show yourself to be systematically motivated by results.
- Stress your sense of responsibility.

Say:

- Some tasks become automatic and the work becomes sort of humdrum.
- I manage to treat even the boring tasks with equal dedication because I believe there is value in everything if you are open to doing the tasks.
- Very few things. I like to work. I would say my least favorite thing was ____ .
- Every job involves a little routine. Fortunately, the tasks that most excite me will be plentiful in this job.
- I wanted to enrich my job by taking on some additional responsibilities, but the workload did not allow for that. I was disappointed at first, so I tried to look at the tasks I had in a new light to keep them interesting.

BEST ANSWER ✓

The challenges I faced compensated for any negative elements. My least favorite thing was ____ but it helped me to ____ .

What are your interests or hobbies?
How do you spend your vacations?

✓ Choose the Best Answer

- ❑ I like _____ a lot. I am on a team and we play twice weekly.
- ❑ That belongs to my private life. I'd rather keep it to myself because I don't see how it could possibly have an influence on getting this job.
- ❑ I like to take it easy: a little siesta now and then. I love lazy Sunday mornings.
- ❑ I participate in sports. What I love most at the moment is bungee jumping.
- ❑ I don't go very far on vacation because I've only got two weeks.

? What They Really Want to Know

- ■ Are you attracted to cultural/club/sports events?
- ■ In what context or circle do you like to be involved?
- ■ Do you know how to re-energize yourself? Do you respect the need to recharge your batteries?

! Watch Out!

Don't:
- ■ Go into your activities/hobbies in a way (time, enthusiasm) that is disproportionate to your professional motivation for the job.
- ■ Reveal any lack of continuity in terms of your image.
- ■ Mention any activities/hobbies that contradict the job profile.
- ■ Talk about dangerous activities that show a wanton disregard for your safety.

Don't Say:
- ■ Just how does your question relate to the job in question?
- ■ I have few interests outside my work.
- ■ I have no particular hobby that thrills me.
- ■ I do not like vacations. They are a waste of money and cost too much.

- I plan everything in advance. I hate surprises—in sports as well as on vacation.
- I'd rather keep that my own little secret.
- Surfing is my passion. I spend all my free time waiting for the perfect wave.
- My interests are not at all related to my work.
- I like to race cars at 120 mph!
- I love to do crafts and spend all my nights and weekends doing that.

Try This!

Do:

- Mention activities/hobbies that have a direct implication for the needs of the job.
- Mention briefly only what you are very familiar with and enjoy.
- Point out the explicit links between the knowledge, know-how, and self-knowledge developed in your activities/hobbies and those required by the job.
- Mention something about your last vacation and what you learned from it.

Say:

- Having friends over for dinner and conversation about current events.
- I like tennis, a sport that develops anticipation.
- I read a lot. The last book I read was _____ .
- I use my vacation time to get to know people from all over. I love the diversity of cultures in our world.
- I play golf [or other activity]. It teaches me how to focus my energy.
- My hobby/activity is related to my work in that _____ .
- I've been biking for 10 years now, and have done several long trips (details, if relevant). I believe in keeping fit.

BEST ANSWER

I like _____ a lot.
I am on a team and we play twice weekly.

9

Professional Goals

AN INTERVIEWER ASKS QUESTIONS about goals to see if a candidate is able to look to the future and plan ahead. Life will go on regardless of whether a person makes plans for it, but most interviewers want to have a sense that a candidate does not just let life happen willy-nilly. Since most jobs require planning to make sure everything that needs to be done, gets done, it's an easy leap to recognize that a person who makes plans, sets goals, and works toward reaching those goals is a better "catch" that someone who just lets life happen to them. We've all heard those expressions, "If you don't know where you are going, any road will get you there" (Lewis Carroll) or "If you don't know where you are going, you will probably end up somewhere else" (Peter Laurence). Most employers want to think that their employees have more purpose than this. By setting goals, a person shows a real commitment to getting what they most want out of life. People who set realistic and measurable goals are generally more positive about life, as they see progress from year to year. They are not afraid of challenges. They know they must plan and take steps—they are able to ask themselves:

- What skills do I need to achieve this?
- What information and knowledge do I need?
- What help, assistance, or collaboration do I need?
- What resources do I need?
- What can block my progress?
- Am I making any assumptions that will deter me?
- Is there a better way I could do things?

By setting goals, people can achieve greater success.

Professional goals questions included here are:

- How do you see yourself progressing with us?
- Describe one of your most recent goals.
- Where do you hope to be five years from now?
- Why do you want to change jobs?
- How would you describe the direction your career is presently taking?
- What is your career plan? What are your short-, middle-, and long-term goals? What do you wish to become in our company?
- What are your long-term goals?
- How would you react if your present boss made you a counter-proposal for you to stay with them?

What the Interviewer Wants to Know About You

By asking questions about goals, the interviewer is trying to find out:

- Do you have a career plan or do you just let things happen?
- Do you see the big picture and set your goals accordingly?
- How are you managing your career and life?

- Are you good at setting goals? Are you a person who strives to make plans and pursue them?
- Can you prioritize your goals and then take the necessary steps to reach them?
- Are you ambitious?
- Do you have long-term vision?
- Are you going to stay on with us if we hire you?
- Do you want to pursue a career with us?

How to Answer

A candidate should demonstrate their purpose and their ability to make and strive for goals, and use examples as proof of their claims. Outline a goal you set two to five years ago and tell how you reached it. Demonstrate enthusiasm about your own life and show how you strive to better yourself over time. Talk about goals you have reached in your jobs and how you went about setting and reaching them.

Use your answers to these questions to show how you want to work with the company. Show them you have done enough research so you know some of their needs and goals. Show them that you are a person who makes long-term commitments and doesn't job-hop at the drop of a hat. Show that you learn from past mistakes and are not a quitter.

Let them know that you have ambition. Use examples to demonstrate your honesty, persistence, and enthusiasm as you plan for the future.

How do you see yourself progressing with us?

✓ Choose the Best Answer

- ❑ It all depends. In the right direction, I hope!
- ❑ I would like to sit in your chair someday.
- ❑ Harmoniously, within the framework of the work to be done.
- ❑ I don't really work to advance my career. Life is too short!
- ❑ Slowly but surely!

? What They Really Want to Know

- ■ Are you going to stay on with us if we hire you?
- ■ Do you have a career plan or do you just let things happen?
- ■ Are you ambitious?

! Watch Out!

Don't:

- ■ Say too little or suggest you don't know how to progress.
- ■ Let yourself be intimidated by the question and act as though all the power for your future rests in their hands and not in your own.
- ■ Indicate that you will immediately be taking over and moving up.

Don't Say:

- ■ I can see myself as boss!
- ■ I wouldn't dare put myself in your shoes.
- ■ I don't understand the question.
- ■ I don't imagine I'll stay here long!
- ■ I just want to do my job.
- ■ My goal is to move up fast in the company.

Do: →

- Say that you hope to be among the 10% of employees who move up rapidly.
- Make it clear that you are reasonably ambitious.
- Stress that you intend to pursue a career, not just find a job.

Say: 🙿

- By investing in the job, I hope to master it and in time move up to a position of more responsibility.
- I'll do this job, and then when the time is right, talk about the future with my boss.
- What are the opportunities for advancement as you see them?

BEST ANSWER ✓

Harmoniously, within the framework of the work to be done.

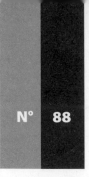

Describe one of your most recent goals.

✓ Choose the Best Answer

- ❑ I don't set goals. I react on the spot, according to the occasion.
- ❑ I would like to get this job.
- ❑ To lose seven pounds in two months.
- ❑ I wanted to run a marathon but after training for two months, I hurt my foot and couldn't do it.
- ❑ What do you mean by "goals"?

? What They Really Want to Know

- How are you managing your career and life?
- Are you good at setting goals? Are you a person who strives to make plans and pursue them?
- Are you committed and trustworthy?

! Watch Out!

Don't:

- Take too long to come up with an answer, as if you had never thought about your goals.
- Hint that salary is what really matters to you.
- Be so discreet and careful in your answer that you make them think you do not set goals that are difficult to reach.

Don't Say:

- I listen to my boss. That's the person who sets goals for me.
- From now on, I intend to set fewer and fewer goals. I get too stressed out when I don't reach them.
- I haven't set any goals lately. I've been too busy.
- I don't know how to set a goal, but I'm ready and willing to learn.

Do:

- Choose, from among your list of achievements, the one most appropriate to describe a goal you set for yourself and reached.
- Describe one of your projects that was well done.
- Highlight your planning skills, using an example.
- Present the results you obtained from a goal you set in your personal life, only if it illustrates a characteristic needed for the job.

Say:

- It's good to find out immediately how to better meet your clients' expectations and then work toward that.
- Six months ago, I started intensive German classes, and now I can actually have a real conversation.
- I created a risk prevention plan at work to bring things in line with new legal requirements.
- I found a way to analyze our clients' position with respect to our direct competitors.
- One of my recent goals was to get an interview with you!

BEST ANSWER

I would like to get this job.

Where do you hope to be five years from now?

✓ Choose the Best Answer

- ❑ Five years? That's a long time from now!
- ❑ Perhaps abroad, perhaps at one of your competitors, perhaps in a different field altogether, perhaps I'll be the president of the country!
- ❑ Surely in the head office.
- ❑ Still with you, faithful to the job.
- ❑ Still with you, in a position that reflects my achievements and motivation.

? What They Really Want to Know

- ▪ Have you got much ambition?
- ▪ Do you have long-term vision?
- ▪ Can we count on you to make to make your career with us?

! Watch Out!

Don't:

- ▪ Appear too ambitious and say you will be running the company.
- ▪ Show that you have fixed ideas with no flexibility.
- ▪ Show a lack of ambition by saying you will be at the same job in five years.
- ▪ Appear hesitant or doubtful, as if to say you don't think about the future.

Don't Say:

- ▪ In pre-retirement on some exotic island.
- ▪ I'm a clever old fox—I'll be moving up for sure.
- ▪ The head office is what I'm after.
- ▪ If you and I get along, I'll still be here.

Do: →

- Describe goals that are feasible and yet still challenging.
- Give examples of projects that you would like to lead.
- Show how you could adapt one of your ambitions to opportunities for job advancement within their company.

Say: 🔊

- I have always been appreciated and sought after by our clients, and I think this ability will help me move into positions of more responsibility over time.
- Could you tell me what it takes to be ranked in the top five in your organization?
- I like to invest in the long term. I can see myself with you five years from now, moving up in a way that allows me to broaden your goals and mine.
- Hoping to carry out all these projects, I can imagine a great career here with your company.
- What would be an ideal career plan for someone who is successful in this position?

BEST ANSWER ✓

Still with you, in a position that reflects my achievements and motivation.

Why do you want to change jobs?

- ❑ My boss wasn't able to offer me the responsibility that corresponds with my competence.
- ❑ Everybody should change jobs once in a while. It usually turns out to be a good thing salary-wise.
- ❑ I'm fed up with my job. They don't give me enough responsibility and they don't recognize my talent. That's why I decided to change.
- ❑ I'm not changing jobs. I'm unemployed.
- ❑ I don't feel my boss understands me, and I think I would do better with a different kind of boss.

? What They Really Want to Know

- Do you have some hidden weaknesses that make it necessary for you to change jobs?
- Are you unstable? Can I carry on with this interview without fearing that you might want change jobs in a few months?
- What is the true incentive behind your application? Is there some problem in your present job that is pushing you to look elsewhere?

! Watch Out!

Don't:

- Speak negatively about the company you would like to leave or have left.
- Be without a precise objective that changing jobs would meet.
- Lack a precise professional goal that you can outline to the interviewer.
- Want to change jobs without having a valid reason why you are doing it.

Don't Say:

- I quit for personal reasons.
- I was fired and would rather not talk about it.
- I just felt like a change. I've been at this job forever.

- I tend to say what I think, and that doesn't sit well with everybody.
- I need a change because I've lost all my motivation.
- The promotion I've been waiting for three years was given to someone who arrived after I did.

Try This!

Do:

- Assure them that your desire to change is the result of serious analysis of your priorities.
- Present well-founded reasons for your decision to make this change.
- Show that, after having done serious research on the companies that appear to match your present goals, you have selected this one to pursue.
- Stress your desire to meet new challenges.
- Show your ability to question your own ideas.

Say:

- I decided to make a career change, and your firm is one that I have identified as best to meet the new challenges I have set for myself.
- I have lost motivation for my present job because _____. I feel like I might find it again with you.
- I'm looking for a job where those skills I most enjoy using will be put to use. For example, I like _____.
- The responsibilities you listed in your ad correspond better with my motivation than those I have in my current position.

BEST ANSWER

My boss wasn't able to offer me the responsibility that corresponds with my competence.

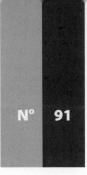

How would you describe the direction your career is presently taking?

✓ Choose the Best Answer

- ❏ I haven't got a goal, but I'll be broke in a month, so I've got to make some money somehow. I don't just want any old job though, so I picked you.
- ❏ I certainly don't want to keep working in a factory!
- ❏ I'd like to start my own business someday.
- ❏ My goal is to develop my skills and make a contribution in a firm like yours.
- ❏ My career is stalled. I don't really see it going anywhere. You're the only ones who have given me an interview!

? What They Really Want to Know

- ▪ Do you like challenges? Risks?
- ▪ Do you see the big picture and set your goals accordingly?
- ▪ Do you want to pursue a career with us?

! Watch Out!

Don't:

- ▪ Stray too far from a realistic plan,
- ▪ Give stereotype goals, such as "make more money," "move up the ladder," etc.
- ▪ Show that you've given up and don't care about your career.
- ▪ Find yourself without an answer.
- ▪ Be vague and act like you don't understand what they are asking.

Don't Say:

- ▪ What's important is that I find some work.
- ▪ I plan as I go along. Whatever happens, happens.
- ▪ I don't have a career plan. I've been lucky so far.
- ▪ I don't like taking risks so I've stayed at my current job for over 10 years.

Try This!

Do:

- Anticipate how this job could match your career direction and talk about that.
- Let the interviewer know you are on track by outlining your five- to 10-year plan.
- Show enthusiasm and ambition.
- Speak about realistic goals and time frames.
- Ask questions about the job's objectives and demonstrate your know-how.

Say:

- I am committed to further education. Do you support continuing education?
- I would like to acquire new skills and let you benefit from those I possess already.
- I would like a long-term commitment with opportunities for progressing and developing.
- My goal is to progress continually with an eye to moving toward a management position.

BEST ANSWER

My goal is to develop my skills and make a contribution in a firm like yours.

What is your career plan? What are your short-, middle-, and long-term goals? What do you wish to become in our company?

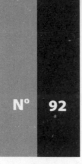

✓ Choose the Best Answer

- ❏ It's up to you to let me know what your goals are!
- ❏ I would like to become head of the _____ Department in a few months.
- ❏ In your company, I would hope we could combine your objectives with mine into common goals that are achievable and measurable.
- ❏ I don't have a real career plan. I just try to adapt. Anyway, I don't want to say anything stupid that I can't live up to later.
- ❏ I haven't thought about it yet. We'll see when I've started working. These things are always so complicated.

? What They Really Want to Know

- ■ Did you really understand what's at stake here, what our concerns are?
- ■ Can you prioritize your goals and then take the needed steps to reach them?
- ■ Are you coming for a better salary, for a better job, or to pursue a career?

! Watch Out!

Don't:
- ■ Announce that your only goal is to make money.
- ■ Admit that you don't have any goals.
- ■ Say you are going to revolutionize things.
- ■ Scare off the recruiter/interviewer by stating goals that are too ambitious or inappropriate.
- ■ Show too little incentive to involve yourself in the company's goals/needs.
- ■ Mention goals that are not in line with the company's strategy.

Don't Say:
- ■ I'm looking for a solution to my employment problem.
- ■ I haven't got goals! I have to earn a living!
- ■ I can do everything. Your goals are my goals.

- I would like to have your job as soon as possible.
- You need me to clean things up here. That's what I'm good at.
- My goal is to earn as much as possible in as short a time as possible.

Try This!

Do: →

- Show that, in your previous jobs, you were always on the same page as your boss.
- Show you are not one-dimensional and can only offer one specialty.
- Make it clear that you are interested in the company's development strategy.
- Show that you understand the recruiter's/interviewer's concerns and worries.
- Prove that you like to grow/learn/develop by using concrete examples.
- Outline your short-, middle-, and long-range goals succinctly.

Say: 🙶

- I fully understand your concerns and hope to be able to meet your expectations very quickly.
- In the short term, I am hoping to get this job. My mid-range goal is to move into a management position within five years, and my long-term goal is to continually strive for positions with more authority and autonomy.
- I am interested in, and well informed on, your strategy, and while we're on the subject _____ .
- I am ready and willing to undergo any training that would benefit my work.
- In my last job, I always met my goals.
- My previous achievements correspond with what you expect of me today. For example, _____ .

BEST ANSWER .... ✓

In your company, I would hope we could combine your objectives with mine into common goals that are achievable and measurable.

What are your long-term goals?

✓ Choose the Best Answer

- ☐ To become your boss!
- ☐ Start up my own business and become the main man.
- ☐ I haven't got any. I just go with the breeze.
- ☐ The sky's the limit! I think I'm capable of becoming a good leader someday.
- ☐ From a professional standpoint, my overall goal is to stay on a course where I keep on expanding my knowledge and experience while moving toward a job with more responsibility and accountability.

? What They Really Want to Know

- ■ Do you plan to pursue a career with us?
- ■ Do you plan ahead or just let things happen to you?
- ■ Are you ambitious?

! Watch Out!

Don't:
- ■ Announce that you plan to take a long trip around the world.
- ■ Disclose that you do not have middle- or long-term vision.
- ■ Be too ambitious (for the job in question).
- ■ Indicate that you are happy with this job while you wait for a better one to come along.
- ■ Indicate that you're just looking for a job that pays the bills.
- ■ Speak only about yourself, showing a lack of concern about the company's needs.

Don't Say:
- ■ I don't have a long-term goal. I am too busy just getting through the day.
- ■ I'm open to anything. I'm adaptable.
- ■ My long-term goal is to be the CEO of Apple Computers.

Do:

- Start off with the middle term, and then build to the long-term goals with several options.
- Show by giving an example that you are achieving the goals set for you in your present job.
- Insist on your enthusiasm for the company and the job, and your strong desire to pursue a career there.
- Underline your incentive to meet the company's needs.
- Demonstrate that you want to progress, without seeming overly aggressive—like you might be tempted to jump a few steps or even take her/his place.
- Ask questions about if/how this job might develop.
- Prove your incentive and willingness to develop/progress/learn.
- Reassure the recruiter/interviewer about your desire to progress/develop without making her afraid of losing you when something better comes along.
- Turn the question around by asking about the firm's perspectives and plans for growth.
- If you have a very specific goal, state it.

Say:

- I will do everything I can to fully satisfy your customers.
- I will live up to the company's demands/reputation.
- I want to be able to progress in the area of _____.
- I will meet the goals that you disclose to me and evaluate them on a regular basis with you.
- My long-term goal is _____.

BEST ANSWER

From a professional standpoint, my overall goal is to stay on a course where I keep on expanding my knowledge and experience while moving toward a job with more responsibility and accountability.

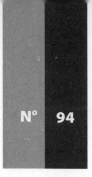

How would you react if your present boss made a counter-proposal for you to stay with them?

✓ Choose the Best Answer

- ❑ That would surprise me.
- ❑ I would discuss the conditions with her in detail to make sure some things would be different in the future.
- ❑ I'd be honored but I really want to work with you because I can offer you _____.
- ❑ I'd accept it right away!
- ❑ I really don't know. I would ask for time to think about it.

? What They Really Want to Know

- ▪ Did you act on an impulse when you approached us?
- ▪ What attracts you—the position or the salary?
- ▪ What is your real incentive to work with us?

! Watch Out!

Don't:
- ▪ Be pretentious and act like your current employer can't live without you.
- ▪ Say that it would depend on the salary.
- ▪ Reveal that you are actually in the processs of negotiating with your boss now.
- ▪ Flatly refuse while criticizing the other firm.
- ▪ Act like you don't care if they want to retain you.

Don't Say:
- ▪ He was so despicable to me; it's out of the question.
- ▪ It's always reassuring to deal with someone you know.
- ▪ I would ask her, "Are you crazy?"
- ▪ I think I would accept, because it's closer to where I live.
- ▪ It's too late. I'm moving on.

Do:

- Give a short answer on why you are interested in this company and change the subject.
- Offer a response that proves that you did not act on impulse, but rather according to genuine guidelines.
- While maintaining focus on the positive aspects of your experience, explain that you need a fresh professional challenge and reiterate why you are intereested in this job.
- Use humor to get the point across that you arr interested in making a professional change.

Say:

- It's not my style to go backwards.
- I would always be suspicious of a counter-proposition. What would you offer me in its place?
- I made my decision. I want to work with you.
- I feel I mastered that job and now am ready to take on new and difficult responsibilities

BEST ANSWER

I'd be honored but I really want to work with you because I can offer you _____.

10

Motivation

S IMPLY SUMMED UP, THIS AREA of questions speaks to the "fire in your belly." The interviewer wants to know what is it that motivates you, not only to work, but also to do your best work. They need to have some sense of why you want to work and what makes you successful at that work. Motivation is generally thought of in terms of traits and benefits and not in terms of skills and abilities. Motivation is intrinsic and therefore deeply rooted within each individual's makeup. It has to do with how people relate to the world. Motivation guides a person to do what they most enjoy and which gives them a sense of fulfillment. In other words, people engage in these activities for the sheer benefit of doing them without thought of some external reward.

There are also external motivators that are outside of the individual that cause a person to value certain things. These external motivators are often tangible rewards like money or benefits. They can also be intangible rewards such as praise from others or the satisfaction of helping someone in difficulty.

In most surveys of what motivates people to do their best, it's no surprise that money doesn't come up as the number one motivator. It's far more often things such as achievement, competition, working with others, recognition, control, helping others, and a variety of interesting duties that help people find their work meaningful and motivate them to strive to do better. People's core values often dictate what their primary motivators (not just in their work, but in all areas of their life) will be.

Not only do interviewers want to know what motivates you in general, but they also need to know very specifically, "Why do you want to work here?" They need to get a sense of what you know about their company and the job in particular that caused you to contact and interview with them. If they can't get a sense of what motivates you the most and whether the job is a good match, they won't feel good about hiring you. They have to make the link between what it is you say that motivates you and how this job will offer those things to you. Interviewers know that if there is a mismatch here, job productivity and satisfaction will not be sufficient to sustain you (and hence them) for very long.

Motivation questions included here are:

- Would you accept a non-paying job?
- Would you like to live in (country/state/city)?
- Would you be willing to work here in our city?
- How long are you going to stay with us?
- After studying our proposition, how do you evaluate this position?
- Do you think you would be better off in a smaller/larger/different type of company?
- Why did you choose to become _____ ?
- What made you choose a large/small company? What attracted you to a regional/national/multinational office?
- What made you answer our ad or decide to contact us?
- Why would someone with your experience/profile want to work for us?
- What do you like most about this job? What do you like least?
- What should we do to support your interest/motivation for this job?

- How well do you know us—our company, our products, our market, our clients, our competitors?
- What do you see as the negative aspects of coming to work for us?
- How determined are you to have this job?
- What is your impression/feeling about our company?
- If you could, what would you change about the job in question?
- If you could choose any company to work for, which company would it be?

What the Interviewer Wants to Know About You

By asking questions about motivation, the interviewer is trying to find out:

- Are you truly determined to work with us?
- What area/branch do you want to work in?
- What do you think of our products/services?
- What opinion do you have about us? What do you really think about us?
- Would you be proud to work for a firm like ours?
- Do you share our values? Are you aware of our company's culture?
- What is it about our specific company that interests or motivates you?
- Why did you choose us?
- What more do you think we can offer you than another company?
- To what extent are you willing to invest yourself in this job?
- Are you really familiar with the job responsibilities for this position?
- What about the job really grabs you?
- Do you really want this job, or simply any job that comes along?
- Is your choice haphazard or well thought out?
- Do the responsibilities motivate you?

- Can you make thoughtful judgments about what is satisfying to you and what isn't?
- Are you able to adapt?
- Do you immediately try to change things?
- Can you prove your qualifications?
- Does the job description suit you?
- Are you able to discuss the negative aspects clearly?
- Are you motivated enough for the job that you would be willing to move?
- Would you accept a training course or a trial period without pay?
- What company would best suit you?
- Is the salary the primary motivation?
- Would you have chosen another field of work if things had been different? Did you have a plan or did you just fall into this?
- What is it about your field of work/profession that you like?
- What are your key assets for this kind of work/profession?

How to Answer

The good news about motivation questions is that individual responses are unique to the person answering the question, and right and wrong don't usually enter in (unless what motivates you is in such direct opposition to what the job offers). What motivates one person to do a great job can be very different from what motivates another person, and both people can still do outstanding work.

The key to answering questions about your general motivation is to be sincere. Make sure you are truthful about what motivates you the most. Before any interview, think carefully about the times in your past when you felt most satisfied and successful and see if you can discern overlapping themes in those times. Summarize what motivators are most important to you. Write up a few examples of things you did that made you feel happy and productive and identify the underlying motivators.

Don't think these questions aren't important. Motivators are vitally important to an interviewer. They must establish that your primary motivators will not only allow you to do the job you are interviewing for, but to do it in a way that benefits everyone. The success of your efforts at any job will hinge deeply on what motivates you. You can understand that if you are applying for a job which doesn't pay that much and probably won't even if you move higher up the ladder, and you say that you are motivated by money, the interviewer will know immediately there isn't a good fit. Conversely, if you are applying for a job where salary is based on commission, and you say you are motivated by cooperation among team members, you might not be stressing the motivator that shows how you are right for the job. An employer probably won't want to hire for a customer service position a candidate who most enjoys working alone. Motivation in the candidate must meet the job requirements.

Interviewers must find out about your motivation to join their particular company and do this particular job. You must show that you have done research on both the company and job and that you have a real desire to work for them doing this job! If you can't show that you are (almost) single-minded in your quest to work for them, you might lose out. Companies don't just want any warm body—they want people who genuinely want to work for them, who know something about them, cared enough to do some research, and have made a determination after finding out this information, that there is a good match. When you are asked, "Why do you want to work for us?" think of this as the time to show what *you* are going to do for *them*. Show them that you cared enough to find out about them—you are motivated to work there and you spent time researching them; this kind of effort and proof of your motivation will carry more goodwill than you can imagine.

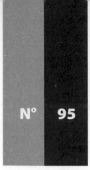

Would you accept a non-paying job?

✓ Choose the Best Answer

- ❑ It depends.
- ❑ That's a funny question. Are you serious? I think all work deserves some kind of pay.
- ❑ Yes, for a short period of time to prove my competence, sure.
- ❑ It's out of the question!
- ❑ Were you considering not paying me?

? What They Really Want to Know

- Would you accept a training course or a trial period without pay?
- Are you ready and willing to involve yourself here?
- What importance do you attach to salary?

! Watch Out!

Don't:
- Make fun of the interviewer's question.
- Appear outraged and act like working without pay is impossible.
- Burst out laughing.
- Reject the idea out of hand without first getting some more details.

Don't Say:
- Are you kidding? Did you have a good look at me?
- I don't know. That's kind of a strange question.
- I wouldn't work under those conditions.
- I refuse to be exploited!
- Of course! No problem!

Do: →

- Give an example of a situation where you would accept working without pay.
- Pursue the subject showing your interest.
- Ask a question to get the interviewer to clarify her idea.
- Stay calm.

Say: 🙮

- Volunteer work? Is that what you mean?
- I am willing to offer you my services for _____ days.
- The incentive to work for no pay should be based above all on mutual aid and increasing skills.
- Perhaps! Work that is worthwhile yet not visible can serve to prepare you for a promising future.

BEST ANSWER

Yes, for a short period of time to prove my competence, sure.

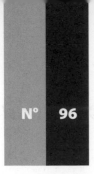
Would you like to live in (country/state/city)?

✓ Choose the Best Answer

- ❏ I will if I have to, but it's not a place I'm attracted to.
- ❏ I don't know. Never been there.
- ❏ I'd rather not move. I like where I am.
- ❏ I would. I like _____ a lot. It has a lot to offer and the lifestyle suits me.
- ❏ Why not? Where would I have to live exactly?

? What They Really Want to Know

- ▪ Are you curious about new things, or are you rigid?
- ▪ Are you truly determined to work with us?
- ▪ Can you adapt quickly? How entrenched are you in your current lifestyle?

! Watch Out!

Don't:

- ▪ Waver and say you don't know.
- ▪ Put an end to the discussion with a flat "No."
- ▪ Reveal that you know nothing about the place.
- ▪ Admit to having a problem with the mobility issue for private reasons.
- ▪ Say "Yes" without expanding on why you would be willing to live there.
- ▪ Say "Never" and list what's wrong with the place.

Don't Say:

- ▪ I'll have to ask my spouse first. She's/he's the one who makes the decisions in our household.
- ▪ I'll go there if it's necessary because the job is interesting.
- ▪ I don't know. I'd have to think about it.
- ▪ My kids have started school in _____ and my mother-in-law is bed-ridden. You can see I need to think about it.
- ▪ No.
- ▪ It's all the same to me.

Try This!

Do:

- Stay positive, particularly if this question comes early in the interview. It might not mean that moving is a primary condition for getting the job.
- Show your interest but be realistic, admitting the consequences of such a change.
- Negotiate the conditions (move, language course, salary, etc.).
- See how such a move might fit with your career plan.
- Prepare how you can return before leaving (if the time period is limited).
- Find out about the conditions by asking questions.

Say:

- I imagine you will be able to convince me with more information!
- Yes, What conditions do you propose to help me make this move?
- Can we predict a middle/long term career plan?
- Yes, most certainly. Could you give some more information about the job?
- I've been there and I liked it. I could see myself living there.

BEST ANSWER

I would. I like _____ a lot. It has a lot to offer and the lifestyle suits me.

Would you be willing to work here in our city?

✓ **Choose the Best Answer**

- ❑ Absolutely! The job really interests me. I am ready to move if you make me a firm offer!
- ❑ I don't particularly like your city. To work in, sure, but not to live in.
- ❑ I'm not very familiar with this city. I just don't know yet!
- ❑ That would mean a big change. I'll have to think about it.
- ❑ Oh, yes. I'm dying to work here, but I don't want to move here. Is a move really necessary?

? **What They Really Want to Know**

- ▪ Are you motivated enough for the job that you would be willing to move?
- ▪ How are you going to organize your move?
- ▪ Are you aware of this city's attractions and features?

! **Watch Out!**

Don't:

- ▪ Ask for some extreme benefit to compensate you for moving.
- ▪ Explain that you just moved and that you are not ready to do it all over again.
- ▪ Insist that the moving costs be reflected in the salary.
- ▪ Waver and show ambivalence about the job.
- ▪ Give the impression that your family is not ready to accept this move.
- ▪ Indicate that moving is out of the question.
- ▪ Act overjoyed before taking the time to really think it over.

Don't Say:

- ▪ Do you have provisions for moving costs?
- ▪ I don't particularly like this city.
- ▪ Of course. What are the housing arrangements?

- I won't consider that. I own my house where I live now.
- It's all the same to me.

 Try This!

Do:

- Make it clear that your companion/family is also willing to move.
- Show that moving will not be a problem.
- Suggest that it would be to your advantage.
- Show your familiarity with and/or interest in the place.
- Make it obvious that you are already fully informed about the city.
- Act as if you are ready to move.
- Ask questions about how a move would be accomplished.

Say:

- Is this city as dynamic as you are?
- I'm ready and willing to make the move.
- I'd love to read some more about what this city has to offer me in addition to this job. Do you have a favorite resource to suggest?
- I've researched the city and found several neighborhoods that are in school districts with high ratings, which is important to me.
- I'd be willing to move but would like to know how you structure these details.

BEST ANSWER

Absolutely! The job really interests me. I am ready to move if you make me a firm offer.

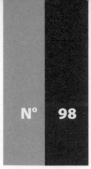
How long are you going to stay with us?

✓ Choose the Best Answer

❑ I suggest we talk about continuing to work together in a year's time, which will give us a chance to review the situation.

❑ There's no limit, as long as I feel that I am developing/advancing and that you are satisfied with my performance.

❑ Perhaps longer than you think! I've got pile of debts and can't afford the luxury of quitting on a whimsy.

❑ Why do you ask? Don't you trust me?

❑ A while, anyway.

? What They Really Want to Know

▪ Do you have a career plan?

▪ Are you stable? Are you impulsive?

▪ Do you make commitments you plan to keep?

! Watch Out!

Don't:

▪ Suggest you can't possibly know.

▪ Make them think it depends on their offer.

▪ Act like you don't care and that only time will allow you to answer the question.

Don't Say:

▪ If there is always a heavy workload, I might not last long here.

▪ I don't know. We'll see if the job is as good as it seems.

▪ If the atmosphere is no good, I'll get out of here.

▪ As long as you want me.

Do:

- Insist on your desire and willingness to develop within the framework of the job you are being offered.
- Use this question to state your three main incentives for the job.
- Remind the recruiter/interviewer of your ambition for the job.
- Reassure the recruiter/interviewer of your intention to fully involve yourself in the job and company.

Say:

- I like the stability and variety of tasks and responsibilities this job involves.
- I'm looking for a job I can invest in for the long haul.
- I am a stable person. I like to carry through with things I start.

BEST ANSWER

There's no limit, as long as I feel that I am developing/advancing and that you are satisfied with my performance.

After studying our proposition, how do you evaluate this position?

✓ Choose the Best Answer

- ❑ It's very interesting, but I've got to think about it. I see advantages and disadvantages. I'm going to have a hard time deciding.
- ❑ It seems just as interesting as all the others.
- ❑ It seems to suit me.
- ❑ I fulfill four of your main requirements, and the job corresponds perfectly with my own goals. Can we sign the contract today?
- ❑ The most important thing for me is to work again. So, if you make me an offer, I'll accept.

? What They Really Want to Know

- ▪ Why did you choose us?
- ▪ What more do you think we can offer you than somewhere else?
- ▪ Are you good at analyzing the ins and outs of each proposition?

! Watch Out!

Don't:
- ▪ Make rash comparisons before you really know the facts.
- ▪ Criticize other jobs on the market and say that nothing suits you.
- ▪ Say that you have no other job in sight.
- ▪ Criticize other competitive job(s).
- ▪ Pretend that this is the only job you're interested in or applying for.
- ▪ Idealize this job and run down all the other ones.
- ▪ Appear too enthusiastic, as if there could not possibly be anything negative about the job.

Don't Say:

- This work suits me because it's less demanding.
- I haven't got any choice but to like it.
- I'll take what I can get. I don't have any other offers.
- Just as long as I can work. Whether it's this job or another, it doesn't matter.
- I'm not sure I have all the qualifications you are looking for.

 Try This!

Do: →

- Have two jobs in sight, in different companies if possible, so real comparisons can be made.
- Explain how your skills fit in with the values and needs of this job.
- Show how this job represents the next logical step on your career path.
- Feel free to admit that you are tempted by other positions and that it will be difficult to choose.
- Fully inform yourself ahead of time in order to focus on the most pertinent aspects of the job.

Say:

- This job suits me perfectly, as it offers me the opportunity to use the assets essential to my career path.
- This job is in line with my career path.
- I think I could easily identify with your company's culture. I see compatibility in _____.
- I know your reputation and appreciate your professionalism.
- I think this job would let me have more responsibility than I had before.
- I would be proud to have this job.

BEST ANSWER

> *I fulfill four of your main requirements, and the job corresponds perfectly with my own goals. Can we sign the contract today?*

Do you think you would be better off in a smaller/larger/different type of company?

✓ Choose the Best Answer

- ❑ It's possible, but I can only answer after a trial period.
- ❑ I'm perfectly at ease in any company of any size.
- ❑ Yes, but I haven't found anything else. I need to earn a living, so I will adapt.
- ❑ Your company is a little small/large, but I'll get used to it.
- ❑ It seems to me that the way you are structured offers an ideal environment for this kind of work.

? What They Really Want to Know

- ▪ Did you make the right choice by applying at our company?
- ▪ Do you think our company offers you enough opportunity to grow and advance?
- ▪ Do you feel comfortable in a small/large firm, having worked only in small/large firms?

! Watch Out!

Don't:

- ▪ Criticize small or large firms.
- ▪ Act as if you don't understand.
- ▪ Get upset and act like you are being attacked by the question.
- ▪ Give the impression you don't have any choice since you've got to earn a living.

Don't Say:

- ▪ Absolutely, but you are the only ones who have agreed to interview me.
- ▪ Possibly, but I could only hope to get the salary I need in a company like yours.
- ▪ I hate large/small companies!

- Possibly, but your hours are perfect for me.
- No, why?
- Possibly, but you are only 10 minutes away from home.

Try This!

Do:

- Explain the thought process involved in your decision to apply.
- Use examples to demonstrate your future contribution.
- Talk about some of the firm's accomplishments that have particularly interested you.
- Support yourself with goals that are similar to the firm's.

Say:

- I've always wanted to be part of a company of this size, which allows for ____.
- The advantage of your company is that it offers a chance to grow, develop, and advance professionally.
- I really prefer working in a company of your size, as I like the ____ it affords.

BEST ANSWER

It seems to me that the way you are structured offers an ideal environment for this kind of work.

Why did you choose to become _____ ?

✓ Choose the Best Answer

- ❏ It's my family tradition.
- ❏ All my professional choices have been made with a job like this in mind.
- ❏ I took the first opportunity out there, particularly the one most in demand.
- ❏ I thought about it, then, by the process of elimination, decided on (this job/profession).
- ❏ I just sort of fell into this kind of work since I had to earn a living somehow.

? What They Really Want to Know

- Would you have chosen another field of work if things had been different? Did you have a plan or did you just fall into this?
- What is it about your field of work/profession that you like?
- What are your key assets for this kind of work/profession?

! Watch Out!

Don't:

- Base your choice on ideals or high-minded aspects.
- Bring up the disadvantages.
- Admit it was your parents who pushed you in the direction you took.
- Indicate that you really wanted to do something else but failed your exams.
- Indicate that it seemed like the least boring of your choices.
- Use a professional or academic failure in another field to justify your motivation.
- Mention purely personal interests.
- Appear to doubt your choice.

Don't Say:

- This work is, for the moment, strictly to pay the bills.
- Doing anything else seemed too risky.

- I like the pay and five weeks vacation.
- It doesn't take much effort and leaves me time for my own life.
- I don't really have a choice. I do what I can.

Try This!

Do:

- Bring up concrete achievements you have made in the field.
- Point to your potential for creativity as the factor that drives you.
- Mention the profession's values that you have incorporated into your day-to-day activities.
- Explain what you like about this field of work.
- Share your enthusiasm for this kind of work.
- Indicate that you went through several stages in making up your mind.
- Show the link between your professional incentives and your experience.
- Describe the enrichment and stimulation this field of work has provided.

Say:

- It is currently a priority among my professional goals, which include _____
- I am sure the job you are offering will inspire me to invest myself 100% in my professional activity. This is very important to me.
- Precision and analysis are two of my qualities that would be put to use in this field.
- It's a passion because _____ .
- Because I am fascinated by the potential for development in this field.

BEST ANSWER

All my professional choices have been made with a job like this in mind.

What made you choose a large/small company? What attracted you to a regional/national/multinational office?

✓ Choose the Best Answer

- ❏ The mentality in a small regional office is narrow-minded.
- ❏ I am attracted by a company whose average salary is above the norm.
- ❏ I come from a big firm and got fed up with all their rules and regulations.
- ❏ Your social benefits are very attractive.
- ❏ I've studied about your company and think I have a good idea how it operates. It's just what I'm looking for.

? What They Really Want to Know

- ▪ Are you geographically mobile?
- ▪ What are your real aspirations?
- ▪ What are your ambitions?

! Watch Out!

Don't:

- ▪ Show your indifference or that you don't consider yourself in a position to choose.
- ▪ Neglect to prove your understanding of the firm's priorities, as based on its structure and/or the type of market targeted.
- ▪ Forget to convince them of your desire for the type of structure they have or are aiming for.
- ▪ Defend your preference for one or the other.

Don't Say:

- ▪ I picked this one so I could move up quickly in the hierarchy.
- ▪ There are more advancement opportunities in this kind of company.
- ▪ I feel more confident than in a small/big company
- ▪ The best training is only offered by the big organizations/firms.

- To take advantage of your good fringe benefits.
- Regional, national, or multinational, it makes no difference. A company is a company!

Try This!

Do:

- Support your preference for the type of structure or market targeted, giving logical reasons.
- Point out your previous experience/achievements within similar structures or markets.
- Demonstrate your knowledge of the priorities of the structure in question and your potential to be effective in this type of structure/market.

Say:

- What I want above all is to find a job that corresponds with my aspirations and skills.
- I love working in an atmosphere like yours.
- I collaborated with my boss for eight years to transform a small company into one with multiple branch offices.
- I am fascinated by your area of work.
- I'm coming from an international firm where I supervised five regional offices.
- We launched a small company with just three employees. After a rapid expansion, I was promoted to manage a group of 20 employees.
- I value pure dedication, which appears to be strong here.

BEST ANSWER ✓

I've studied about your company and think I have a good idea how it operates. It's just what I'm looking for.

N° 103

What made you answer our ad or decide to contact us?

Choose the Best Answer

- ❑ I've been job-hunting for a year, for anything in my field.
- ❑ I systematically answer all ads.
- ❑ You are near my home.
- ❑ This job corresponds exactly to what I'm looking for because _____.
- ❑ You are on the lists I have from the Internet.

What They Really Want to Know

- ▪ Are you really attracted by our company or this kind of job?
- ▪ Can you prove your qualifications?
- ▪ Do you really want this job, or simply any job that comes along?

Watch Out!

Don't:
- ▪ List the job's advantages from the ad.
- ▪ Be incoherent about connections and reasons.
- ▪ Show that you didn't particularly aim for this firm.
- ▪ Forget to emphasize your actual job search.

Don't Say:
- ▪ I saw the ad and answered because I have the profile you're looking for.
- ▪ I systematically answer all ads for jobs in my geographical area.
- ▪ I am available and so I have written to all companies in this field.
- ▪ You offer training, and that's just what I need, as I didn't finish my degree. I am stuck as far as my career is concerned.

Do:

- Avoid bluffing about your other negotiations/offers (interviewers might talk among themselves).
- Mention positive information you have gathered while job hunting.
- Use this opportunity to show your interest in the company you are negotiating with. List some relevant factors about the company that really interest you.

Say:

- After studying your ad, I noticed that what I can offer you corresponds closely.
- I found out about your goals and your philosophy on your website and it is exactly what I am looking for.
- I am a satisfied user of your products and services; therefore I would be very convincing in representing your company.
- Fascinated by the field your company covers, I arranged to talk it over with one of your colleagues. She encouraged my decision to develop my career in this field.
- Your know-how is recognized all over the county/state/country, and I want to be part of that.

BEST ANSWER

This job corresponds exactly to what I'm looking for because _____ .

Why would someone with your experience/profile want to work for us?

✓ Choose the Best Answer

- ❏ I've been job-hunting for 19 months. My field is saturated. I'm going to have to change direction.
- ❏ Your company interests me for two precise reasons: _____ and _____.
- ❏ I heard that you have a generous salary policy.
- ❏ I am convinced that I am your ideal person. Besides, I don't have any other offers. I'm all yours!
- ❏ I've been told you offer excellent benefits. This is something to consider at my age.

? What They Really Want to Know

- ■ Are you really attracted by our company?
- ■ Is your choice haphazard or well thought out?
- ■ Do you know yourself?

! Watch Out!

Don't:

- ■ Be presumptuous or overconfident and act like you are doing them a favor to consider them.
- ■ Imply that you have tried everything to find a job and that nothing has panned out until now (this interview).
- ■ Imply that you are applying at random.
- ■ Only show your interest in the perks/benefits offered by the company.
- ■ See the company merely as a potential paycheck.
- ■ Appear to be unsure of what you can bring to the company.

Don't Say:

- ■ I need to work.
- ■ I've had it with responsibility. I just want a nice comfortable job.

- Your company is right close to my house.
- You are nice and I congratulate you.
- You need me!

Try This!

Do:

- Show how you can bring opportunity and development to another clientele.
- Tell why you chose this company, among all the others, for what it is.
- Mention three reasons for wanting this position, in this company.
- Show that you have done some research about the company and its goals/aims.

Say:

- I have specific knowledge/experience/skills that would benefit your company! I can _____.
- To gain new experience in a job I would love.
- Your firm is known to be the best in the field. I want to work with you because _____.
- I am attracted by the opportunity you offer to _____.
- Simply put, your values and goals are in line with mine.

BEST ANSWER

Your company interests me for two precise reasons: _____ and _____.

What do you like most about this job?
What do you like least?

✓ Choose the Best Answer

- ☐ In the end I think the task of _____ is going to bore me to tears. This job has more negative things than positive.
- ☐ I like the fact that _____; on the other hand, _____ and _____ sound terrible.
- ☐ Absolutely everything. I love this job!
- ☐ About a third of the tasks.
- ☐ I only see the positive aspects because the job tasks match my goals and skills so well. As time goes on, I imagine I will see what doesn't excite me as much.

? What They Really Want to Know

- ▪ Are you really familiar with the job responsibilities for this position?
- ▪ What is your preferred working style (independent or team)?
- ▪ Can you make thoughtful judgments about what is satisfying to you and what isn't?

! Watch Out!

Don't:

- ▪ Base your answer only on positive working conditions (such as salary, cafeteria, closeness to home).
- ▪ Paint too glossy a picture of the job.
- ▪ Speak of it only in negative terms.
- ▪ Talk about things that motivate you that you will not find in the job you are interviewing for.
- ▪ Ignore half of their question (by not answering what you like least).

Don't Say:

- ▪ I like to have free time and the possibility of delegating.
- ▪ I don't know.

- There are stores nearby.
- The salary you offer is good. I like that!

Try This!

Do:

- Mention what kind of tasks you enjoyed, which are included in responsibilities for the job in question. Mention something routine which all jobs include but qualify it by saying you understand the need for it.
- Describe concrete achievements.
- Start off mentioning what you like and then mention one thing as the least interesting and move quickly to another topic.
- Mention the quality of the work accomplished.
- Underline the positive relational aspect—the good team spirit.
- Talk about your accomplishments as they relate to the job duties, to show you understand what the job involves. Mention something you dislike that is not central to the job duties.
- Point out your skill at multitasking, your energy.
- Emphasize your skills/competencies useful for the job in question.

Say:

- The independence that you offer is something I appreciate! On the flip side, I hope there will be opportunities for some interaction with other departments.
- The most? Responsibilities. The least—a longer commute but perhaps I can take the train and use that time for reading.
- I appreciate your value system and regret that certain clients don't and therefore they don't realize what they're missing out on. As for the least, I imagine the same as most people—paperwork!

BEST ANSWER

I only see the positive aspects because the job tasks match my goals and skills so well. As time goes on, I imagine I will see what doesn't excite me as much.

What should we do to support your interest/motivation for this job?

✓ Choose the Best Answer

- ❏ Don't worry. I'm always motivated.
- ❏ Pay me well.
- ❏ Let me pursue my career with you.
- ❏ Leave me alone because I like to work independently.
- ❏ Let me have time for a good lunch.

? What They Really Want to Know

- ▪ Should we let you set your goals?
- ▪ Do the responsibilities motivate you?
- ▪ Is the salary the primary motivation?

! Watch Out!

Don't:
- ▪ Say, "Give me the job."
- ▪ Focus on the salary aspect of the job.
- ▪ Act like there is nothing that would help you be motivated.

Don't Say:
- ▪ I would like to have a raise on a regular basis.
- ▪ I don't know.
- ▪ I would like to work in a well-structured and sociable environment.
- ▪ Motivation comes from above.
- ▪ As far as I am concerned, motivation comes from a decent salary.

Try This!

Do: →

- Remain open in your attitude and say what motivates you to do well.
- Show enthusiasm for the job.
- Express your satisfaction with the job content and particulars.
- Smile while maintaining eye contact.
- Lean forward slightly to show your interest.

Say: 🙶

- I like working toward goals. Knowing that our goals are similar, I think it is a good match.
- I appreciate having a periodic meeting with my supervisors.
- I identify with the company. Its motivation is my own.
- I will do everything in my power to uphold the company's image by ____.
- I am able to find my incentive in each goal/mission I am entrusted with.
- For me, training is an extremely motivating factor.

BEST ANSWER ✓

Let me pursue my career with you.

How well do you know us—our company, our products, our market, our clients, our competitors?

✓ Choose the Best Answer

- ❑ As well as everyone else!
- ❑ I appreciated your website, in particular where you point out these two things: first of all ____, and ____.
- ❑ Not much, in fact, and I'm curious to find out more. Tell me everything I need to know!
- ❑ I know all kinds of things!
- ❑ Nothing at all. I like to come to an interview with a clear mind and no expectations.

? What They Really Want to Know

- ▪ Do you share our values? Are you aware of our company's culture?
- ▪ Have you given sufficient thought to your career development?
- ▪ What is it about our specific company that interests or motivates you?

! Watch Out!

Don't:

- ▪ Admit that you don't know anything/much about the company.
- ▪ Say negative things about any company.
- ▪ Kowtow to your recruiter/interviewer.
- ▪ Ignore the trends/developments/priorities of the area in question.
- ▪ Talk too much and try to tell them everything you know in one breath!

Don't Say:

- ▪ I'm waiting for you to tell me about it.
- ▪ I don't like the way you ____.
- ▪ I'm dying to find out more about your company.
- ▪ I studied everything I could find on your company, but I'm still confused about ____.

Do:  →

- Refer to the company in a positive light and offer two facts you have learned.
- Show that you know the market and the competition.
- Initiate a dialogue about the company's goals, and ask questions.
- Prepare your questions in advance so you are prepared to talk intelligently about the company's products, competitors, etc.
- Ask about ongoing projects or goals.

Say: 🔢

- I read your annual report last year and was impressed by your ____.
- I particularly liked the "Vision" page on your website because ____.
- I closely followed the launching of your last product. I loved it because ____.
- I like the way you manage your stores. By the way, I'd like to know ____.

BEST ANSWER ✓

I appreciated your website, in particular where you point out these two things: first of all ____, and ____.

What do you see as the negative aspects of coming to work for us?

✓ Choose the Best Answer

☐ For the moment I am very positive. That's my nature.

☐ The job seems interesting. I suggest we discuss the negative aspects at the end of the trial period.

☐ It's too hard to say. You've undoubtedly got some hidden flaws that I won't find out about until later.

☐ The general atmosphere seems a little tense.

☐ Why did my predecessor quit?

? What They Really Want to Know

■ Does the job description suit you?

■ Are you able to discuss the negative aspects clearly?

■ Would you have any objection to having a [male/female/older/younger] supervisor?

! Watch Out!

Don't:

■ List only the negative aspects.

■ Make a face as if to say you can't answer.

■ Stay silent too long like you are thinking which (of many) negative things to bring up.

Don't Say:

■ I'm used to wearing jeans and a T-shirt, and I see here everyone's wearing a tie.

■ I don't know yet.

■ I don't see any.

■ What do the other candidates say about this?

Do:

- Show that you have gathered enough convincing information on the company.
- Say the job corresponds exactly to what you're looking for (if it's the case).
- Toss it off with the idea that all jobs have negative as well as positive aspects, though, in the final analysis, the positive dominates.
- Reply quickly mentioning a slightly negative point and two or three positive ones.

Say:

- I would like to have details on the three key tasks for this job. I think that will convince me even further that it is a good match.
- I see mainly positive things which reconfirm my interest in this job. For example, _____ .
- The positive information I found has been confirmed during this interview. You seem to offer _____ .

BEST ANSWER ✓

For the moment I am very positive. That's my nature.

How determined are you to have this job?

✓ Choose the Best Answer

- ❑ Since the job corresponds to my profession/trade/craft, I am obviously determined.
- ❑ The tasks and responsibilities you offer correspond exactly to what I'm looking for. I believe this job would be a great match for both of us because _____.
- ❑ I thought I proved that to you in my application letter.
- ❑ Since I have to work, it's obvious that I'm serious!
- ❑ That depends on your offer.

? What They Really Want to Know

- ▪ Are you really motivated?
- ▪ To what extent are you willing to invest yourself in this job?
- ▪ What about the job really grabs you?

! Watch Out!

Don't:

- ▪ Rummage around in your files to furnish an answer.
- ▪ Appear surprised and stammer and say you aren't sure.
- ▪ Point at your resume or your letter indicating that you mentioned your motivation in writing.
- ▪ Give it some thought and then act like it's not that important whether you get the job.

Don't Say:

- ▪ I admit I would have to accept pretty long hours.
- ▪ My determination will depend on the salary and benefits.
- ▪ Do you plan to open up a branch in my area?
- ▪ Can the hours be modified?

Do:

- Mention your own goals and how they match the job.
- Give examples of what you like about the job.
- Show that you are perfectly familiar with the tasks and responsibilities of the job.
- Suggest a two- or three-day trial period, with no strings attached.
- Show the link between your determination and the firm's vision and goals.
- With the actual job offer ad/description in hand, point out how your skills and experience correspond with the stated requirements.
- Hand over some documents from your portfolio that illustrate your motivation.

Say:

- Take me on for a trial period and I'll prove my determination.
- I have given this job a lot of thought. I am very determined to have it. I have thought of a few ideas on how I could enrich the position to show you my motivation.
- You have made your objectives clear and I agree with them. That's what motivates me.

BEST ANSWER

The tasks and responsibilities you offer correspond exactly to what I'm looking for. I believe this job would be a great match for both of us because _____.

What is your impression/feeling about our company?

✓ Choose the Best Answer

- ❏ I think you are a good firm. My friends remind me that at least I'll have a good business card and the job would look good on my resume!
- ❏ The salaries are good.
- ❏ Somebody I know told me about this company.
- ❏ The article that made me decide to apply for this job presented a very stimulating development plan. I particularly liked _____.
- ❏ You have a good retirement plan.

? What They Really Want to Know

- ▪ What do you think of our products/services?
- ▪ What is your opinion of us? What do you really think about us?
- ▪ Would you be proud to work for a firm like ours?

! Watch Out!

Don't:

- ▪ Act surprised and not say something positive.
- ▪ Be trivial or talk about money/benefits.
- ▪ Say anything negative or tell them their "problems."
- ▪ Be evasive.

Don't Say:

- ▪ Now, that's a tough one!
- ▪ I think your firm is a little too big/small.
- ▪ Your company has some problems but will probably work them out.
- ▪ Doesn't everyone get a company car?

Do:

- Praise some very specific points about the company.
- Show that you did some research on the company before the interview.
- Talk about something you learned from their website.

Say:

- I gained confidence in you after all that I read and heard about you. I am particularly interested in _____ .
- I picked up on three interesting characteristics.
- Your loyalty to your employees and your commitment to growth and innovation.
- Your company favors communication between management and personnel, and that's a major point for me.
- You are the best at what you do. I've studied your competitors and I see that you are far and away the leader in this field.

BEST ANSWER

The article that made me decide to apply for this job presented a very stimulating development plan. I particularly liked _____ .

If you could, what would you change about the job in question?

- ❏ I would propose a better salary.
- ❏ Quite a few things!
- ❏ I would need a few weeks to get to know the job in its entirety and then we can talk about it.
- ❏ Could I ask you a few more questions about the position [salary, vacation, retirement, etc.]?
- ❏ Nothing.

? What They Really Want to Know

- ▪ Is the job description clear to you?
- ▪ Are you able to adapt?
- ▪ Do you immediately like to change things?

! Watch Out!

Don't:

- ▪ Criticize the job without knowing more about it.
- ▪ Suggest things that go against company policy.
- ▪ Impose your ideas and try to completely revamp the job description.
- ▪ Make up things in desperation.
- ▪ Say "nothing."

Don't Say:

- ▪ In the job, nothing. However, the way the office is decorated isn't very appealing.
- ▪ I'm full of ideas. I'll give you a complete list.
- ▪ I don't know enough about the job.
- ▪ I have no ideas on the subject.

Do:

- Show your acceptance and knowledge of the job description.
- Be constructively humble yet dynamic.
- Be proactive and present one or several projects prepared in advance, if it seems appropriate that these would enrich the job rather than criticize it.
- Speak in terms of working together and suggest having brainstorming sessions.
- Turn the question around and ask if anything needs to be changed.

Say:

- I would need some time to fully analyze the situation before saying what could be improved.
- I would rather give you an answer in a few weeks when I'm more familiar with things.
- The best way I could give you an answer would be for you to give me the job and then we can talk about it in a couple of months.
- I believe this job is responsible for _____ and I think it might be a good use of time and energy if _____ were added to that particular function.

BEST ANSWER

I would need a few weeks to get to know the job in its entirety and then we can talk about it.

If you could choose any company to work for, which company would it be?

✓ Choose the Best Answer

- ❑ Yours!
- ❑ It's all the same to me as long as I have a job.
- ❑ Whichever pays best.
- ❑ Maybe one of your competitors known for their efficiency.
- ❑ An organization that has goals similar to yours.

? What They Really Want to Know

- How serious are you about working for us?
- What area/branch do you want to work in?
- What company would best suit you?

! Watch Out!

Don't:
- Say another company that is their competitor.
- Hesitate too long before giving an answer.
- Show your interest in benefits.
- Speak only about yourself.

Don't Say:
- I don't know because I don't know enough about other companies to decide.
- I'd lean toward the one closest to my house.
- I would love to work for _____ because I know they have a great retirement plan.

Do: →

- Stick to the company's culture and what attracts you about it.
- Respond in terms of the company's goals.
- Talk about your values and how the company meets them.
- Underline your interest in the work that is offered.

Say: 🙿

- Yours is the one I am most interested in working with because _____.
- An organization that supports the greater community by sharing some of its resources like you do with _____.
- An organization whose values I share, particularly _____.
- I researched many companies and truly feel yours is the best one for me because _____.

BEST ANSWER

Yours!

11

Previous Professional Experience

O NE OF THE MAIN THINGS an interviewer has to establish is how well you can actually do the job in question. If they fail to understand how you can meet their needs at this most basic level, they will not want to hire you. At this stage of the game, the interviewer is in the driver's seat. It's true that an interview is a conversation and a two-way give-and-take, with both parties trying to decide if it's a good fit, but until the basics have been established (Do you have the skills for this job?) there isn't much real reason for an interviewer to invest much time and energy in you. It is imperative for a candidate to make sure an interviewer is left with no questions regarding how your skills, abilities, and past performance show that you are qualified for the position. If you can't do this during an interview, it's going to be hard for the interviewer to know why he/she should hire you.

These questions are generally aimed more at eliciting information about your transferable skills, than your personality traits and characteristics. This is the meat-and-potatoes section of the interview! Various kinds of transferable skills are listed on the next page to help you understand what these skills are:

- Analyzing
- Coaching
- Cooperating
- Coordinating tasks
- Counseling
- Counseling
- Creating ideas
- Decision making
- Delegating
- Expressing ideas
- Gathering information
- Identifying problems
- Implementing decisions
- Managing
- Managing groups
- Negotiating
- Organizing
- Persuading
- Selling ideas or products
- Setting and meeting deadlines
- Solving problems
- Teaching

Previous professional experience questions are designed to find out what you have done in the past so the interviewer can determine what you will be able to do in the future, as it relates to the job you are interviewing for.

Previous professional experience questions included here are:

- In your past, what projects/tasks/assignments/missions were you unable to carry out, which you would like to have completed?
- Describe the organization of your present/last job.
- Describe a real contribution you made to your company.
- There seems to be a six-month gap in your resume. What did you do during this time?
- Tell me about your professional experience (former jobs, employers).
- Can we contact your present/last employer for information about you?
- Can you describe a typical day in your last job?
- What was the highest point in your career?

- What do you consider as your most important achievement?
- What is/was your workload in your present/past job?
- Tell me about the most important decisions you have made in the context of your work?
- How was your relationship with your last employer?
- What duties/tasks/assignments did you carry out in your last job and how much time did you spend on them?
- What are the most important assignments you carried out in your last job?
- Tell me your "story." Describe your career track.

What the Interviewer Wants to Know About You

By asking questions about your previous experience, the interviewer is trying to find out:

- What do you know how to do?
- What are your main competencies/skills?
- Do you have a good idea of your tasks and responsibilities?
- Are you able to describe the techniques you use to get work done?
- How do you manage a project? Are you results-oriented?
- What responsibilities have you assumed in the past?
- Do you involve yourself personally in the tasks you are given?
- How do you organize your days? Do you make yourself a daily task list?
- Are you good at prioritizing your tasks?
- How big a workload are you capable of assuming? Are you adaptable/versatile?
- Did you accomplish all your tasks? If not, why?
- Are you aware of the priority of the tasks assigned to you?
- How do you fully invest yourself in what you do?
- Are you experienced in the duties I'm thinking of assigning to you?

- In your career, have you reached all your goals?
- Do you have professional goals and ambitions?
- How are you building your career?
- Is your career path coherent and logical?
- How well do you know yourself?
- What do you value most?
- What is the most important thing you have accomplished during your career?
- What is it that motivated you in your professional choices?
- Do you have an analytical mind?
- What are your strong points?
- Are you efficient?
- Are you mature?

How to Answer

When asked about past performance you are being given the opportunity to make your case about your skills and abilities. Talk in very specific language here. Demonstrate by example what you have done in the past, as it relates to this job. Don't spend time talking about skills (even if you like them) that don't have much to do with the job you are interviewing for. It won't advance your case. The interviewer is single-minded at this stage. They need to know in no uncertain terms, "Can you do this job?" Show them that you possess the skills and abilities to handle what they consider the most important aspects of this job.

To do this, you are going to have to do some research before attending the interview. You better have a good idea of the kinds of tasks, duties, and responsibilities that make up the job – you won't be able to focus your answer on these particular criteria if you haven't a clue what will likely be expected. So, use the Internet and any other means of information you can, to make a list of the likely skills needed, and then make sure you have an example (more than one is okay!) on how that you can meet their needs in these areas.

Write down examples where you have successfully used the skills you've acquired. Take the time to compile a list of responses that itemize your skills, values, and abilities. Be sure you emphasize what you can do to benefit the company rather than merely what interests you.

You'll find in many instances, especially when talking about past performance and your skills, that you will be asked questions in a behavioral format. (See Chapter 19, *Behavioral Interviewing,* for more information.) Become familiar with the format of this kind of question so you are not stumped when it's time to give an answer. These questions are based on the premise that past behavior is the best predictor for future behavior. The answer to this kind of a behavioral question demands that you talk about what you did, how you did it, and what the measurable outcome was. Answers must be detail-oriented and explain thoroughly how you have the skill or ability in question. Responses to these kinds of questions don't leave much room for bluffing or canned answers because they are unique to you and concern a very specific event or action that occurred.

N° 113 In your past, what projects/tasks/assignments/ missions were you unable to carry out, which you would like to have completed?

✓ Choose the Best Answer

- ❑ Lots. You have to make choices. That's everybody's problem.
- ❑ I'm not in the habit of dropping a project that has been given to me, but it happens occasionally.
- ❑ When I commit myself to a project, I do everything humanly possible to carry it out. However, there were two cases where it wasn't possible because unexpected circumstances arose.
- ❑ Unfortunately, I have quite a few examples I could give you, since the projects given to me were often impossible.
- ❑ Several, since my supervisors never gave me the means to carry out the projects.

? What They Really Want to Know

- ▪ Did you accomplish all your tasks? If not, why?
- ▪ In your career, have you reached all your goals?
- ▪ How do you fully invest yourself in what you do?

! Watch Out!

Don't:

- ▪ Drag out a written list of all the principal missions given to you.
- ▪ Give examples of setbacks/failures you have experienced that suggest the failure was your fault.
- ▪ Explain that the fault often lay with an incompetent supervisor.
- ▪ Hint that you might just give up if you run up against a difficulty.
- ▪ Give the impression that you're not good at supporting a project when faced with criticism.
- ▪ Mention examples from your private life.
- ▪ Mention examples without including concrete and measurable elements.
- ▪ Turn the question around in an aggressive manner.
- ▪ Make excuses or try to justify yourself.

Don't Say:

- I was fired, so I couldn't finish much.
- I've never had projects or missions to complete where I was in charge.
- Projects I alone was responsible for.
- No one's ever given me a project/task/mission.
- Yes. Some work was suspended because of a lack of personnel.
- I completed everything I ever undertook.

 Try This!

Do:

- Mention a couple of projects you managed to complete despite some difficulty.
- Demonstrate that you are able to defend a project.
- Demonstrate that you manage your time, even under stress.
- List the causes for the setbacks and what lessons were learned.
- Know all (the paragraphs you have written on) your competencies well.
- Prepare a portfolio with visuals of your accomplishments.
- Underline your ability to prioritize activities.

Say:

- There were some, but I willingly gave up all the different project files to another team so the job would get done.
- I had started the setting up of a distribution system to enhance communication with my marketing service; it was brought to a successful conclusion a few days after my transfer.
- My projects are in a constant state of development. Each experience creates a new project.
- In my last job I started a renovation of the IT structure and wasn't able to finish it. I left all the plans with my successor, who successfully finished the job.
- I started _____ but, due to cutbacks in our resources and staff, we had to move the project to the back burner for some time.

BEST ANSWER ✓

When I commit myself to a project, I do everything humanly possible to carry it out. However, there were two cases where it wasn't possible because_____.

Describe the organization of your present/last job.

✓ Choose the Best Answer

- ❑ Its three strongest points were _____.
- ❑ It was a mess.
- ❑ It was confusing. Nobody knew where we were going!
- ❑ I'd rather not talk about it!
- ❑ My last job consisted of too much paperwork.

? What They Really Want to Know

- ■ Do you have a good idea of your tasks and responsibilities?
- ■ Do you have an analytical mind?
- ■ Are you able to describe the techniques you use to get work done?

! Watch Out!

Don't:

- ■ Criticize your former employer.
- ■ Say that organization was not the prime quality of your last employers.
- ■ Go into too much detail.
- ■ Complain about too much work.

Don't Say:

- ■ It's a little complicated and delicate to talk about. It was a huge firm!
- ■ I would describe it as "fire fighting."
- ■ My last company could sure stand some training on the subject.
- ■ I would just organize my work from day to day.
- ■ Organization? It was total chaos!

Do:

- Be honest and describe the functions/responsibilities that worked.
- Bring attention to your skills/accomplishments/past responsibilities.
- Prove that the work you accomplished was made possible thanks to reliable techniques or strategies.
- Bring attention to your latest responsibilities.
- Talk about the hierarchy and how responsibilities were assigned.

Say: 🙶

- We're talking about a particularly effective kind of organization that recognized and took advantage of each colleague's skills.
- The organization that was established allowed us to reach the goal of _____ .
- I'd like to point out three particulars.
- I worked mostly alone, but reported to my boss every week via an email describing my accomplishments for the week and the priorities for the next week.

BEST ANSWER ....

Its three strongest points were _____.

Describe a real contribution you made to your company.

✓ Choose the Best Answer

- ❑ You should ask my former boss. There would be so many examples.
- ❑ There are so many! But they weren't all easygoing!
- ❑ I do the work they give me and just hope my contribution is recognized.
- ❑ Would you like me to describe the projects I have managed alone or with a team?
- ❑ Can't think of a concrete example just offhand. I have to admit that I left my last job several months ago, so I don't remember, nor would they, probably.

? What They Really Want to Know

- ■ How do you manage a project? Are you results-oriented?
- ■ What kind of responsibility have you assumed in the past?
- ■ Do you involve yourself personally in the tasks you are given?

! Watch Out!

Don't:

- ■ Hesitate in forming your answer, as if you can't remember a contribution you made.
- ■ Neglect to give a concrete answer by replying in generalities.
- ■ Underestimate your contribution, opting for humility instead (which will not serve you well in this instance).
- ■ Overestimate your contribution by neglecting to give credit to others when it is due.

Don't Say:

- ■ I didn't have enough time or resources to really do anything great.
- ■ The project I started was abandoned.
- ■ My contribution was not given the recognition it deserved, so I quit!
- ■ To tell you the truth, I was the only person in my group who was involved.

Do: →

- Mention a past contribution that corresponds to the level of the position in question.
- Give the results obtained in numbers. For example: a rise in sales of 15%.
- Elaborate on your real role in this contribution, the result obtained, what you learned.
- Offer to make a short presentation of a previous contribution.

Say: 🙿

- I developed the project from A to Z.
- I established strong links with the suppliers during the negotiations.
- I got excellent results from teamwork, by not imposing myself too strongly.
- I was instrumental in the establishment of the _____ process in our department.
- I am one of the main planners in the establishment of an internal helpline.

BEST ANSWER

Would you like me to describe the projects I have managed alone or with a team?

There seems to be a six-month gap in your resume. What did you do during this time?

✓ Choose the Best Answer

- ❏ I used this time to take a break.
- ❏ Are you able to pull yourself up by your bootstraps when necessary?
- ❏ I didn't find another job right away.
- ❏ When I got fired, I ended up on welfare.
- ❏ Nothing in particular. It took me a while to get over being fired. I'm better now, though.

? What They Really Want to Know

- ■ Did you really do something during those six months?
- ■ Are you able to pull yourself up by your bootstraps when necessary?
- ■ Do you know how to use your free time to learn something new or improve your skills?

! Watch Out!

Don't:

- ■ Ramble on vaguely.
- ■ Try to avoid the question or be evasive.
- ■ Let it be known that you didn't do anything constructive during that time.
- ■ Say you used the time to work on something trivial (i.e., organizing recipes, building a bird house, etc.)

Don't Say:

- ■ I caught my breath and recuperated.
- ■ I got to know myself. Everybody should have that right, shouldn't they?
- ■ I was depressed.
- ■ Nothing special. I worked on my tan.

Try This!

Do: →

- Compliment the recruiter/interviewer for her alertness in noticing the gap.
- Be prepared with a proactive answer showing something constructive you accomplished.
- Stay calm and smile. Point to something practical you accomplished during that period.

Say: 🔢

- After taking stock, I defined my aims and started out on my job search campaign.
- I got my priorities in order and then launched myself into my job hunt.
- I'm one of those people who need to gather a certain amount of information before making an important decision.
- I used the time to build up my network and reestablish connections with several professional groups.

BEST ANSWER

✓ *I took advantage of this lapse in time to take a Spanish course, knowing it would be useful/necessary for practically any job.*

Tell me about your professional experience (former jobs, employers).

✓ Choose the Best Answer

- ❏ What kind of experience do you want to hear about?
- ❏ I've done so many things, I wouldn't know where to begin.
- ❏ I have to admit I've been unlucky in the past. In fact, I've had some pretty bad experiences.
- ❏ My former employer was not an easy person, but I survived. I know how to let things slide.
- ❏ I think these three achievements best illustrate my professional choices.

? What They Really Want to Know

- What is it that motivated you in your professional choices?
- What kinds and what level of goals/responsibilities were entrusted to you?
- Is there a logic/coherence in your professional path?

! Watch Out!

Don't:

- Bluff, lie about, or exaggerate your real experience.
- Go back and forth in time, thus losing sight of the sequence of the steps.
- Focus on inconsistencies on your career path without following the thread that motivated these choices.
- Get lost in details about your life and include personal information. Don't go on and on.

Don't Say:

- What kind of experience do you want to hear about?
- I've done so many things, I don't know where to start.
- I have all the experience I need for this job.
- Everything's in my CV; by the way, here's a copy.
- I've just seemed to fall into the jobs I've had without any real plan.

Try This!

Do:

- Support your examples with facts and figures.
- Be concrete and specific as you outline your career path.
- Put your achievements/successes up front.
- Connect your experience to an aspect of the job profile.
- Summarize. Go for the "big picture" and point out the main turning points.

Say: "

- What is the main competency/skill this job requires? This will allow me to give you more appropriate information.
- Reorganizing my tasks allowed me to _____.
- My professional experience in relation to this job is _____.
- Here is my portfolio. May I comment on it?

BEST ANSWER

✓ *I think these three achievements best illustrate my professional choices.*

Can we contact your present/last employer for information about you?

Choose the Best Answer

- ❏ I wouldn't be thrilled. Why don't you contact the references on my resume?
- ❏ I'm not sure my last boss would appreciate being disturbed, just for a reference.
- ❏ Certainly! I've already told my former boss you might contact him. He was happy to serve as a reference.
- ❏ I don't think he could inform you objectively since he hardly appreciated the fact that I quit.
- ❏ What do you want to ask him? I'm afraid I'd have to say "No"—for personal reasons.

? **What They Really Want to Know**

- ▪ Are you someone to be trusted?
- ▪ Did you leave on good terms? Is there a red flag I will find if I call him/her?
- ▪ What kind of information might I be able to get about you? Will it impress me?

! **Watch Out!**

Don't:

- ▪ Criticize your last employer.
- ▪ Try to impose on another reference instead of your present/last employer.
- ▪ Be ill at ease, and show you are afraid of what might be said about you.
- ▪ Give the impression you are hiding something.
- ▪ Avoid answering.
- ▪ Say no to the request.
- ▪ Blush/stammer/lower your gaze and show that you are uncomfortable.
- ▪ Go into long explanations about why your present/last employer won't speak well of you.

- Be on the defensive and suggest there is some reason your present/last employer should be bypassed.

Don't Say:
- That bothers me!
- I think I lost her address.
- I'd rather not.
- No!
- We didn't get along. He won't have anything good to say about me.

 Try This!

- Tell the recruiter/interviewer you are still working there and would prefer they don't contact them yet.
- Give the contact information for your boss/ex-boss to the recruiter/interviewer.
- Indicate the person in your current/former company who could best talk about you.
- Show how your ex-boss appreciated you.
- Accept, looking the recruiter/interviewer straight in the eye.
- Act enthusiastic and encourage the recruiter/interviewer to call him/her.

- Of course. I don't see any problem.
- She's a frank and impartial person who will give all the information you need.
- Of course. He will most probably confirm my principal traits.
- Yes. You can contact her at _____ .
- Here's the contact information for the people who know me best.

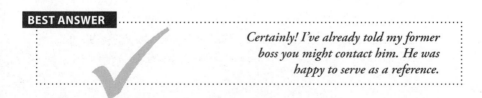

BEST ANSWER

Certainly! I've already told my former boss you might contact him. He was happy to serve as a reference.

Can you describe a typical day in your last job?

Choose the Best Answer

❑ I set my priorities every day and defined the tasks first thing in the morning. I then _____ .

❑ That's difficult. I don't remember much. I haven't worked for 13 months!

❑ That's impossible! There was never any such thing as a typical day.

❑ I'm a little uncomfortable about that. I don't know what to tell you. It was monotonous, every day the same thing being done.

❑ We had practically nothing to do, which is why the company ended up being restructured. But I'll try to describe a typical day.

? **What They Really Want to Know**

- How do you organize your days? Do you make yourself a daily task list?
- Are you good at prioritizing your tasks?
- How big a workload are you capable of handling? Are you adaptable?

! **Watch Out!**

Don't:

- Mention your difficulty in getting going in the morning.
- Run down your ex-colleagues, claiming that you did everything.
- Go into too much detail. Don't take more than a minute to answer.
- Find yourself incapable of remembering and defining what you used to do every day.
- Mention days when there was nothing to do.
- Neglect to talk about the team.
- Fail to talk in terms of concrete results.
- Present your work as completely routine, with no relief.
- Forget to mention the responsibilities you had that would be useful for this job.
- Give an example of an atypical day.
- Get carried away talking about things you didn't like.

Don't Say:

- There is no connection between my old job and the job in question.
- I'd rather not talk about my old job.
- Every day was the same—of absolutely no interest.
- Just like in your firm, we had to work on a shoestring, with no structure.

Try This!

Do:

- Describe this day on a scale of priorities, importance, or urgency.
- Show your flexibility (schedule, tasks, unexpected things).
- Make the link between the goals of the old job and those of the new one.
- Mention the solutions you found to the day-to-day problems.
- Show the pleasure you have meeting your daily goals.
- Present the main points and avoid getting lost in detail.
- Use this opportunity to talk about your past tasks and missions that would be important for the new job.
- Underline the variety of your tasks and your enthusiasm for them.
- Briefly structure the description of a day.

Say:

- I have really learned to manage my stress, thanks to the variety of problems we had every day. My typical day was organized around the top three priorities I had. For example _____ .
- I never had a typical day. I gave of my best every single day in order to deal with all the problems that would come up.
- I organized my day around the priorities, without forgetting to allow for unexpected urgencies, and then I would adapt! I would usually work on projects first, return calls, answer emails, attend meetings, finish up needed paperwork, meet with my boss on a regular basis, and plan for the next day.

BEST ANSWER

I set my priorities every day and defined the tasks first thing in the morning. I then _____ .

What was the highest point in your career?

✓ Choose the Best Answer

- ☐ Today! Because you are offering me a new chance. Until now, things have been pretty calm. That's why I am expecting a lot from you.
- ☐ It will be when I will have helped you advance to a higher position and I take your place!
- ☐ I have a few nice points already, but we have everything to look forward to.
- ☐ There have been several. Each time, I manage to go beyond the goals I have set and acquire new responsibilities. For example, in my last job, I _____.
- ☐ I'm not a career person.

? What They Really Want to Know

- ▪ Are you ambitious?
- ▪ What is the most important thing you have accomplished during your career?
- ▪ What are you proud of?

! Watch Out!

Don't:

- ▪ Mention an insignificant point.
- ▪ Get lost in detail and go on too long.
- ▪ Boast about yourself in terms that make you seem arrogant.

Don't Say:

- ▪ I don't know.
- ▪ I have never actually "enjoyed" my work.
- ▪ I have never had a chance to reach my highest point.
- ▪ I never did anything exceptional.
- ▪ I don't remember.

- I'm good in all areas.
- My career is not essential for me.
- It was when I won the award at work for the best dancer.

Try This!

Do:

- Demonstrate your ability to manage a situation and show how you excelled.
- Be clear and precise.
- Furnish an example, a real experience, of what made you proud.
- Indicate a point that is connected to the job in question.

Say:

- Would you like an example in a precise situation? I once _____.
- I hope I'll reach it with you.
- Getting my specialized degree while I was working.
- The improvement I have made thanks to all my years of experience.
- When I was in external technical service _____.
- When I was in charge of _____.
- When I was involved in very inspiring continuing education courses.
- When I was selected over 25 other applicants for the position of _____.
- When I was given an award for Outstanding Employee of the Year.

BEST ANSWER

There have been several. Each time, I manage to go beyond the goals I have set and acquire new responsibilities. For example, in my last job, I _____.

What do you consider as your most important achievement?

- ❑ I've done many little things. If you add them all up, you'll see I have had major achievements.
- ❑ The creation of _____, which has become the "reference" in the trade.
- ❑ I've often helped out, so there are tons of things my friends appreciate me for.
- ❑ I've never really asked myself that question. I don't know what to say.
- ❑ Getting up early to get here on time for this interview.

? What They Really Want to Know

- ▪ What are your strong points?
- ▪ Have you been invested with responsibility?
- ▪ How well do you know yourself and what do you value most?

! Watch Out!

Don't:

- ▪ Mention all kinds of tasks you've done, with no specific results.
- ▪ Suggest you have never done anything "major."
- ▪ Talk about a failure.
- ▪ Be vague and appear to be the victim of circumstances.
- ▪ Be unable to prioritize what you consider most important.
- ▪ Give an example from your personal life, unless you can link it to a characteristic needed for the job.

Don't Say:

- ▪ I did the same work as everyone else.
- ▪ I was a thorough worker, yet the praise went to the others.
- ▪ I've never been given the opportunity to achieve anything very important.
- ▪ I once saved a person from drowning.

Do:

- Provide proof of what you say by telling the specific outcome.
- Choose the achievement most pertinent to the job.
- Describe your achievements in terms of concrete results and examples—use facts and figures to illustrate how your achievement impacted others.

Say:

- I developed a concept that is still being used today. It is the _____.
- I perfected a technique during my last job to _____.
- I was given a pay raise for the good work I did in _____.
- I was able to _____, even when faced with a downturn in the market and shrinking revenues.
- I brought my file along, which includes my latest achievements. May I show you the one I consider most important?

BEST ANSWER

The creation of _____, which has become the "reference" in the trade.

What is/was your workload in your present/past job?

✓ Choose the Best Answer

- ❏ It was okay!
- ❏ I sort of feel I'm being exploited by my boss and that I'm working 150%.
- ❏ I managed to reach the goals that had been negotiated with my supervisor. I do a lot of planning and following up. There was always something exciting and challenging on my desk!
- ❏ The job was fascinating, but the stress got to be too much. That's what made me decide to look around for a change.
- ❏ I'm not afraid of work!

? What They Really Want to Know

- How do you manage your time?
- Are you efficient?
- Do you know how to prioritize?

! Watch Out!

Don't:
- Invent extra work to make yourself look better.
- Lie about your schedule.
- Claim to deserve all the merit for managing a stressful job.

Don't Say:
- There are days when I have nothing to do.
- I never manage to finish all the work I'm supposed to do.
- I can't seem to manage to get things done on time.
- I pick out the things I like to do and try to delegate the others.
- I'm often overwhelmed by my goals.

Do:

- Mention the goals that affect(ed) your present or past workload.
- List activities planned for your weekly schedule.
- Give an example of planning from your last job.
- Describe your schedule for one day, one week, one month.
- Mention some positive feedback you received on your efficiency.
- Describe the kind of work where you are most efficient.
- Describe how you plan a busy day.
- Explain what technique you use to make your work productive.

Say:

- My workload was full because my boss believed I could get my work done in a timely fashion and made sure to keep the pipeline flowing!
- I usually had about five hours of work on daily projects and about two hours of work meeting and talking with others on my team. I used the rest of my time to finish critical paperwork, respond to emails, and brainstorm plans and ideas for the future.
- I rarely got to work on one project or task at a time, so I had to be sure to manage things properly and prioritize my tasks to get the most important things done first.
- My boss always complimented me on how well I managed my workload. I am good at prioritizing what must be done first, and I pay attention to detail and organize things so they don't slip through the cracks. These skills allow me to handle my workload well.

BEST ANSWER

I managed to reach the goals that had been negotiated with my supervisor. I do a lot of planning and following up. There was always something exciting and challenging on my desk!

Tell me about the most important decisions you have made in the context of your work.

✓ Choose the Best Answer

- ❑ Wait a minute. I'll have to think about it.
- ❑ I always talk to my boss when there's a decision to be made, and she's the one who makes it. You need that kind of discipline.
- ❑ I don't really like making decisions in the professional area. I have so many to make in my private life!
- ❑ I took everything about my work seriously.
- ❑ Decisions involving the hiring and firing of colleagues. For example, I once had to _____.

? What They Really Want to Know

- ■ What were your real responsibilities? What do you consider important?
- ■ Are you mature?
- ■ How well do you manage stress?

! Watch Out!

Don't:

- ■ Explain that you took over your supervisor's work.
- ■ Give the impression that you impose your ideas with no or little regard for the ideas of others.
- ■ Give the impression that you make no decisions at all.
- ■ Indicate that decision making is just too hard for you to do.

Don't Say:

- ■ I just did what I was told. I didn't make the decisions.
- ■ I had no responsibility whatsoever.
- ■ I don't know. I've had several jobs.
- ■ I didn't make any. They were all made according to the hierarchy.
- ■ I made decisions that involved how to keep my boss happy.

Try This!

Do:

- Give concrete examples.
- Offer accomplishments useful for the field of work you are being interviewed for.
- Highlight your successful professional decisions.
- Talk about the decisions in a positive light by stressing their complexity.

Say:

- Establishing the use of communication charts to track the impact my work had on my clients. May I show you an example?
- Innovating a friendlier working system by _____ .
- Making sure information concerning my work was systematically passed on to my colleagues so they could _____, and implementing a new procedure for _____ .

BEST ANSWER

Decisions involving the hiring and firing of colleagues. For example, I once had to _____.

How was your relationship with your last employer?

✓ Choose the Best Answer

- ❏ She was a person who never kept a promise, so I never trusted her.
- ❏ Excellent. You can contact her. Would you like her number?
- ❏ I'd rather not say, because if I get going I'm likely to criticize him.
- ❏ Bad. I've had to go to court, but my lawyer says I have an excellent case.
- ❏ Very mediocre.

? What They Really Want to Know

- ▪ Have you had problems/conflicts with your bosses?
- ▪ Were you laid off or did you quit? Why did you leave?
- ▪ Do you criticize the people you worked with?

! Watch Out!

Don't:

- ▪ Belittle your last employer.
- ▪ Put down your ex-colleagues.
- ▪ Go into too much detail and list what was wrong with him/her.
- ▪ Exaggerate the praise for your ex-boss.
- ▪ Tell a professional secret.
- ▪ Put yourself in the position of being a victim.
- ▪ Justify yourself by acting embarrassed.
- ▪ Complain.

Don't Say:

- ▪ I've suffered so much.
- ▪ I can't stand working for that kind of person any longer.
- ▪ We're on bad terms.
- ▪ I loved her. We were great friends.

Do:

- Mention one to three good points about your last boss.
- Choose your words truthfully and carefully, avoiding too much detail (especially if there has been a problem).
- Give reasons if you were caught in a reduction in force.
- Be loyal to your former employer.
- Highlight your ability to communicate with the hierarchy.
- List the best of what you learned from working with this employer.
- Point out that you have remained on good terms with him/her.
- Remain discreet and not discuss personal issues.

Say:

- It was an interesting relationship. I particularly liked the way he _____ .
- I learned a lot about people from her. Specifically, _____ .
- We had many lively and productive discussions. Our relationship was good.
- A certain balance of power can be motivating. I find his direction to be very well thought out.
- My last boss was terrific. We had clear lines of communication and each knew what to expect from the other. There was a high level of trust between us.

BEST ANSWER

Excellent. You can contact her. Would you like her number?

What duties/tasks/assignments did you carry out in your last job and how much time did you spend on them?

✓ Choose the Best Answer

- ❑ I had too many administrative duties and was not put to use well.
- ❑ I had a huge number of duties. I can't even begin to tell you how much time I spent on each task. The work was irregular but fascinating.
- ❑ My duties were divided into three groups [similar to those in the job description for this job] and took about _____ time each.
- ❑ I carried out all the normal tasks relevant to the position of _____.
- ❑ The tasks assigned to me were not always interesting. I wouldn't like to run into the same ones in my new job.

? What They Really Want to Know

- ▪ Are you aware of the priority of the tasks assigned to you?
- ▪ Are you experienced in the duties I'm thinking of assigning to you?
- ▪ How well do you manage your time?

! Watch Out!

Don't:

- ▪ Give vague information that makes it seem like you're not good at the tasks at hand and that you're not aware of your own level of (in)competence.
- ▪ Make up duties that you have not actually fulfilled.
- ▪ Show a lack of interest in your past duties.
- ▪ Spend too much time talking about duties that are not relevant to the job in question.
- ▪ Go into too much detail.
- ▪ Forget to talk about the time you spend on each.

Don't Say:

- ▪ I can't tell you just offhand how much time I spent on each task.
- ▪ I plan to forget the past and concentrate on the interesting assignments you offer.

- Tasks related to _____ took up 50% of my time. I hope that won't be the case with you.
- My supervisor assigned hardly any interesting tasks.

Try This!

Do:

- Evaluate in percentage form the time spent on each type of task.
- Point out the tasks common to those of the job in question.
- Be explicit about what the tasks are.
- Briefly describe your main tasks and your management structure.
- Concentrate on three to five types of key duties and talk about the time you spend on each.

Say: 🙿

- Three types of tasks were almost exactly like those in your job description. They represented about half of my activity. Those tasks involved _____.
- Most of my duties were slightly different from those we're talking about. However, in these three assignments I used the skills you're looking for. I would say I spend _____ percent of my time on _____ and _____ percent on _____.
- The assignments/tasks that I carried out and that will probably interest you represented 70 percent of my last job's activity. They are _____ .

BEST ANSWER

My duties were divided into three groups [similar to those in the job description for this job] and took about _____ time each.

What are the most important assignments you carried out in your last job?

✓ Choose the Best Answer

☐ None of the projects that have been assigned to me so far have offered as much interest as the job you are offering.

☐ The best projects ever assigned to me gave me the opportunity to put to use the three key competencies for your own organization. They were _____.

☐ I find it hard to say. Can we come back to that later?

☐ Each project I was ever assigned was important and I carried them all out successfully.

☐ I've never been assigned an important project. My last boss had a hard time delegating. I was on a team where we never worked on a very important project.

? What They Really Want to Know

■ What do you rate as important?

■ What makes you tick? What motivates you?

■ What are your main competencies/skills?

! Watch Out!

Don't:

■ Mention a project of no interest to the recruiter/interviewer.

■ Hesitate.

■ Mention projects you weren't able to finish.

■ Get lost in detail describing complicated projects, using jargon inappropriate for the recruiter/interviewer (overly technical, scientific, etc.).

Don't Say:

■ None of the projects assigned to me ever really motivated me. It just seemed like they were projects nobody else wanted.

■ I've done a great variety of things. It's hard to remember exactly.

■ I carried out a project, contrary to everyone's advice.

- I've never had any important assignments.
- I think I could modestly say that I helped save my company.

 Try This!

Do:

- Talk about some of your favorite assignments and explain why you think they were important [what you learned].
- Briefly explain, in concrete terms, how you carried out a project.
- Mention projects that illustrate the skills/results useful for the job you are interviewing for.

Say:

- I completed all my assignments, but here are a couple I'd like to mention.
- The projects I most recently completed are all in line with the kind of goals that you are thinking of entrusting me with for this job. For example, _____.
- Here are two projects I completed that gave me the incentive to aim for a position like the one we're talking about today. First, _____.
- Here are two projects I completed and their profitable consequences for a company that, like yours, is very concerned about the quality of its client service. First, _____.

BEST ANSWER

The best projects ever assigned to me gave me the opportunity to put to use the three key competencies for your own organization. They were _____.

Tell me your "story."
Describe your career track.

✓ Choose the Best Answer

- ❏ I was born in _____ , in 19xx. My father _____. My mother _____.
- ❏ I didn't have an easy life. When I was a kid, _____.
- ❏ When I finished my apprenticeship in August 1985, it was hard to find a job, so I took whatever came by and ended up as a salesperson at _____. Then in 1986 I got married, then _____.
- ❏ Everything is on my resume. What more can I tell you?
- ❏ Shall I talk about my entire career path or just develop a few specific points relevant to the job in question?

? What They Really Want to Know

- ■ Do you have professional goals and ambition?
- ■ How are you building your career?
- ■ Is your career path coherent and logical?

! Watch Out!

Don't:

- ■ Act defensive or try to justify yourself.
- ■ Act pretentious.
- ■ Elaborate on your life, your entire career path, or on private areas.
- ■ Be evasive, aimless, or lacking in enthusiasm.
- ■ Give the impression that your career path is defined solely in terms of the moneymaking jobs you have had.
- ■ Imply that you take life as it comes!
- ■ Talk about your weaknesses or negative things.
- ■ Talk about difficult moments in your life, such as prison, divorce, being fired, etc.
- ■ Get lost in details that have nothing to do with the job.

Don't Say:

- ■ After I was fired, _____.
- ■ I have to earn a living so I took a job doing _____.

- I'd rather we talk about the job [in question].
- I don't know if this will interest you.
- I just started working, so I don't really have a career path yet.
- The situation at home made me _____.
- My path has been extremely chaotic. I've jumped from job to job. I guess you could say I have a lot of interests.
- My path might seem surprising for someone interested in this job, but I can explain.
- Following the financial crisis and the restructuring of my company, I decided to go into _____.
- Can't you ask me questions that are a little more precise?

Try This!

Do:

- Stick close to the future job for the entire discussion and show how your career path relates to it.
- Show the link between the skills and experience you have developed with the needs of the new job.
- Stay focused!
- Express yourself in positive terms.
- Limit yourself to your career path only.

Say:

- I acquired the skills for the position of _____ mostly during these last six years.
- I'll give you a couple of themes and you can tell me which ones you'd like me to talk about.
- I'd like to tell you about my last experience, which has a direct link with what you do.
- My career path reflects a logical evolution toward this position.
- My past is fascinating, but working for your firm seems even better. My road to get here involved _____.
- I'd be glad to. I think these three key experiences fit with the qualities required for this position.

BEST ANSWER

Shall I talk about my entire career path or just develop a few specific points relevant to the job in question?

12

Organizational Hierarchy

QUESTIONS ABOUT HIERARCHY GENERALLY REFER to the relationships you have had in the past with your bosses and others above you in levels of authority. The interviewer may also ask about your interactions with those below your level in the hierarchy. Depending on the size of a company and the jobs you have had, there might have been no one between you and your boss, or there might have been as many as five to 10 levels of authority between you and the top of the organization. An employee should be able to interact properly with all levels if needed.

A candidate who doesn't recognize that it is his/her job to understand and try to help his/her boss is a candidate that might not be a good employee. Like it or not, almost every company with more than one employee has a chain of authority. It is the employee's role to support the boss even if the boss is difficult or unfairly demanding. What's important to remember is the person with the most power is usually the person who will win if a battle breaks out between employee and boss.

Employers expect a certainly loyalty from their employees. It goes with the territory, whether it's deserved or not. If problems do arise between a boss and subordinate, very few bosses ever think they are the problem—they will blame the employee, and the employee will pay the price, either by having to leave the job (voluntarily or by being fired) or they will suffer in attitude and work output, which may haunt them when they go to look for another job and don't get the kind of recommendation they think they deserve.

So, the bottom line is that an interviewer wants to know that the candidate understands and respects the levels of authority and can get along with people at all levels in an organization.

Organizational hierarchy questions included here are:

- How often do you meet with your boss? What do you talk about?
- With how many levels of the hierarchy have you had to communicate? On what kinds of subjects or issues?
- How well do you accept hierarchy?
- Describe the best boss you have had.
- What do you think of your present boss? Your former boss?
- What skills/talents do you think your boss or supervisor should have?
- What kind of person manages you the best?
- Who is the most difficult boss/supervisor you've ever had and why?
- You have met the person who will be your boss if you are hired here. Do you think you will like working for him/her?
- How do you feel about working for someone who is much younger than yourself?

What the Interviewer Wants to Know About You

By asking questions about the hierarchy/boss, the interviewer is trying to find out:

- Have you had good relationships with your former boss(es)?
- What would you like from your boss or supervisor? What do you expect?
- What would you name as the principal qualities for a chief/boss?
- Do you ever see your boss outside of work?
- Have you ever had a problem with other employers in the past?
- Do you equate age with expertise?
- Do you follow company procedures?
- Would you rather make the final decisions or run the show?
- How have you interacted with the hierarchy?
- Do you understand how authority works in an organization? Do you respect that?
- Do you get along with authority figures?
- How do you behave when you have difficulties with a higher-ranking person?
- Are you sensitive enough so you won't rock the boat here?
- What characteristics in others do you respect?

How to Answer

The first rule (and the golden one at that) is to never talk badly about a former boss when asked about your previous jobs. If you speak badly about a former boss, a potential new boss is likely to wonder if you might talk about him/her in similar terms at some point in the future. And no boss, going in, wants to risk that. So, no matter what the situation (even if you had the boss from hell), find a creative way to talk about what you got from your boss that has helped you to be a better worker or allowed you to develop new skills or knowledge. If you can look at every job as a stepping stone to the next job (and one without which you could not have progressed), you will realize that even in bad situations, good can be found. That is what must be stressed.

If you were lucky enough to have good bosses in the past, these questions will be easy for you. Make a list of the characteristics you appreciated about your former bosses and be ready to name some of those characteristics. Frame your answers so you show what it is you learned from each boss that helped you do your job(s) better and will help you be the right person for this new job.

Interviewers also want to know in what ways you were proactive in nurturing your relationships with your bosses. Show how you took responsibility for mistakes when you made them and explain what you learned so that the mistake was not repeated. Explain that you worked to understand your boss's style and adapt your own accordingly to meet it. Talk about taking initiative to solve problems without first burdening your boss. Tell the interviewer how you understood that by furthering the mission of the organization and your boss, you were helping everyone achieve success. If you can demonstrate to an interviewer that your job, in part, was to advance the goals of your boss, you will go a long way in convincing them that you are a team player with the big picture in mind and someone who doesn't get bogged down by petty jealousies and complaints. If you want something from your boss, look inward first to see what you can give your boss. If you can show yourself to be an employee like this, you will convince your interviewer you are a person worth taking seriously.

How often do you meet with your boss? What do you talk about?

✓ **Choose the Best Answer**

- ❑ He was always so busy I never had a chance to see him.
- ❑ I don't see my boss often enough to talk about anything other than work.
- ❑ As seldom as possible. I don't know what to say to her.
- ❑ As often as possible. We have lunch once a week. We have the kind of relationship that allows us to talk about many different things from work to family to political opinions. There is mutual respect.
- ❑ What for? I have the feeling that I'm bothering him.

? **What They Really Want to Know**

- ▪ Do you have a good relationship with your boss?
- ▪ Do you ever see your boss outside of work?
- ▪ Do you work together well?

! **Watch Out!**

Don't:

- ▪ Explain that your professional and private life are two separate elements.
- ▪ Hint at the fact that you hesitate to seek out the company of your boss or supervisor.
- ▪ Say anything to suggest that you consider your boss inferior to yourself and that you would just as soon avoid him/her.
- ▪ Suggest that you should be in the job your boss has.
- ▪ Let it be known that you have never run into your boss outside the workplace.
- ▪ Appear to be reticent to talk to your boss/supervisor.
- ▪ Act like you are afraid to talk to your boss—that you're afraid of him/her.

Don't Say:

- ▪ I only talk about work with my boss.
- ▪ She was always gone.

- I never see my boss outside of work.
- I don't see my boss often enough to have a chance to talk about anything other than work.
- My employer was very busy and had little time to spend on relationships with his employees.
- My boss made it clear that she does not wish to talk to her employees in any meaningful way.

Try This!

Do: →

- Explain that you get along with your boss, even outside work.
- Mention that you suggested to your boss having regular review meetings.
- Talk about your boss in a positive light.
- Stress that you communicate with your boss often enough and well and can talk about issues other than work-related ones.

Say: „

- We have interesting conversations on all kinds of subjects. For example, ____.
- Sometimes I would invite him/her to lunch and we'd talk about what's going on in the world in general.
- We used to carpool together so we had time to visit outside of work hours.

BEST ANSWER

As often as possible. We have lunch once a week. We have the kind of relationship that allows us to talk about many different things from work to family to political opinions. There is mutual respect.

With how many levels of the hierarchy have you had to communicate? On what kinds of subjects or issues?

✓ Choose the Best Answer

- ❑ None. I did everything my way.
- ❑ Too many for my liking.
- ❑ With three levels, both above and below my level, in particular for situations that had to do with workplace improvements.
- ❑ It would depend. It's hard to answer that. Sometimes two, sometimes five, sometimes even more.
- ❑ What exactly do you mean by "levels of hierarchy"?

? What They Really Want to Know

- ■ Are you procedural?
- ■ Would you rather make the final decisions or run the show?
- ■ How have you interacted with the hierarchy?

! Watch Out!

Don't:

- ■ Adopt a haughty attitude with the people lower down on the ladder.
- ■ Avoid answering, even if you haven't had much interaction with others in the past.
- ■ Appear too ambitious and suggest you played a bigger role than you did.
- ■ Object to or criticize the hierarchy.
- ■ Suggest that your superiors didn't know what they were doing.

Don't Say:

- ■ I really prefer dictating memos.
- ■ I hate it when I'm told exactly what to do.
- ■ I don't know. I never thought about it.
- ■ I have a hard time with hierarchy because I don't think they know what I can really do.
- ■ I want to advance my career, so I try to get along with the hierarchy.

Do:

- Show your ease in communicating with the different levels of the hierarchy.
- Indicate your desire to interact with the different levels of hierarchy.
- Show that you value the exchange and circulation of information.
- Talk of your respect for all levels of hierarchy.

Say:

- It's important to know how to adapt yourself to whomever you are dealing with, regardless of their position.
- I worked on several committees and the experience was always good.
- I never forget to inform my colleagues who are involved with mutual projects.

BEST ANSWER

With three levels, both above and below my level, in particular for situations that had to do with workplace improvements.

How well do you accept hierarchy?

❏ It depends. If my boss is intelligent, there's no problem.

❏ I respect the roles each person plays in an organization like this, and feel comfortable interacting with co-workers at every level.

❏ I don't let myself be bossed around by someone younger than me.

❏ I don't know yet. I've been working in a company where there were only three of us.

❏ I try to deal directly with my boss, if only to save time.

? What They Really Want to Know

■ Have you ever had a problem with other bosses (or employees) in the past?

■ Are you sensitive enough so you won't rock the boat here?

■ Do you understand how authority works in an organization? Do you respect that?

! Watch Out!

Don't:

■ Bring up any questionable past experiences.

■ Ask if it is absolutely necessary to follow hierarchal procedure.

■ Express arrogance by suggesting you don't respect those around you.

■ Show that you consider an organizational chart superfluous.

■ Demonstrate your ignorance about the internal functioning of an organization.

Don't Say:

■ That's not a problem for me, but _____.

■ I'm used to being told what to do, being bossed around.

■ I don't really like having to answer to anybody.

■ I appreciate having someone in charge of my responsibilities as long as they leave me alone to do my job.

■ If it's a woman/man, I can't guarantee anything.

Do:

- Give some recent successful examples of how you interacted with your boss/colleagues/subordinates.
- Discuss an example of a successful common effort.
- Demonstrate that you are not biased and that you respect all people.
- Describe a case where your hierarchy was of considerable help.

Say:

- A manager must respect the hierarchy and work within it so everyone can do their job well.
- I've studied your organizational chart and understand who's in charge of what. It suits me.
- I know how to recognize a good boss/manager and so have no problem with hierarchy.
- I respect the tasks and responsibilities of each person. It takes everyone to get the job done well.

BEST ANSWER

I respect the roles each person plays in an organization like this, and feel comfortable interacting with co-workers at every level.

Describe the best boss you have had.

❑ I can talk about all my former bosses, because each one contributed to my experience and the fine-tuning of certain skills. For example, from _____ I learned _____.

❑ He was a friend of mine.

❑ I don't think I can describe one, because up to now, I've never had the luck of having a good boss. With you that could change, though!

❑ There have been so many! All my bosses have been good.

❑ I've never met one in my life. Something tells me it could be you, though.

? What They Really Want to Know

- Do you get along with authority figures?
- What would you like from your boss/supervisor? What do you expect?
- What would name as the principal qualities for a supervisor/boss?

! Watch Out!

Don't:

- Criticize your former employers.
- Show a lack of respect for your former job and those you worked with.
- Overly exaggerate or overly flatter former bosses.
- Tell sob stories about former bosses.

Don't Say:

- That's hard to say. Each boss has his faults.
- There's no such thing. I've had disagreements with all my bosses.
- He always wore a suit and a striped tie and came to work with his dog. He was great!
- I couldn't tell which one I liked better.
- I think it'll be you!

- My former boss was so neat! She was irreplaceable!
- I had a real cool boss. We could do anything we wanted.

Try This!

Do:

- Underline the good relationship(s) you had with a former boss(es).
- Stress the importance of respecting the hierarchy.
- Speak well of your boss. Use concrete examples of why your former boss was a good boss. Show what you valued about him/her.

Say:

- She was a demanding person, but fair. I learned a lot.
- Each boss from my last three jobs has given me something valuable to take with me. For example, _____.
- I appreciate a boss who treats her employees like people, rather than numbers.
- I appreciate people who have a gift for authority and encourage the best in others.
- The boss at my last job encouraged us to share our ideas with him, and when he liked them, he made sure they were implemented and always gave us credit. For example, I suggested we _____.

BEST ANSWER

I can talk about all my former bosses, because each one contributed to my experience and the fine-tuning of certain skills. For example, from _____ I learned _____.

What do you think of your present boss? Your former boss?

✓ Choose the Best Answer

☐ One thing I can say is that my present boss is a little nicer than the last one. I've never been very lucky in this area.

☐ I'd rather not discuss that. We got along but I never liked him.

☐ She never offered me any career development opportunities or any challenges.

☐ I've been around. I've had quite a few. There are good ones and less good ones.

☐ We have a good relationship based on trust and respect. He often asks me to fill in for him when he's absent.

? What They Really Want to Know

- Do you have good relationships with your bosses?
- Are you sad or angry over leaving your last job?
- Are you faithful and loyal? Are you trustworthy when you speak of your previous boss or company?

! Watch Out!

Don't:
- Criticize or make negative judgments about anyone.
- Talk badly about your ex-boss. Avoid mentioning his/her faults.
- Excessively flatter your last boss.
- Go into detail about the conflicts you had with your boss.
- Show yourself as rebellious to authority or hierarchy.
- Get lost in details and take too long to answer the question.

Don't Say:
- He screwed me.
- He didn't respect me.

- She didn't respect my work.
- He didn't give me enough responsibility.
- She didn't have confidence in me.
- I hope you will be more understanding than he was.
- I was much better than him. I should have been the boss.

Try This!

Do:

- Be discreet when you talk about a former boss. Mention the things you learned from him/her.
- Mention three qualities you recognized that showed their strengths, and stop there.
- Mention only positive things. Show how they helped you become the person you are today.

Say:

- I learned a lot from that boss [note: you may say this even if the relationship was contentious]. For example, _____.
- I really like her a lot. We were a very good duo. We often_____.
- I appreciate three things in him: efficiency, honesty, and vision.
- We were able to build a relationship of trust, which served as the basis for good organization and efficiency.

BEST ANSWER

We have a good relationship based on trust and respect. He often asks me to fill in for him when he's absent.

What skills/talents do you think your boss or supervisor should have?

✓ Choose the Best Answer

- ❏ Generosity!
- ❏ Being sensitive to my sensitivity.
- ❏ The same qualities I have.
- ❏ Natural authority, willpower, and a good sense of humor.
- ❏ He shouldn't be too rigid about the hours. That's an area where bosses are lacking in flexibility.

? What They Really Want to Know

- ▪ Do you accept taking orders? What's your relationship with the hierarchy?
- ▪ What do you expect of me?
- ▪ What do you fear in a boss or supervisor?

! Watch Out!

Don't:

- ▪ Announce a long list of things that have been wrong with previous bosses.
- ▪ Criticize a former boss.
- ▪ Dramatize a past conflict so your response is only negative.
- ▪ Appear to be hurt by your ex-boss.

Don't Say:

- ▪ A boss should always think of her subordinates first.
- ▪ I would have liked a boss who appreciated me.
- ▪ My boss was useless! He only got his job because he was related to the CEO.
- ▪ An understanding attitude when people make mistakes.

Try This!

- Give the three key competencies of a supervisor.
- Discuss the positive aspects of your former bosses.
- Show you understand the difficulties a boss faces.

Say: "

- I've always had good working relations with my bosses and colleagues. I particularly appreciate _____.
- I'm pretty flexible and I adapt easily. I like a boss who wants me to use my full potential by _____.
- What kind of boss are you?
- Three things: _____.

BEST ANSWER ✓

Natural authority, willpower, and a good sense of humor.

What kind of person manages you the best?

✓ Choose the Best Answer

- ❑ My family members.
- ❑ The best boss for me is one who appreciates my strengths and brings out the best in me by communicating honestly. I respond well to a person who stresses fairness and respect in their dealings with others.
- ❑ My ex-boss. She was nice and knew how to handle me.
- ❑ I'm easy to manage, as long as I am shown respect.
- ❑ An understanding boss, who recognizes my weaknesses and knows how to work with them.

? What They Really Want to Know

- ■ What kind of boss are you hoping to find?
- ■ What attitude should a boss have to make himself respected?
- ■ What characteristics in others do you respect?

! Watch Out!

Don't:

- ■ Suggest that you can't stand being given orders by your superiors.
- ■ Show any nervousness and have nothing to say.
- ■ Take too long to answer without offering at least two characteristics that a boss you admire would have.
- ■ Drag out the subject into a boring monologue.
- ■ Take the negative approach by saying what doesn't work for you.

Don't Say:

- ■ I don't like taking orders, especially from a boss I don't respect.
- ■ I'm easy to manage and get along with everybody.
- ■ No one has ever asked me that before. I'll have to think about it.
- ■ To give orders effectively, you need to know how to follow them.

Try This!

Do:

- Be spontaneous and answer positively.
- List characteristics of people with whom you have had excellent relationships.
- Just smile and let a few seconds go by before answering with one or two characteristics you respond well to.

Say:

- The kind of person who has had my kind of experience and understands how I might approach a problem.
- It's important to be able to adapt to all kinds of people.
- I can work on my own, but I appreciate the advice of others, especially those who have the necessary experience.
- A person who knows what she wants and is willing to bend when needed.
- Someone respectful and responsible who is capable of motivating me.

BEST ANSWER

The best boss for me is one who appreciates my strengths and brings out the best in me by communicating honestly. I respond well to a person who stresses fairness and respect in their dealings with others.

Who is the most difficult boss/supervisor you've ever had and why?

✓ Choose the Best Answer

- ❑ I've never had trouble. I'm everybody's buddy.
- ❑ There was real incompatibility with my boss. He never admitted when he had made a mistake!
- ❑ It depends on what you mean by difficult!
- ❑ I've had a few difficult cases above me. Listen to this: _____.
- ❑ I had a difficult boss at one job, but I learned a lot from him. For example, I learned that it is important to defend my ideas in an assertive, but not aggressive way. He taught me that when I did defend my idea in a way that strengthened the team, he had respect for me.

? What They Really Want to Know

- How you would describe the boss/supervisor you liked the least.
- How do you behave when you have difficulties with a higher-ranking person?
- What criteria do you use for judging a boss/supervisor as difficult?

! Watch Out!

Don't:
- Run down or make derogatory remarks about a former boss.
- List the reasons you didn't get along with a former boss.
- Hesitate answering or get tongue-tied.
- Use the real name of the person in question. The interviewer may know him/her.
- Laugh nervously and act like the question is a joke.

Don't Say:
- I can't think of an example, but I suspect everything's going to work with you.

- It was a woman and, between you and me, with her lack of competence, she must have pulled a few strings to get her job.
- I've had a few problems, but I know perfectly well how to command respect.
- Never had any difficult bosses.
- I'd rather not say. I hate to speak badly of anyone.
- A younger boss who got his job because he was related to someone else in the company. I had more experience and had been there longer.

Try This!

Do:

- Show that certain delicate professional situations can be excellent learning opportunities.
- Give a direct/spontaneous/positive answer and show how you benefited from the experience.
- Choose your words carefully so you avoid insulting people.
- Remember that every difficult experience brings the chance to gain something, if you are open to the bigger picture.

Say: 🎙

- A difficult boss gives me incentive to learn and grow.
- The only thing my boss and I disagreed about was the sport we played!
- I suppose I can be difficult at times too. Everyone has some aspect that is difficult for someone else.
- When a boss seems demanding, he may simply be testing your boundaries/character.
- A demanding boss is often a necessary element in a smooth running firm to keep things moving along.

BEST ANSWER ✔

I had a difficult boss at one job, but I learned a lot from him. For example, I learned that it is important to defend my ideas in an assertive, but not aggressive way. He taught me that when I did defend my idea in a way that strengthened the team, he had respect for me.

You have met the person who will be your boss if you are hired here. Do you think you will like working for him/her?

✓ Choose the Best Answer

- ❑ It's hard to say just now. I'll need a little time to know for sure.
- ❑ I enjoyed meeting him immensely. Do you know if the feeling was reciprocal?
- ❑ What's most important for me is to get along with my colleagues.
- ❑ When you're on a job, you get along with your boss. It's always been that way for me.
- ❑ Of course I will like her. That's my job!

? What They Really Want to Know

- ▪ Do you accept authority?
- ▪ How do you feel about authority?
- ▪ Do you make snap judgments?

! Watch Out!

Don't:

- ▪ Either act indifferent or over-react by saying what a great person he/she was.
- ▪ Suggest that you can't know how you will respond with such a short meeting.
- ▪ Look up in the air avoiding eye contact with the recruiter/interviewer as if to say you don't know.

Don't Say:

- ▪ Oh, that must have been the guy in the red necktie!
- ▪ I could never work for that person.
- ▪ Oh, I don't think there would be any problem.
- ▪ I always trust my first impression.

Do:

- Give some solid examples illustrating your ability to work together based on your past experiences with bosses.
- Show that you understand the meaning of "team spirit."
- Keep eye contact with the interviewer and smile!

Say: 〝〝

- I am looking forward to working with him. I believe we will have a good working relationship.
- I've never had any particular trouble with a boss. I think that will be true here too.
- I have pleasant memories of my relationships with previous bosses and so am always eager to learn from a new boss.
- I welcome the opportunity to be part of her team.

BEST ANSWER ✓

I enjoyed meeting him immensely.
Do you know if the feeling was reciprocal?

How do you feel about working for someone who is much younger than yourself?

✓ Choose the Best Answer

❑ I have worked for a younger people before. I find their energy and enthusiasm refreshing and it brings out the best in me.

❑ It depends. If my boss is intelligent, there's no problem.

❑ I don't like being bossed around by someone younger than me.

❑ I don't know yet. I've been working in a company where there were only three of us.

❑ That's not a problem for me, but it could be for someone else.

? What They Really Want to Know

- Will your ego suffer because you have a younger boss?
- Do you respect authority?
- Do you equate age with expertise?

! Watch Out!

Don't:
- Adopt a haughty attitude because you think younger people are inferior.
- Make it clear that you don't like being given orders by younger people.
- Question how decisions are made about who gets promoted.
- Act like age is an issue for you.

Don't Say:
- I've never had a younger boss so I can't honestly say how I will feel.
- It won't be a problem.
- I'm easy to manage and get along with everybody.
- I'd rather not say.
- I once had a boss who was younger than me who was a favorite of the CEO, whereas I had more experience and had been there longer.
- I like young people. They have good ideas sometimes.

Try This!

- Give some examples illustrating your ability to work with younger people.
- Show your respect for the hierarchy.
- Show that you know what cooperation means.
- Discuss an example or two of what you bring to the table that has nothing to do with age.

Say:

- I am looking forward to working with a new boss who is full of energy and ideas.
- I've never had any particular trouble with any of my bosses, regardless of their age.
- I respect expertise. Age doesn't determine that.
- The most important thing for me in a boss is someone who is respectful and responsible and is capable of motivating me.
- Everyone adds something to the mix. The best teams are those who are made up of diverse people, all of whom contribute to the end goals.
- I have always respected good leadership and don't feel threatened by age—either my own or others.

BEST ANSWER

I have worked for a younger people before. I find their energy and enthusiasm refreshing and it brings out the best in me.

13

Workplace Relationships and Communication

Q UESTIONS ABOUT YOUR RELATIONSHIPS in your past jobs generally refer to how you have interacted with your co-workers and whether you prefer working alone or in a group/team. Since most jobs have some element of interaction with other people, be it with co-workers, customers, clients, suppliers, competitors, etc., an interviewer needs to establish whether you are a person who gets along with others, and if there have been problems, what has caused them. There is certainly a correlation between how you have co-existed with others around you in a job and how you will get along at this new job. This isn't to say that you have to like everyone you meet and work with, but you do have to know what it is in others that causes problems for you. Once you know this about yourself, you can work to correct any problems or, at the very least, try to position yourself so you are not working continually with those who cause you difficulty.

In addition to knowing your preferred style of working (alone or in a group/team), an interviewer will try to establish how you best communicate with others. It's a rare job when you don't talk or interact with another person at least some of the time, and the key to successful relationships is how effectively you communicate. Are you able to get your thoughts across in a way that others can understand you? Are you able to keep your head about you and respond tactfully when faced with a conflict? Can you speak and write in an organized fashion so people aren't left wondering what you are really trying to say? Are you able to share responsibilities (both the good stuff and the not-so-good stuff) when working in a team? Do you know how to respect everyone's contribution to a team effort? Can you empower others to bring out the best in your team members?

If you can't communicate well, it's hard for others to engage with you and feel confident that there is an understanding and agreement about what is said and what is heard. If this goes on too long, ultimately the productivity of everyone is compromised.

Workplace relationships and communication questions included here are:

- Do you like working in a group? How do you fit into a team?
- Have you ever had people problems or difficult relations with others?
- How do you contribute to team spirit?
- How do you think you will integrate into our company?
- How did you get along with your last team?
- How do you position yourself among your peers?
- In your last/current job, what percentage of your time was spent working in a group or alone?
- Describe a team you were on. How did it function? What did you bring to it?
- I'm going to describe a team that you might join. How do you think you would go about fitting in?
- When you start working with new people, how do you go about it? Are you good at predicting their reactions?
- What type of people do you get along with best? Least?
- How important for you is communication at work?
- How do you relate to others?
- Do you think it is important to communicate with others at work?

What the Interviewer Wants to Know About You

By asking questions about your relationships and communication style, the interviewer is trying to find out:

- Can you establish and maintain good relationships with people?
- Can you identify the values others hold, and fit in?
- Do you have a preference for working with specific kinds of people?
- Do you prefer working alone or on a team?
- Are you sociable?
- Do you make contacts easily or are you shy?
- Are you more or less a leader, a team member, or a loner?
- How well are you able to perform on a team? What do you like to contribute?
- How well can you fit in? Are you easily accepted?
- What kind or relationships do you have with others in the workplace? Do you value your peers?
- Are you aware of which you prefer to work with: data, people, or things?
- Are you used to working on a team or independently?
- What's your working style?
- How do you feel about taking orders? Are you pretentious and full of yourself?
- Do you have a confrontational side?
- Will you adapt to the team without rocking the boat, or will you disturb it?
- Will you fit in with us? Do you make trouble for others?
- Can we fit you into our team? How well or easily do you become integrated?
- Would you respect an established team, or would you tend to impose your views/style from the beginning?

- What is your communication style?
- What makes you decide when it might be useful to communicate?

How to Answer

You must show that you understand and value good working relationships with others. Give examples of how you have worked to promote positive relationships with your co-workers, clients, customers, etc., showing that you realize efficiency is improved when people communicate clearly and honestly with one another.

Talk about your interpersonal skills and how you best interact with others. Be sure that you are honest here. Don't give yourself qualities you don't possess.

Give examples of how your communication skills have helped you avert problems with others. Show that you can make your points even when there is disagreement with others. If you have had conflicts in the past, the important thing to be shared is what you learned from those conflicts that now allow you to avoid them or deal with them more positively. It is not the problems we encounter in life that keep us from moving forward, it is how we respond to them and learn from them. Show that you are a person who knows that wisdom and changing behaviors that don't work are the true measure of growth.

Give examples indicating that you understand the importance of building relationships and your contact base. Talk about how you reach out to new people and foster collaboration between others. Show by your examples that you are willing to take initiative to reach out to others.

Have an example ready of how you joined an existing group and were able to fit in quickly. Talk about the qualities you think most important in others (and yourself). Give an example to show that you have respect for different personal styles and don't expect everyone to behave exactly as you do. The bottom line for an interviewer many times is just as simple as, "Will you fit in here?" If you can show that you will, you have cleared this important hurdle.

Do you like working in a group? How do you fit into a team?

✓ Choose the Best Answer

- ❏ You don't have to worry about me. I'm rather popular.
- ❏ I just quit my last job because of the atmosphere in the team.
- ❏ I often find it difficult to fit into a team when the people aren't much fun.
- ❏ Having a little disagreement with my colleagues doesn't keep me from doing my job.
- ❏ I find teamwork stimulates me.

? What They Really Want to Know

- ■ Can you establish and maintain good relationships with people?
- ■ What's your working style?
- ■ Will you adapt to the team without rocking the boat, or will you disturb it?

! Watch Out!

Don't:
- ■ Go into any misfortunes/conflicts you had in the past.
- ■ Go on and on about teamwork if the prospective job doesn't depend on it.
- ■ Act surprised and say you never have conflicts with anyone.

Don't Say:
- ■ "No" or "Not at all."
- ■ I prefer working alone.
- ■ More or less well. But, certain working methods are just incompatible.
- ■ I love working in a team. I get too lonely if I have to work alone.

Try This!

Do:

- Give examples of group projects or tasks you managed well.
- Describe a precise and concrete element that you brought to the group.
- Underline your sincere interest in interpersonal relationships—in particular, your skill at meeting new people and getting along with others.

Say:

- Thanks to the group effort, I managed to exceed the objectives of the XYZ project.
- I find that group work helps bring out the strong points in each collaborator.
- Group work develops creativity.

BEST ANSWER

I find teamwork stimulates me.

Have you ever had people problems or difficult relations with others?

✓ Choose the Best Answer

- ❏ It depends! "*C'est la vie.*"
- ❏ Me? Never!
- ❏ Yes, but it didn't come from me. People are just more and more stressed out.
- ❏ Naturally, like everyone. But I always managed to smooth things out.
- ❏ Rarely, but during my last job I had a couple of problems.

? What They Really Want to Know

- How well do you manage conflict?
- Do you like group work?
- Will you fit in with us? Do you make trouble for others?

! Watch Out!

Don't:

- Blame others.
- Give no answer at all.
- Go on and on in detail about a conflict.

Don't Say:

- I have a problem with authority!
- Sometimes I have a hard time making myself accepted.
- I'm good at using psychology! You'll be able to count on me!

Try This!

Do:

- Speak only briefly about this.
- Show you know how to cooperate with others.
- Give an example of a time you had a conflict and how you remained calm and resolved it.
- Mention how you best relate to others.
- Show how you overcame a conflict with someone else.

Say:

- In teamwork I appreciate open and clear communication.
- I like working on a team and exchanging ideas.
- I get along well with people. I have an outgoing personality.
- I always try to be receptive so that everyone gets along.
- Teamwork allows us to multiply our ideas. That is something I like!
- When I had a conflict with someone, I tried to learn from it so I would not repeat the experience—and I haven't!

BEST ANSWER

Naturally, like everyone. But I always managed to smooth things out.

How do you contribute to team spirit?

✓ Choose the Best Answer

- ❏ I was the one who did everything on my old team and they were grateful. I think I've got what it takes to be a manager. You can trust me.
- ❏ I am respected because I get things done!
- ❏ I really like teamwork. I try to be as involved as possible in group decisions and then carry out the projects with attention to detail and a sense of purpose.
- ❏ I do my best in spite of working fairly independently.
- ❏ I always make an effort to be part of the team. I'm good at it.

? What They Really Want to Know

- ▪ Do you like to take initiative?
- ▪ How do you fit in a team?
- ▪ Do you prefer working alone or on a team?

! Watch Out!

Don't:

- ▪ Humiliate your other team members.
- ▪ Act like you were always the best member of the team.
- ▪ Make negative judgments about the team members.
- ▪ Reveal that you are in fact a loner and rather reserved.

Don't Say:

- ▪ I always think it's smarter to let the others say what needs to be done.
- ▪ Actually, I can do everything myself.
- ▪ I am pretty much a loner.
- ▪ Team spirit? Fantastic, especially during halftime!
- ▪ I am a natural leader so it's easy for me to be on a team. I usually take over.

→ *Try This!*

Do: →

- Insist on listing your social skills that make you a good member of a team.
- Show you have a positive impact on a team using examples from past experience.
- Insist on the importance you attach to communication and demonstrate with an example how you do it.
- Present your methods for planning resources and time.
- Underline your sense of solidarity with the group.
- Offer praise of the group members and the outcomes you achieved.

Say: "

- I love group work for building a project. For example, we once were asked to ____.
- I love to work as part of a team because I appreciate all the skills and different viewpoints that come from being part of a team.
- I fit in well on a team and participate actively. For example, ____.
- I am open by nature and appreciate exchanging skills. Teamwork lets each person bring their best skills to the forefront.
- Working in a group allows a project to move forward quickly because the best ideas can be shared and then acted upon.
- I like being part of a team and find that when called upon to lead the team I am at my best. I value collegiality and the give-and-take that happens when people are working to meet the same goals.

BEST ANSWER

I really like teamwork, so I try to be as involved as possible in each group decision and then to carry out the projects with attention to detail and a sense of purpose.

How do you think you will integrate into our company?

✓ Choose the Best Answer

- ❏ I am good at sizing up a department/company and finding out how to be accepted.
- ❏ I don't know. It depends on the bosses and the colleagues. It's up to them!
- ❏ I'll go around to all the departments, then we'll see.
- ❏ I'll just observe for a while. Then I'll tell you.
- ❏ Don't worry. I know how to impose myself. People usually respect me right away.

? What They Really Want to Know

- ▪ Can you identify the values others hold, and fit in?
- ▪ How do you see our working together?
- ▪ What could you bring us?

! Watch Out!

Don't:

- ▪ Give the impression that you intend to revolutionize the place.
- ▪ Neglect to show any incentive.
- ▪ Forget to highlight your talents/skills/competencies relevant to the job.
- ▪ Act as if a team would be lucky to get you as one of its members.

Don't Say:

- ▪ I couldn't care less. What's important is that you hire me.
- ▪ I can't really see that far ahead yet.
- ▪ I'm not familiar enough with your company to answer that.
- ▪ I don't know. It's too early to say.

- I'll need a certain amount of time to adapt.
- I'll have no problem integrating. I get along with everyone.

Try This!

Do:

- Illustrate how well you integrated into your last job by giving an example.
- Show your curiosity. Ask questions.
- Show a link between your competencies and the company's needs and how you will add to the company in a short time.
- Give an example of how you integrated into your last company.
- Find out how the firm operates by asking questions so you will know how you can fit in.

Say:

- I'm a very sociable person and adjust easily.
- I hope to be able to meet your expectations rapidly. I am____ and____.
- What do you expect from a candidate? I will do everything in my power to satisfy you.
- Right away!

BEST ANSWER

✓ *I am good at sizing up a department/company and finding out how to be accepted.*

How did you get along with your last team?

✓ Choose the Best Answer

❑ The team didn't like me much because I was the most recent one on board/ the youngest/a man/woman.

❑ We used to go eat together.

❑ We hardly ever had the same viewpoint. Things used to heat up, but somehow it still worked.

❑ We got along perfectly.

❑ We were a united team with different personalities that allowed us to look at the many sides of an issue. We worked well together.

? What They Really Want to Know

▪ Are you respectful?

▪ Are you sociable?

▪ Can we fit you into our team? How easily/well do you become integrated?

! Watch Out!

Don't:

▪ Criticize your colleagues.

▪ Suggest you didn't get along and place the blame on others.

▪ Express criticism or slip into personal feelings.

▪ List all the problems, such as disputes.

▪ Act like everything was always perfect.

Don't Say:

▪ There were certain colleagues I didn't appreciate.

▪ There was no rapport.

▪ I don't like belonging to a group. I prefer working alone.

▪ I loved my team so much that I can't bear the thought of not working with them any longer.

Try This!

Do:

- Move quickly onto something else if you experience was negative. Keep details to a minimum.
- Show that effort is an essential element in the success of any business.
- Stay positive and mention the good things that come from being part of a team.

Say:

- As a whole, the atmosphere was great. We respected each other and worked together nicely.
- I entirely enjoyed working with them. We were particularly good at _____.
- I always had a good relationship with my team. I think that was because _____.
- I would hope to be lucky enough to always work with a team of such quality.

BEST ANSWER

We were a united team with different personalities that allowed us to look at the many sides of an issue. We worked well together.

How do you position yourself among your peers?

✓ Choose the Best Answer

- ❑ At meetings I tend to sit back. Maybe I should talk more.
- ❑ I like a good exchange. I have respect for others and new ideas and welcome the chance to accomplish goals with my team members.
- ❑ I often find I am smarter than they are.
- ❑ I don't like to compare myself, but I am a natural leader.
- ❑ I'm fairly timid by nature so I tend to be a loner.

? What They Really Want to Know

- ■ Are you ambitious/modest/self-centered?
- ■ How good are you at teamwork?
- ■ What kind of relationships do you have with others? Do you value your peers or colleagues?

! Watch Out!

Don't:
- ■ Belittle or criticize others.
- ■ Show too much ambition, too much willingness to go it alone.
- ■ Talk about conflict resolution in the team you worked with.
- ■ Play the individualist and suggest you need no one else.

Don't Say:
- ■ I had a hard time finding my niche.
- ■ I avoid my peers as they talk too much.
- ■ I appreciate neither the comparison nor the competition.
- ■ They make me uncomfortable.
- ■ The less I see them, the better I feel.
- ■ I love working as a leader.

Try This!

Do:

- Describe your friendliness and your ability to listen.
- Indicate your willingness to be part of a team.
- Show self-confidence and tell of good experiences in the past with co-workers.
- Talk about team spirit in general, about the importance of cooperating to reach goals.
- Speak in terms of "We" instead of "I."
- Turn the question around: "As a boss or subordinate?"
- Emphasize your entrepreneurship.

Say:

- They are an inexhaustible source of new ideas and learning opportunities.
- I am on very good terms with them. I enjoy sharing our experience.
- I appreciate their feedback.
- I need them to carry out my job.
- Team energy is always stronger than the lone energy of each member.
- I like working with others. In my last job I was extremely lucky to be part of a team of bright, dedicated people who enjoyed our work together.

BEST ANSWER

I like a good exchange. I have respect for others and new ideas and welcome the chance to accomplish goals with my team members.

✓ Choose the Best Answer

- ❑ I couldn't say. It used to depend on _____.
- ❑ I used to always work alone because I didn't get along with everyone. But if it's necessary, I can work on a team.
- ❑ If I take a typical day/week/month, I'd say 1/3 on a team and 2/3 time alone.
- ❑ If you want something done right, do it yourself.
- ❑ Teamwork wears me out!

? What They Really Want to Know

- How well do you manage tensions and conflicts?
- Are you aware of how you prefer to work when it comes to data/people/things?
- Are you used to working on a team or independently?

! Watch Out!

Don't:
- Admit not knowing how you spent your time.
- Act blasé, as if it didn't matter.
- Point out your preference for working alone/in a group.
- Suggest that you are the only one who can do things right and therefore spent all your time correcting others.

Don't Say:
- I like to be there all the time to correct other people's mistakes.
- I have a preference for a chief who takes things under his/her control.
- All the others can get along without me.
- You can only count on yourself.
- Without me, nothing will work.

Try This!

- Offer concrete examples to illustrate your work split between the team and alone.
- Give "for" and "against" arguments for both situations.
- Prove that both formulas suit you by referring to past achievements where you worked alone/on a team.
- Try to get the recruiter/interviewer to tell you what's behind the question. Does this job involve a great percentage of time one way or the other?

Say:

- I can get used to any situation. I like working on a team because I enjoy the creative energy that flows but I also like working alone so I can really focus and get things done.
- Working on your own allows for distance, whereas a group allows for creativity.
- It would seem ideal to me to divide the time between individual consideration and a group exchange.
- All their situations had advantages. I appreciated the diversity of these moments. I like _____ about being on a team and I like _____ about working alone.
- I split my time 50/50 because many of our decisions were made in group meetings.
- I would say I spent about five hours of the day working independently and about four hours working in a team/group situation.
- I spent most of my time working alone but would like to change the balance to spend more time as part of a team.
- I spend most of my time working on a team, and would like to change the balance a bit to work independently more.

BEST ANSWER

If I take a typical day/week/month, I'd say 1/3 on a team and 2/3 time alone.

Describe a team you were on. How did it function? What did you bring to it?

✓ Choose the Best Answer

- ❑ Teamwork allows you to find new ideas and new solutions. In my last job, for example, _____.
- ❑ I need to know the members of a team before I can really invest in it.
- ❑ I did my work like my supervisors wanted, so no problem. Besides, the teams were practically always the same.
- ❑ I showed interest in my co-workers when I used to ask them about their weekend.
- ❑ We operated according to the house policy.

? What They Really Want to Know

- ▪ How well are you able to perform on a team? What do you like to contribute?
- ▪ How well can you fit in? Are you easily accepted?
- ▪ How do you feel about groups? Are you basically a person who wants to go it alone?

! Watch Out!

Don't:

- ▪ Describe any conflicts you might have experienced in a group.
- ▪ Give the impression you prefer working on your own.
- ▪ Suggest that teamwork is hard for you.
- ▪ Show you are very selective.
- ▪ Go into detail about your experience.

Don't Say:

- ▪ I need to know the people well before I am comfortable working on a team.
- ▪ Sometimes I find it difficult to fit in, but it usually ends up working out okay. In my last job, I was on a team that was decent.
- ▪ I was double-crossed before, so now I'm careful.

- I was wary about my team. We didn't communicate well.
- I'm more or less a loner.

 Try This!

Do:

- Bring up an example of a successful team effort.
- Demonstrate your adaptability to working with a team by using an example from your past.
- Explain that group cohesion is important to you.
- Talk about how you helped your team move forward, using an example.
- Prove that the energy of a group of five is greater than the total energy of five people working alone.
- Emphasize that teamwork stimulates everyone's creativity.

Say:

- Thanks to a successful team effort, we were able to _____.
- I have often worked on a team. For example, _____.
- I love teamwork. It's stimulating to me because _____.
- I really like teamwork. How many are on your team? I once worked with a team to _____.
- Teamwork always creates new ideas and solutions. My last team was put together for a special project by the president of the company, and we traded duties and ideas. I was able to offer substantial input, and together we finished our project ahead of the deadline.

BEST ANSWER

Teamwork allows you to find new ideas and new solutions. In my last job, for example, _____.

I'm going to describe a team that you might join. How do you think you would go about fitting in?

✓ Choose the Best Answer

- ❏ These people seem perfectly ready to include someone of my value.
- ❏ Well, the team's not really important. I do my job even when the atmosphere is not so good.
- ❏ First of all, by observing how the team works together, then by offering my own experience from the field.
- ❏ I've already encountered people like that; they don't scare me.
- ❏ I think it depends more on them than on me. I'm sure I'll be respected, if that's the way I have to go.

? What They Really Want to Know

- ▪ Do you prefer working on your own or on a team?
- ▪ How easily do you adapt? What do you bring to the team?
- ▪ What problems in your past experience have you encountered?

! Watch Out!

Don't:

- ▪ Forget to listen to the description of the team given by the interviewer.
- ▪ Abruptly change the subject without answering how you could fit in.
- ▪ Give the impression you're a marginal type, a "Lone Ranger."
- ▪ Talk about some bad experiences you had with other teams.
- ▪ Act pretentious, claiming to know how to adapt to any situation.
- ▪ Bring up all kinds of problems that might arise if you were in fact to join this team.

Don't Say:

- ▪ This would be my first experience, so I don't know.
- ▪ I think it's more for them to adapt to me. There's not much I can do.
- ▪ I'm an individualist. I like working alone more than in a group.
- ▪ I've never been on a team like you described. It would take me some time to figure out my role.

Try This!

Do:

- Demonstrate your appreciation of one of the team's qualities.
- Give a couple examples of successful teamwork from your professional or non-professional past.
- Point out the advantages of teamwork after listening to what is described.
- Draw a parallel with a recent team-building situation.
- Ask questions and show your interest in this team and its achievements.
- Get out your day planner and make an appointment to get acquainted with the team.

Say:

- I look forward to having some rewarding exchanges with my co-workers. I think I bring _____ .
- I am anxious to work with them, and I think they will appreciate someone who really wants to learn something and who has my expertise in _____ .
- I think it's equally important for them to make my acquaintance. When could I meet them?
- Before trying to make a worthwhile contribution, I will need to take advantage of their experience to teach me what I need to know.
- My general knowledge makes me comfortable on a multicultural team.
- I know how to listen, a quality much appreciated by my previous bosses and co-workers.
- Such as you have presented this team, I would be delighted to meet them. I believe my experience in _____ would allow me to fit right in.
- Everything leads me to believe that we are going to be able to accomplish some fruitful work together. I am particularly interested in _____ .

BEST ANSWER

First of all, by observing how the team works together, then by offering my own experience from the field.

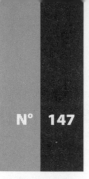

N° 147 — When you start working with new people, how do you go about it? Are you good at predicting their reactions?

✓ Choose the Best Answer

- ☐ They should adapt to me and not the opposite.
- ☐ Getting to know each person by talking with them individually to find out what makes them excited. I listen carefully to what they say.
- ☐ I'm tolerant with the older ones, but not so much with the younger ones.
- ☐ I don't listen to my colleagues, because if I do, we don't make any progress.
- ☐ New people have to adapt. That's just basic management.

? What They Really Want to Know

- Do you make contacts easily or are you shy?
- What are your interpersonal qualities? Do you have good people skills? Do you use a particular strategy?
- Would you respect an established team, or would you tend to impose your views/style from the beginning?

! Watch Out!

Don't:

- Act like you are pretty much of an individualist and do not like teamwork.
- Show that you have a hard time respecting systems established by others.
- Talk about conflicts.
- Appear to be imposing/overbearing.
- Suggest that you never have a problem with anyone.

Don't Say:

- I like to just get on with it. I let the getting-to-know-you process happen naturally.
- I do what I have to and it seems to work.
- I don't do anything in particular.
- I am friendly. I don't think it takes more than that.

Do:

- Consider the skills of others and show you appreciate them.
- Ask if you can meet your future co-workers.
- Show how you can become an additional resource for the team.
- Point out what the company expects of you.
- Highlight your listening and analytical skills.
- Explain that your style is to first observe and respect, with no criticism, what was done before you joined the company.
- Avoid being labeled as a "know-it-all."
- Prove your ability to adapt to a new corporate culture, to listen to a new team.
- Question your future co-workers in a friendly way to find out about them.

Say:

- I have learned a lot from others. When new to a group, I watch and ask questions so I can learn what has gone on before. I will offer my ideas but don't react if they are not all adopted. I believe in give and take.
- In my last job, I really appreciated being able to organize group projects. For example, _____.
- My style is to listen and learn and trust that my expertise will present itself in a non-threatening way. I like talking to others to find out about their work and their lives.
- I hope to invite them to lunch to break the ice and begin the "getting to know each other" process.
- I am careful to watch how others interact so I can adapt my style to theirs. I like to fit in with the team on their terms and not mine.

BEST ANSWER

Getting to know each person by talking with them individually to find out what makes them excited. I listen carefully to what they say.

What type of people do you get along with best? Least?

✓ Choose the Best Answer

- ❑ I like people who are frank with me. I don't appreciate the kind of bosses who think they're so superior and step all over everyone else. By the way, I know just how to put them in their place, when it's necessary.
- ❑ People I get along with inspire me to give my best. As for the others, I try to get the best out of them. I think I'm good at adapting to all kinds of people.
- ❑ I don't like people who take advantage of others.
- ❑ I don't like people who are slow to understand things.
- ❑ I like people who keep their nose to the grindstone best.

? What They Really Want to Know

- How well do you work in a group?
- What kind of work atmosphere do you thrive in?
- Do you have a preference for working with specific kinds of people?

! Watch Out!

Don't:
- Criticize anyone else.
- Say you're an individualist.
- Be categorical or fanatical and say there is any particular group of people you dislike.
- Express a blunt personal opinion that is negative.
- Show too much independence.
- Say you love everyone.

Don't Say:
- With some people, you know right away that it won't work!
- I've always preferred working alone.
- I like people who have qualities the same as mine.

- I get along with everyone. Never have any problems.
- I get along with everyone. But, I prefer working with women/men/young people/older people.
- I always get along with the pretty girls. Ha, ha!
- Bosses who never leave me alone drive me crazy.

Try This!

- Ask if the question is aimed at the professional domain or outside, or both.
- Highlight your abilities and qualities for working in a group by giving an example.
- Illustrate with concrete examples your ability to work with different types of people.
- Remain neutral and don't put down other people.

Say:

- In what context?
- As team leader or member?
- I was involved in a project on XYZ with a very heterogeneous group of seven people. It was a real pleasure.
- I try to adopt the qualities I admire in people, and simply ignore any weakness they might have.
- I can work with almost everyone, but it helps to have the same objectives.
- They say you get along better with people who don't have the same character as you. So, a little diversity is only beneficial.
- It's rare that you find the ideal situation. What counts is knowing how to get along, even if some people are different from yourself.
- You can always learn something from others if you are open.

BEST ANSWER

People I get along with inspire me to give my best. As for the others, I try to get the best out of them. I think I'm good at adapting to all kinds of people.

How important for you is communication at work?

✓ Choose the Best Answer

- ❑ When each person does his own job, everything goes smoothly.
- ❑ I don't come to work to talk. I do that outside of work.
- ❑ Enormously important! Good relationships make work more effective, and clear communication is essential for establishing and maintaining those relationships.
- ❑ I think it's good to communicate at work even though it takes up a lot of time.
- ❑ It's not important for me. I've always done my job independently of others.

? What They Really Want to Know

- ■ How do you imagine your professional encounters? Do you willingly share ideas with your co-workers?
- ■ Are you more or less: a leader, a team member, or a loner?
- ■ What is your communication style?

! Watch Out!

Don't:
- ■ Appear to be terribly shy so oral communication is hard for you.
- ■ Emphasize your self-sufficiency.
- ■ Show an unsociable side of yourself.
- ■ Pretend that you always communicate clearly and it is others who don't do this well.

Don't Say:
- ■ I only like contact with people outside of work.
- ■ I'd rather work on my own account.
- ■ Of huge importance. I put everything in writing and file all the messages I send my colleagues.

Try This!

Do:

- Bring up real experience. Explain how you prefer to communicate.
- Give an example of how you value clear communication.
- Show that you know how to build and keep up a strong network.
- Show your regard for communication as an essential element in the effectiveness of a team.

Say:

- The quality of one's work is proportional to one's ability to communicate.
- Communication [exchanging/sharing information] plays a major role in all kinds of continuous learning.
- I believe in communicating clearly. I say what I mean and I mean what I say.
- Without clear communication, it's easy to make mistakes that could have been avoided because directions were not clear.
- Clear communication is essential. I like to write, as it makes it easier to know if I am specific and understandable in what I'm trying to say.
- I am careful to keep in touch with my network by communicating often.

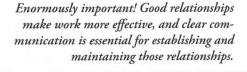

BEST ANSWER

Enormously important! Good relationships make work more effective, and clear communication is essential for establishing and maintaining those relationships.

How do you relate to others?

- ❏ I appreciate meeting new people; it's always been rewarding and is one of the main things that has allowed me to grow. I like to share information and experiences with others.
- ❏ I willingly accept orders from my boss as long as they are not stupid.
- ❏ I get along with everyone. No problem!
- ❏ I am an independent person. I can accomplish a task without having to consult/bother anybody else.
- ❏ I am an open person. I can talk for hours with my co-workers about almost anything under the sun.

? What They Really Want to Know

- ▪ How do you feel about taking orders? Are you pretentious? Full of yourself?
- ▪ Do you have a confrontational side?
- ▪ How do you feel about hierarchy?

! Watch Out!

Don't:

- ▪ Mention or criticize a previous boss or co-workers.
- ▪ Criticize a specific kind of person.
- ▪ Pretend that everyone likes you.
- ▪ Make believe that if you are out of work, it's somebody else's fault.
- ▪ Show bitterness or resentment toward other nationalities.
- ▪ Show that you are very independent and don't need others.
- ▪ Come across as a person with no personality who tends to take a back seat and accepts everyone.
- ▪ Display your collection of work certificates to prove your good relations.
- ▪ Focus on a bad relational experience or a past conflict.

Don't Say:

- ▪ No problem. I get along with everybody.

- I am a quiet person who gets along with others.
- I love making new acquaintances.
- I have excellent relationships with good-looking women/men ____
- I don't like being told what to do.
- I'd rather work alone than in a group.
- I am more or less a loner.
- I don't particularly like working with foreigners.

Try This!

Do: →

- Mention what you have achieved in a group.
- Demonstrate that you live in a balanced social and family environment.
- Give an example of an outside activity you do with colleagues from work.
- Explain your interest in different cultures and your openness to others.
- Mention other activities, such as volunteer work.
- Highlight your team spirit.
- Reveal your skill as a moderator and a good listener.
- Speak in terms of a balance between individual and group work.
- Offer an example of working together and adapting well.

Say: 🙶

- Thanks to my familiarity with his culture, I managed to ____.
- My intervention in a disagreement proved to my boss and co-workers that my negotiation skills were helpful and allowed me to relate to everyone involved.
- When a problem came up, my co-workers would all turn to me because they knew I could troubleshoot the problem.
- Working with others allows knowledge to be shared and improvements made.
- I accept people for who they are and look for the positive in everyone.
- I respect authority and I value input from others so I can constantly learn and grow in my skills.

BEST ANSWER

I appreciate meeting new people; it's always been rewarding and is one of the main things that has allowed me to grow. I like to share information and experiences with others.

Do you think it is important to communicate with others at work?

✓ Choose the Best Answer

- ❏ It's my boss's role to pass on any information.
- ❏ Yes, communication is at the basis of the synergy created in good teamwork.
- ❏ Communication doesn't seem essential in my particular case/job.
- ❏ I work on my own and prefer to send reports out to everyone instead of wasting time talking to them.
- ❏ Yes, I do, but without succumbing to "meeting fever."

? What They Really Want to Know

- How do you get along with your co-workers?
- What makes you communicate with your co-workers?
- What makes you decide when it might be useful to communicate?

! Watch Out!

Don't:

- Criticize your former bosses for not interacting enough in your meetings.
- Describe a situation where you felt isolated from your colleagues.
- Explain that you work better alone.
- Show that interaction is not of primary importance.
- Talk about problems with your co-workers.

Don't Say:

- It's not important and doesn't interest me. I don't talk when I'm working.
- I'm not paid to communicate, but rather to be productive.
- Most of my co-workers are men, and they don't like to talk.
- I think interaction is important at business get-togethers, but at work I think we should all be discreet.

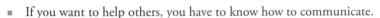

Try This!

Do: →

- Show that you enjoy communicating through your outside activities as well.
- Let it be known that you have kept in touch with co-workers from different companies where you have worked.
- Show that you know how to build and keep up a strong network.
- Show your regard for communication as an essential element in the effectiveness of a team.

Say: 🙶

- If you want to help others, you have to know how to communicate.
- Communication leads to new ideas.
- Communication should be honest and frank, and create an atmosphere of confidence.
- 90% of the success of a corporation is due to good communication.
- To be effective in the workplace, communication should be brief but regular. This makes it easier to remember things and helps keep the staff stimulated.
- Good communication is very important for keeping everyone informed.

BEST ANSWER

Yes, communication is at the basis of the synergy created in good teamwork.

14

Vision

I NTERVIEWERS WANT TO KNOW if candidates can see the "sum of all the parts." Can you think strategically with an eye to the future? It's not that they expect you to be a person who can see exactly what the future will hold as if you had a crystal ball; it's just that they want to know that you have vision that extends beyond today. Often a "best guess" about what will or should happen is the most that can be realized. People with vision are willing to make those "best guesses" and act on them by using all the information, reasons, and clues that are at hand. People with vision are constantly striving to look at things in a new light or a different light and see what might be possible. They are not content with the status quo—they want to push the envelope and see what's possible. They are not people who ask, "Why?" but, rather, people who ask, "Why not?" They are willing to risk trying new things. They are honest, and when they see a way to improve something, they speak up.

Vision questions included here are:

- Where do you think our greatest opportunity lies? What is our biggest asset with regard to our competitors?

- Illustrate how your (last) job corresponds with the general goals of our department/organization.
- What trend or major change do you see in our sector?
- What is your employer's current major project?
- After looking at our website, what recommendations would you make to improve it?

What the Interviewer Wants to Know About You

By asking questions about vision, the interviewer is trying to find out:

- When you look at your job, do you see the big picture or do you focus on the details?
- Do you have vision? Are you strategic?
- Are you analytical? Do you notice small details?
- Are you going to bring a breath of fresh air, new ideas, to our firm?
- Can you look to the future?
- What do you know about our sector?
- What could we improve right now?
- Can you be diplomatic and still offer suggestions?
- Are you going to help us to achieve our goals, to exceed them?
- What is it about our firm that attracts you? Why are you here?
- Do you have a thorough understanding of our sector?
- Have you kept up with what's happening in your field?

How to Answer

Make sure you do your homework before going to an interview. It will be hard to answer questions about what a company or sector might do to improve, without having done some research on what makes the company/sector tick. You cannot answer intelligently if you don't know the basic history and past trends. It is okay to make educated guesses about how things might change in the near and far future. You do not have to be right; you only have to show that you can think strategically with an eye to the big picture.

If you are asked what improvements can be made to something, and feel your ideas offer a new twist, speak up and give your opinion. Don't be rigid in your suppositions, but show that you know how to analyze and evaluate problems and solutions.

Where do you think our greatest opportunity lies? What is our biggest asset with regard to our competitors?

✓ Choose the Best Answer

- ❏ I should be asking you this question!
- ❏ I'm not too sure who your competitors are.
- ❏ In comparison with your competitors, your distinctive advantage/ competence is _____. As for your greatest opportunity, I'd have to spend some more time with you to know all the factors affecting this.
- ❏ I'm meeting you for the first time. How could I know where your opportunities lie?
- ❏ Have you got a lot of competition?

? What They Really Want to Know

- ▪ Do you have vision? Are you strategic?
- ▪ What do you know about our sector?
- ▪ What could we improve right now?

! Watch Out!

Don't:

- ▪ Let yourself be flustered by such a pointed question, even if it comes early in the interview.
- ▪ Appear to be ignorant about the problems, competition, and trends of the sector.
- ▪ Come to the interview without having a look at their website and/or press articles on the their company, industry, and particular market.
- ▪ Suggest something superficial.

Don't Say:

- ▪ Innovation!
- ▪ There's nothing that needs improvement.
- ▪ I'll wait until you describe your company before I answer.
- ▪ I can't say.
- ▪ The benefits for employees!

Try This!

Do:

- Ask questions to clarify the short- and medium-term goals of the firm.
- Suggest gathering information with an eye on how to make improvements.
- Gather information about their current ongoing projects so you will know the mission of the company.
- Give an example to show you understand who their competition is and how they fit into the market sector.

Say:

- In order to seriously identify your opportunities, I would have to know you better. But just offhand, I see three obvious qualities.
- According to my information, I can conclude that ____.
- Your sector is currently confronted with a great challenge. It would seem to me that due to ____ and ____, you are well armed to meet it.
- Your website points out two quite interesting things that I haven't found elsewhere, namely ____ and ____ .

BEST ANSWER

In comparison with your competitors, your distinctive advantage/competence is ____. As for your greatest opportunity, I'd have to spend some more time with you to know all the factors affecting this.

Illustrate how your (last) job corresponds with the general goals of our department/organization.

✓ Choose the Best Answer

- ❏ I don't know what your department's goals are. You would need to tell me about them first.
- ❏ They were much more ambitious, but I don't want that much responsibility.
- ❏ My previous goals didn't have much to do with yours.
- ❏ Your goals are much more ambitious and I hope to be able to meet them.
- ❏ In spite of a few small differences, you seem to be aimed in the same direction in these three areas: _____, _____, and _____.

? What They Really Want to Know

- ▪ Are you going to help us to achieve our goals, to exceed them?
- ▪ What is it about our firm that attracts you? Why are you here?
- ▪ Is your experience (your present duties or responsibilities) sufficient for the responsibilities we will entrust in you?

! Watch Out!

Don't:

- ▪ Ask for details on their objectives/goals.
- ▪ Run down your former boss or job.
- ▪ Mention objectives you were not able to achieve.
- ▪ Use examples from your last job that are not relevant to this job.

Don't Say:

- ▪ I don't know what your goals are.
- ▪ My last job's goals have nothing to do with yours.
- ▪ My goals were unrealistically high and impossible to achieve.
- ▪ My boss was incapable of setting clear and realistic goals.
- ▪ Since our goals are similar, I can guarantee that if you hire me, I will raise your bottom line by _____ percent.

Do: →

- List the skills you have, and develop those that will be useful for the new job.
- Explain what you can bring to the company in concrete terms.
- Point out which of your skills would be transferable to the new job.
- Speak with enthusiasm about your achievements and goals achieved or exceeded.
- Prove that you fully understand the company's goals.

Say: ""

- The main direction pursued by your company appears to be ___. My last job provided me with ____ and ____. Would you say that these skills will fit the goals of this particular job five years from now?
- The goals of my last job are right in line with yours. These two achievements should serve to convince you of what I can bring to your firm: ____ and ____.
- Although my previous goals were slightly different from yours, this job represents an interesting challenge, and I like a good challenge.
- If you hire me, what are the three results on which you will evaluate me at the end of my first year with you?

BEST ANSWER

✓ *In spite of a few small differences, you seem to be aimed in the same direction in these three areas: ____, ____, and ____.*

What trend or major change do you see in our sector?

✓ Choose the Best Answer

❏ Your guess is as good as mine!

❏ The opinions of the experts are not in agreement and I hesitate to make any predictions. However, I think _____.

❏ That's a hard question.

❏ I'll need some time to immerse myself into the reality of the market and take into account the real factors that affect the situation to give you a thorough answer. At the present time, I see a shift in _____.

❏ Without doubt, the sector is going to grow/shrink in the next six months.

? What They Really Want to Know

■ Are you going to bring a breath of fresh air, new ideas, to our firm?

■ Do you have a thorough understanding of our sector?

■ Do you have vision? Strategic vision?

! Watch Out!

Don't:

■ Push future trends that are only hypothetical.

■ Make a guess without any research to back up your statement, just so you can answer.

■ Make hasty comparisons with another sector you know better than this one.

■ Fail to do any research about this sector.

Don't Say:

■ And what do you see?

■ Progress. I'll bring you that!

■ The sector is in disastrous shape. What's important is to survive.

■ I really can't see that far ahead.

Try This!

Do:

- Report on what you have recently seen/heard in the news or on the Internet.
- Offer to find out and talk about it at a later date.
- Inform yourself about the sector before the interview so you can respond intelligently to this question, even if you can't offer a concrete direction the sector will take.
- Keep up on market trends (through the Internet, print media, associations, etc.).

Say: 🙿

- I would be glad to look into this subject.
- I cannot foresee the future, but would like to remain optimistic. I can get down to work and find out.
- Could we compare our views, since mine is coming from the outside?
- I see _____ based on the research I have done. This seems to me to indicate there is a chance for us to work on a future project.

BEST ANSWER

I'll need some time to immerse myself into the reality of the market and take into account the real factors that affect the situation to give you a thorough answer. At the present time, I see a shift in _____.

What is your employer's current major project?

✓ Choose the Best Answer

- ❏ To make more money. But he doesn't talk about it much.
- ❏ I believe it is to adapt to the changing market and to consolidate the company's profit for the greatest economic growth possible.
- ❏ That doesn't really concern me. It's her problem.
- ❏ To keep the turnover from rising even more.
- ❏ He's got so many projects! I can't pick just one.

? What They Really Want to Know

- ■ When you look at your job, do you see the big picture or do you focus on the details?
- ■ Do you know the firm?
- ■ Have you kept up with what's happening in your field?

! Watch Out!

Don't:
- ■ Criticize your employer.
- ■ Reveal information that could have a damaging effect on your employer, such as confidentialities and malicious gossip.
- ■ Refuse to talk about your boss.

Don't Say:
- ■ I'm not sure how it will help you to know this.
- ■ I couldn't care less.
- ■ I don't know. She never confided in me.
- ■ No comment.
- ■ His project is too ambitious for me!

Try This!

 **Do:**

- Lead the discussion toward what you [for example] brought to the team to promote the priorities of the department/company.
- Talk about strategic solutions that would be more profitable.
- Bounce the question back to your skills.
- Show yourself as motivated by the results and goals you helped achieve at your former/current job.

 **Say:**

- To build up her clientele and create customer loyalty.
- To consolidate the company's/department's growth.
- To expand the company by external acquisition.

BEST ANSWER

✓ *I believe it is to adapt to the changing market and to consolidate the company's profit for the greatest economic growth possible.*

After looking at our website, what recommendations would you make to improve it?

✓ Choose the Best Answer

☐ I liked the graphics on your site, particularly _____. I think the picture of _____ might be a bit bigger to make a stronger impact.

☐ Oh, I didn't look at it.

☐ I liked it. I wouldn't change a thing.

☐ My computer is too slow so I only looked at your home page.

☐ I liked how you listed your new products, but I thought they should be listed alphabetically.

? What They Really Want to Know

▪ Did you do your homework before the interview?

▪ Can you be diplomatic and still offer suggestions?

▪ Are you analytical? Do you notice small details?

! Watch Out!

Don't:

▪ Go to an interview without checking out the company's website.

▪ Criticize the site without offering a suggestion for improvement.

▪ Say you don't have a computer so you didn't look at it.

▪ Say nothing.

▪ Say you liked it without explaining why.

▪ Say you didn't like it without giving a reason.

Don't Say:

▪ I thought the site was too busy—it was hard to figure out what to look at first.

▪ Websites are all the same—they are basically boring.

▪ Who designed your site? I could offer them some help.

- I couldn't figure out how to get to your section on _____. Perhaps my browser doesn't work right.
- I think you need more pictures on your site.

Try This!

Do: →

- Give some concrete examples illustrating what you liked about the site.
- If you see a typographical error, politely point it out [so they can fix it].
- Speak in specifics.
- Mention the use of color/sound/graphics if appropriate.

Say: 🙦

- On the left column, I liked the subject categories that make it so easy for a user to locate their specific concern(s) fast. The center section with the categories is also nicely organized. It's easy to move from category to category very quickly.
- I noticed a typographical error on page 3 (explain the error). I imagine you will want to correct this.
- I liked the clean, crisp look of your site. The left sidebar is particularly helpful because _____ .
- While I liked your section on portfolios, I wonder if using bullets to list the different items might be more visually attractive.
- I found it easy to move around the site. Your services are listed well and the user can see at a glance all that you offer.
- I loved the color on your site. It immediately invites the user in and makes them want to learn more.
- I took the online assessment you offered and found it helpful. I particularly liked _____ .

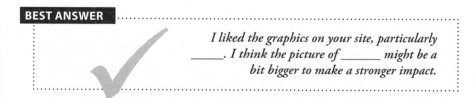

BEST ANSWER

I liked the graphics on your site, particularly _____. I think the picture of _____ might be a bit bigger to make a stronger impact.

15

Job Hunting

Y OU MAY THINK IT ODD that an employer would ask you about your job hunting activities, but it's a good window into your character. Because job hunting produces more stress than almost any other experience, it tells a lot about how you function when things are difficult. Interviewers want to know if you are proactive in your job search or are just sitting back idly hoping that something will land in your lap without much effort on your part. There is a correlation between how you approach your job hunt and how you approach your job(s) and indeed your life. Those who get out on the front lines, who stay with it, who double their efforts when things dry up, and who understand that to have a different outcome they have to try a different strategy, demonstrate personal characteristics that employers value in their employees.

They usually want to know why you have approached them and perhaps even how you came to know about them (unless you are responding to an ad they placed) to see if you take initiative and go after what you want. No company likes to think they were selected without sincere interest in their work/mission or that they were randomly selected from the phone book without any specific or personal reason on the part of the job hunter.

Questions to find out what other organizations you are approaching (if any) are asked to see if there is a pattern or continuity in your interests. If you are all over the map with the kinds of jobs you are pursuing, they might think you are not seriously committed to getting the kind of job you are applying for with them. Your activities with other companies tell an interviewer if you are in demand. Everybody likes to think others want the person they will choose for the job—human nature is drawn to those who are perceived as desirable. If you have other offers in the pipeline, it can also give you a leg up in the negotiating process if they offer you a job down the line.

Job hunting questions included here are:

- Do you like job hunting?
- Do you have any other offers in the pipeline?
- Have you received any firm offers?
- How did you hear about us?
- How did you find your last job?
- Describe your job hunt. How do you go about conducting a job search?
- How long have you been looking for a job?
- What will you do if you are not offered this job?
- When will you be available? What is your current activity level?
- What other organizations/companies have you approached?
- If we offer you this job, what reasons will you give your employer when you resign?

What the Interviewer Wants to Know About You

By asking questions about your job hunting, the interviewer is trying to find out:

- How do you organize yourself?
- Do you get discouraged easily, or are you tenacious and persevering?

- Are you resourceful? Proactive? Do you have initiative? Do you know what works when it comes to job hunting?
- What motivates you in your job hunting?
- Are you truly motivated by the job we're discussing / by our company?
- Have you visited our website?
- Are you familiar with our company/products?
- Are you well informed on our sector/market activity?
- What is your real interest in this job?
- Have you applied for jobs with other firms/organizations?
- Are you a success? If you are attractive, am I going to have to fight to get you? Do I have a little more time to calmly think over my decision? Might a rival company snatch you up?
- If you get other job offers, whom will you pick?
- Are you negotiating any job offers at the moment?
- Do you have other plans?
- How long have you been job hunting?
- Are you ready to sell your soul to the devil by taking any job?

How to Answer

When you are asked questions about your job hunting activities, it's important to be up-front and tell the truth. If you are just starting out in your activities, say so. Tell them what you plan to do and who else you are considering contacting. If you have been at it a while, tell them the companies you have interviewed with and what you like about each job (you can mention one reason why the job doesn't suit you as long as you don't say anything negative about that company). If you have offers, you can say that you are considering one or two (when this is the case) other offers, but will choose this company if you are offered a job, since "this is the company I most want to work for." If you have been job hunting a long time with no concrete results, tell the interviewer what you have been doing that's constructive and shows that you are actively pursuing your goals (job-wise and personally). Show them you are systematic in your approach to job hunting activities.

Whatever you do, don't lie about how much you have been doing or claim that you have offers if you do not have them. You don't know if the interviewer might know someone at the company you mention and check it out. It's better to stick with the truth and demonstrate your commitment to find exactly the right job.

Tell the interviewer of your sincere interest in his/her company and this particular job. Frame your answers so that you show a real desire (backed up by research and planning) to be with them. Tell them what you like about the company and the job. Tell them that you are familiar with their sector/competitors/customers, etc. Let them know you have sought them out for valid reasons. Do not give the impression that you just threw a dart onto the board and came to them with no real passion for the job they offer or the company itself.

Do you like job hunting?

✓ Choose the Best Answer

- ❏ I'm beginning to get used to it!
- ❏ Put yourself in my place and ask yourself that question.
- ❏ I would have to admit that finding the right kind of work is what motivates me, plus the idea that I will be able to do what I love doing.
- ❏ No. But, I'll end up finding something because I answered 64 ads this month and sent out 50 letters.
- ❏ When I'm lucky enough to meet a recruiter/interviewer as charming as you.

? What They Really Want to Know

- ■ How do you organize yourself?
- ■ What motivates you in your job hunting?
- ■ Do you get discouraged easily, or are you tenacious and persevering?

! Watch Out!

Don't:
- ■ Criticize the business world in general as being responsible for the unemployment situation.
- ■ Let your fear for the future show.
- ■ Show you are pessimistic and don't expect good results.
- ■ Get out your thick file of research.
- ■ Admit the reason you haven't found a job is because something is wrong with you.
- ■ Play the victim.
- ■ Act like someone who gives up easily.

Don't Say:
- ■ After being at it for two years, you can imagine what it's like.
- ■ You are the first to offer me an interview in a year!

- I expect to be offered a job.
- Frankly, I am fed up. I'm ready to take anything.
- I prefer to let an agency offer me something.
- No. It's a waste of time. And besides, my resume is now outdated.
- I do sort of like it, but I don't seem to be very good at it!

 Try This!

Do:

- Make clear that this time period has been put to good use.
- Avoid being on the defensive. Job hunting takes time, and you should show that you have been using it wisely.
- Talk about how job hunting stimulates you to find the job that is the best fit for you.
- Indicate your enthusiasm for the current interview.
- Present this time as a chance for a new direction.
- Show yourself as ready for a new challenge.

Say:

- It's an opportunity for me to concentrate on my career plan.
- It's a time of bad and good surprises. Some things have been delightfully interesting and some things are more difficult because it's hard to know which job will be the best fit for my future company and me.
- I'd rather be job hunting than working at a job that doesn't meet my needs.
- Yes and, by the way, it's what allowed us to meet.
- Yes, and it was an occasion for me to take a look at my career and to confirm my interest in the work you are offering.
- Yes. It makes me think about new ways of developing my career. For example, _____.

BEST ANSWER

I would have to admit that finding the right kind of work is what motivates me, plus the idea that I will be able to do what I love doing.

Do you have any other offers in the pipeline?

✓ **Choose the Best Answer**

- ❏ After sending out 50 letters, you are the only one who invited me for an interview. I was desperate! It's revolting! They don't even answer!
- ❏ I'm waiting for an answer from a company similar to yours, who is interested in my profile.
- ❏ No. Maybe that's because I'm not really interested in this sector.
- ❏ Yes. I'm waiting for an answer for a job that seems particularly interesting.
- ❏ Yes. I have a few, but the salary is not good.

? What They Really Want to Know

- ▪ Are you a success? If you are attractive, am I going to have to fight to get you?
- ▪ Are you actively job hunting?
- ▪ Can I afford to take my time to offer you the job?

! Watch Out!

Don't:

- ▪ Reveal confidential information on competitors.
- ▪ Give negative reactions about other companies you have contacted.
- ▪ Be evasive in your answers.
- ▪ Let it be known that you are applying for other kinds of jobs or in other sectors than the one you are interviewing for.
- ▪ Mention that you have other things going without emphasizing that this job/company in question is the one you prefer, and list the specific reasons why you want to work for them.

Don't Say:

- ▪ No. I am immediately available.
- ▪ No. I'm beginning to get worried.

- No. I do not have any other offers.
- Yes. And I would only accept your offer if it is financially attractive, because the other job seems quite interesting.
- Yes. But I would only accept the other job if nothing better shows up.
- You are the only one I wrote to.
- You are the only firm that showed any interest in me.

Try This!

Do:

- Make it clear to the recruiter/interviewer that, in spite of your other moves, you want to work with her/his company.
- Show that you are indeed actively job hunting, yet at the same time are particularly interested in the post you are interviewing for.
- Try to find out if the recruiter/interviewer is hesitating to make you an offer because he/she is trying to decide between several candidates.

Say:

- I've had three interesting interviews in the last month.
- I am waiting for answers from other companies.
- I am currently negotiating with some of your competitors. On your side, have you had many other candidates?
- A headhunter contacted me with some possible positions that might be a good fit.

BEST ANSWER

I'm waiting for an answer from a company similar to yours, who is interested in my profile.

Have you received any firm offers?

✓ Choose the Best Answer

- ❑ In fact, I have. I am in the final phase of negotiations with two firms. I am very interested in your company as well.
- ❑ None at the moment. At my age I scare everyone off because they can't afford me.
- ❑ I have one, but they find me too expensive.
- ❑ Out of 73 applications, it's pretty unlikely not to receive any firm offers.
- ❑ No. I am completely available and can start right away.

? What They Really Want to Know

- ▪ Do I have a little more time to calmly think over my decision? Might a rival company snatch you up?
- ▪ Are you truly motivated by the job we're discussing/by our company?
- ▪ If you get other job offers, which will you pick?

! Watch Out!

Don't:

- ▪ Deceive the recruiter/interviewer by announcing that you have indeed received some firm offers if this isn't the case. You run the risk of being sent back to those rivals without a job offer!
- ▪ Let the question upset you if you haven't received any offers yet.
- ▪ Admit that, in spite of all the efforts you have made, you have still not received a single offer.
- ▪ Use the disastrous situation of the market to justify the lack of offers.
- ▪ Forget to point out that, even if you have received other offers, your preference is for the job in question and state, "For the following reasons: _____."

Don't Say:

- ▪ No other company has shown any interest in my resume yet.
- ▪ You know that the market is in the dumps.

- I hope to receive a definitive answer in the next few days.
- Yes, but I'd prefer not to talk about it.

 Try This!

Do:

- Announce that you have only recently begun actively job hunting, that your choice is very focused, and that their firm is your primary focus.
- Show that the company you are interviewing with at this moment is the one you wish to work for, for the following reasons _____.
- Answer briefly and go on to another subject by asking a question.

Say: "

- If I receive one from yours, that will make two!
- I have contacted very few companies—only those that really match what I'm looking for.
- No, but I'm waiting on two companies I interviewed with last month.
- Yes, I've had a few offers, but everything is still open. I am very interested in this job as my first choice. I am mostly drawn to _____ and _____ that this job would offer.
- Yes, I did receive one, from your direct rival!

BEST ANSWER

In fact, I have. I am in the final phase of negotiations with two firms. I am very interested in your company as well.

How did you hear about us?

✓ Choose the Best Answer

- ❏ My advisor/coach encouraged me to contact you.
- ❏ Another unemployed friend told me you were maybe looking for someone.
- ❏ I picked up the phonebook and started at Z instead of A, unlike most people!
- ❏ By accident/chance!
- ❏ I focused on your sector in my job hunt and aimed my efforts specifically at your company because it has three features that differentiate it from its rivals.

? What They Really Want to Know

- ▪ Have you visited our website?
- ▪ Are you familiar with our company/our products?
- ▪ Are you well informed on our sector/market activity?

! Watch Out!

Don't:

- ▪ Say that you are a neighbor, but you're not quite sure if the job interests you.
- ▪ Go into detail about the friend who told you about the job/company.
- ▪ Suggest that whether it's this company or another, it's all the same to you.
- ▪ Get lost in long, useless explanations that don't add anything to why the company is special to you.

Don't Say:

- ▪ So, what do you make here at your company?
- ▪ I have a friend in this branch who told me you were definitely hiring.
- ▪ I know your company. I've written to you three times.
- ▪ I am aware that you cut down last year. I heard about the layoffs.

Do:

- List two or three products/services that this company furnishes and why it interests you.
- Make it clear that you network in the sector and list those activities, briefly naming organizations and people when appropriate.
- Show that you are well informed on their area of activity.
- Mention their website and what you liked about it.

Say:

- I have always followed the economic developments in your sector with great interest. Thus, I have seen that _____.
- When I learned who the main players were in this sector, it was obvious I had to contact you.
- A company I used to work for was on very good terms with your company and suggested I contact you. I also looked at your website and particularly liked the way you _____.

BEST ANSWER

I focused on your sector in my job hunt and aimed my efforts specifically at your company because it has three features that differentiate it from its rivals.

How did you find your last job?

✓ Choose the Best Answer

- ❑ My friend worked there and got me an interview. I loved the job and we finished on Fridays at 4:30 PM. It was great.
- ❑ By accident. I answered an ad and they told me I could begin right away. I was surprised but happy to find something at last.
- ❑ I saw their ad in the paper.
- ❑ I started my job hunt using all means available, such as the Internet, networking, and job ads, and then selected the companies that best matched my profile as the ones I should contact.
- ❑ Not good at all. I didn't like my boss.

? What They Really Want to Know

- ▪ Did you choose among several offers?
- ▪ Do you have a good network of professional relationships?
- ▪ Are you resourceful? Proactive? Do you have initiative? Do you know what works when it comes to job hunting?

! Watch Out!

Don't:
- ▪ Appear to be a passive person.
- ▪ Show that you let your professional choices just happen to you without any design on your part.
- ▪ Mention pulling any strings or using friends/relatives.

Don't Say:
- ▪ For two months I waited to be offered the job.
- ▪ I was recommended.
- ▪ I took the first one that came along.
- ▪ I didn't have any choice. It was the only thing I could find.
- ▪ Pure chance.

Try This!

Do: →

- Explain that your choice was purposeful and part of a certain design on your part.
- Show that you had a winning strategy in place.
- Point out all the motivation and information gathering that preceded your decision.
- Show that you know how to activate your network and appreciate its help.
- Present the truth as it is. Explain how you came to get the job without acting like you were just lucky or in right place at the right time.
- Display a certain pride in your job hunt, in the self-knowledge and know-how that resulted from the experience.

Say: 🙷

- By sheer determination and hard work. I made a plan and each day did 10 activities to reach my goals.
- Acting spontaneously after identifying the companies that are growing.
- By using my network of acquaintances [headhunters, coaches, etc.] to suggest possible avenues for me. One suggested _____.

BEST ANSWER ✓

I started my job hunt using all means available, such as the Internet, networking, and job ads, and then selected the companies that best matched my profile as the ones I should contact.

Describe your job hunt.
How do you go about conducting a job search?

✓ Choose the Best Answer

- ❏ It's not easy, but I keep at it.
- ❏ Hard work and, above all, lots of luck.
- ❏ I did a thorough assessment of my career up to now, then got information from people out in the field. That allowed me to set some clear and realistic goals. And here I am today in your office.
- ❏ I did a course on it, resulting in some good reference letters and a good resume. But times are difficult. Companies aren't doing well and competition is stiff.
- ❏ You know, the market is saturated, but I'm patient.

? What They Really Want to Know

- ■ Have you applied for jobs with other firms/organizations?
- ■ Are you resourceful/creative and do you take initiative?
- ■ How good are you at taking responsibility for your future?

! Watch Out!

Don't:
- ■ Criticize choices you made along your career path.
- ■ Admit you have been out of work for a long time.
- ■ Complain that nobody appreciates you which is why you haven't gotten a job.
- ■ Talk about your failures.
- ■ Use the economic situation as an excuse for not finding a job.

Don't Say:
- ■ I'm waiting patiently for an offer.
- ■ I'm waiting for the right ad to appear in the paper.
- ■ I go about it haphazardly, just any old way.
- ■ I do my researching at home and wait for someone to contact me.

- I read the ads diligently.
- I've sent 500 resumes to companies on the Internet.
- I'm not exactly sure what I'm looking for.
- I've only been in contact with your company.
- I answer all ads that seem even remotely possible.

 Try This!

 **Do:**

- Describe any projects that you are currently working on that show your skills.
- Highlight any knowledge and/or skills you have recently acquired.
- Explain how you network and how you stay current in your occupation, and in your skills.
- Talk about a recent course, seminar, night class, distance learning you found useful.
- Tell that you have had the opportunity to go on several interviews [if true].

 **Say:**

- I find out things by doing thorough research.
- I go directly to the recruitment office when I am interested in a position.
- I find out about the firm, the potential position, and make contact.
- I am currently participating in a career management seminar.
- I look at professional websites for job vacancies at least twice a week and follow up on those that are interesting.
- Every morning I undertake at least two concrete actions to find a job.

BEST ANSWER

I did a thorough assessment of my career up to now, then got information from people out in the field. That allowed me to set some clear and realistic goals. And here I am today in your office.

How long have you been looking for a job?

✓ Choose the Best Answer

- ❑ It's been two years since I've been offered something of interest.
- ❑ For six months, during which time I have improved my knowledge/skill in _____ by taking classes.
- ❑ Months, but I'm not wasting my time. I am taking some courses at night.
- ❑ For a long time. It's so nice to actually be here in your office!
- ❑ I am really not looking any more. I just jump when a good opportunity comes up.

? What They Really Want to Know

- ■ Have you kept up a professional rhythm?
- ■ Were you able to seize the opportunity to get some training or learn something new?
- ■ Are you ready to sell your soul to the devil by taking any job?

! Watch Out!

Don't:

- ■ Lie and shorten the time you have been looking.
- ■ Act discouraged/fed up and show that you think nothing good is going to happen.
- ■ Pretend that you were involved in an advanced stage of negotiations with another company if you were not.
- ■ Sigh, shrug your shoulders, or shake your head (in desperation).

Don't Say:

- ■ For months and months, and I'd do anything to be working again.
- ■ Does this time factor mean one is bad?
- ■ I'm running out of time and feeling desperate.
- ■ For only two days. I just got fired.

- For six months to be exact, but I'm so discouraged now that I don't do much active job hunting anymore.

 Try This!

Do:

- Mention any training or courses you took during this period, especially if they relate to the tasks of the job.
- Show that you took full advantage of your job-hunting period and made some good contacts.
- Highlight how well you managed your time while doing your information gathering, and tell them some useful information you have learned about the sector/market.

Say:

- For six months, and during this time I improved my Spanish.
- It took me a while to find out what kind of job fit me the best. I took time to do some thorough research. I have found that _____.
- For four weeks. I had several offers, but hoped to work in your sector.
- A short time only. I am always involved in some kind of learning to improve my skills or further my interests so I can excel at my job.

BEST ANSWER

For six months, during which time I have improved my knowledge/skill in _____ by taking classes.

What will you do if you are not offered this job?

✓ Choose the Best Answer

- ❑ I think you're going to give me this job, aren't you? I am a good candidate.
- ❑ I'll be pretty upset. I'll re-apply regularly. You know, I can be very persistent.
- ❑ I'd be surprised if you found anyone better than me.
- ❑ As we have discussed, I believe that I correspond to the profile you are looking for. What would make you prefer another candidate?
- ❑ If I don't get this job, I don't know what I'll do. I really need it.

? What They Really Want to Know

- ▪ Are you negotiating any job offers at the moment?
- ▪ Do you have other plans?
- ▪ Are you really motivated for this position?

! Watch Out!

Don't:
- ▪ Forget to ask for the reasons that you don't fit the job profile.
- ▪ Get angry if you feel you won't be offered the job.
- ▪ Leave without asking for reasons why you weren't selected.
- ▪ Appear as a defeatist, a failure.

Don't Say:
- ▪ So why did you ask me to come for this interview if you didn't want to hire me?
- ▪ I don't know what else you want me to tell you.
- ▪ I'm sorry you don't find me to be the right person.
- ▪ Don't tell me I didn't manage to convince you of my suitability for the job.

Try This!

- Ask what you are lacking to fulfill the conditions to be hired.
- Demonstrate that the job does correspond with your competencies/skills.
- Prove that you're ready and willing to persevere, that this job means a lot to you.

Say:

- Now that things are clear between us, I can say that I would like to offer my services to a firm that has your goals.
- I'm happy for you that you found a candidate who suits you 100%.
- Do you mind my asking what is was exactly that discouraged you from hiring me?
- In what way did I not meet up to your expectations? What point, exactly?

BEST ANSWER

As we have discussed, I believe that I correspond to the profile you are looking for. What would make you prefer another candidate?

When will you be available?
What is your current activity level?

✓ Choose the Best Answer

- ❑ At the moment, I'm out of work. I could start right away if you want.
- ❑ As soon as my boss lets me leave.
- ❑ My present job is boring and badly paid. I could work for you at the beginning of next month.
- ❑ I have to finish my present job and then I intend to go on vacation. I could start after that though.
- ❑ How soon would you like us to start working together?

? What They Really Want to Know

- ■ Are you active, dynamic, motivated?
- ■ Are you in the middle of a job, a course/training, without work?
- ■ Can I depend on you? Are you aware of our needs and our urgency?

! Watch Out!

Don't:

- ■ Drop your present professional obligations and show that you are a person without loyalty.
- ■ Forget to point out the reason, your incentive for aiming for this position.
- ■ Answer too quickly without asking when they might actually hire you.
- ■ Suggest you are just sitting around with nothing else to do.

Don't Say:

- ■ Right away! I've been waiting for so long to get back to work.
- ■ I would be more than willing to adapt to your needs.
- ■ I'm on sick leave at the moment and _____.
- ■ I'm unemployed, so I could start right away.
- ■ As soon as possible.

- The job sounds interesting, but I have to take my vacation first.
- Right now! I need to work.
- Immediately, since I don't have any other offers.

Try This!

Do:

- Assume the position of offering your services within a reasonable time frame.
- Negotiate the starting date.
- Question the possible starting date if it won't allow for you to honor your other commitments.

Say:

- I'm under contract until November, but I'll try to negotiate my departure date with my boss.
- I'll have no trouble adapting to your needs.
- I can free myself up fairly quickly, as soon as we've agreed on a starting date.
- Maybe we can agree on a date that suits both of us?
- What date do you have in mind for us to start working together?
- Right away. When did you have in mind?
- According to my contract I have to give two months notice.
- Depending on when you need me, I could free myself up by the end of the month.

BEST ANSWER

How soon would you like us to start working together?

What other organizations/companies have you approached?

✓ Choose the Best Answer

- ☐ Temporary work companies like Manpower, just to survive.
- ☐ I have sent 50 resumes and I'm full of hope.
- ☐ I've got two other negotiations going. However, your company seems by far the most attractive and I really hope my resume is of interest to you.
- ☐ None for the moment. I've only contacted you.
- ☐ I sent in my resume for a job in Administration.

? What They Really Want to Know

- How long have you been job hunting?
- What are you really looking for? In what field? Who else looks interesting to you?
- What is your real interest in this job?

! Watch Out!

Don't:

- Pretend you have not made any moves toward other companies.
- Lie and say you have interviewed with companies you have not.
- Demonstrate that you don't have a very good job search strategy.
- Appear to be someone with no ambition.
- Show that you have done no research into the field/sector.

Don't Say:

- The ones I think will offer me the best conditions/salary.
- I've sent out 50 letters in the last month, and I'm going to send out just as many next week.
- I've contacted all the companies in this area.
- I've only approached your company.
- Three of your competitors, but there's nothing interesting.

Try This!

Do:

- Show you are a proactive person by telling what initiative you have taken in your job hunt.
- Show, using examples, that the area of activity of the company really matches your aim/expectations.
- Name a few of the competitor firms you have contacted (only if true). Don't discuss whether the contact was negative or positive.
- Specify the type of firm(s) you have contacted and underline your interest in the job you are interviewing for.

Say:

- I'm in touch with several companies in the same sector and am now at an advanced stage of negotiation.
- Since my interest is in logistics, I am in touch with several different types of companies.
- Counting yours, I have interviewed for three jobs, and I am ready to consider an offer from you.
- In the area where I am job hunting, it's your company that attracts me the most.
- You are the first company I've contacted, as my job search is just beginning. I have researched what you do and I feel that I would be a good match because ____ .

BEST ANSWER

I've got two other negotiations going. However, your company seems by far the most attractive and I really hope my resume is of interest to you.

If we offer you this job, what reasons will you give your employer when you resign?

✓ Choose the Best Answer

- ❏ I have found an employer who understands me, and a company with a better working atmosphere than the one here.
- ❏ I have decided to change jobs. What is the deadline for turning in a resignation? How much vacation time do I have left?
- ❏ I'm leaving because I have the right to do as I please.
- ❏ A firm has made me an offer that I accepted since it corresponds to my future goals. I would like to offer you my resignation, allowing you the time you need to find my replacement.
- ❏ I think I've done everything I can in this job, and I submit my resignation.

? What They Really Want to Know

- ■ Are you diplomatic or opportunistic?
- ■ Why do you want to quit your present job? Are you experiencing conflicts in your present job?
- ■ Are you honorable in keeping your commitments, or do you just drop everything and run to the next thing?

! Watch Out!

Don't:

- ■ Criticize your present employer.
- ■ Dramatize the situation you are in and say you can't wait to leave.
- ■ Show arrogance and a lack of sensitivity to your present employer.
- ■ Speak of conflict as the reason you are changing jobs.
- ■ Suggest you don't mind leaving your employer in the lurch by quitting immediately.
- ■ Close any doors from your past.

Don't Say:

- Everybody has a right to do what's best for themselves. I can leave when I want.
- They don't need to know why I'm leaving.
- I'm leaving. That is my decision! Goodbye.

 Try This!

Do:

- Announce that your field of interest has changed and you seek more opportunity for growth.
- Be honest but fair. Allow them time to adapt to your leaving.
- Talk about the personal growth/development a new opportunity will afford you.
- Talk about why you are seeking a fresh professional challenge.

Say:

- I spent an important period of my life with you and I learned a lot in this job. I owe you much gratitude.
- I hope to remain on good terms with you and would like to know how much time you might require before I leave the company?
- My present job no longer corresponds with my goals. I am thankful for the time I spent here and hope you know that I am taking only good feelings with me.

BEST ANSWER

A firm has made me an offer that I accepted since it corresponds to my future goals. I would like to offer you my resignation, allowing you the time you need to find my replacement.

16

Salary

Q UESTIONS ABOUT SALARY ARE USUALLY toward the end of an interview and only then if the interviewer is really interested in the candidate. There is no reason to cover salary/benefit issues in detail if the interviewer is sure they do not want to hire you.

In some cases an interviewer will bring up the subject of salary early on to test the waters and find out if there is compatibility on the money issue between the candidate and the company. Most interviewers will expect a candidate to answer their questions on salary without too much protesting. However, it's usually a mistake to answer any salary question with a concrete and specific dollar figure, especially during the early stages of an interview when the job responsibilities and tasks may not be well defined yet. It is often a good strategy on the part of the candidate to turn the question around, if asked early on, by saying, "What is the salary range you have budgeted for this position?" and see how the interviewer responds. If they won't divulge a number and keep pushing, it's best to respond with a broad range that leaves plenty of room for negotiation at a later point.

Salary questions included here are:

- What kind of salary would make you accept our offer? What are your expectations as far as salary is concerned?
- Is salary important to you?
- We offer a choice between fixed pay and merit pay. Do you have a preference?
- What is the minimum salary you are willing to accept?
- What was your last salary? What is your present salary?
- What ratio between salary and fringe benefits would you like to have?
- Have you ever been asked to accept reduction in pay? Why?

What the Interviewer Wants to Know About You

By asking questions about salary, the interviewer is trying to find out:

- Do you know how much you are worth in the marketplace?
- Do you believe in yourself? Do you think your abilities will allow you to make more money?
- Do you have a positive image of yourself?
- What are your deepest values and motivators?
- How much do/did you earn in your present/last job?
- What was your last salary?
- Are you willing to accept a smaller salary than previously expected?
- How much do we have to pay you to work for us?
- How much are you going to cost us?
- Are you a good deal?
- Do you imagine yourself taking on responsibilities and risks?
- Are you interested in the responsibilities or the job or just the money?
- Are you basically lazy?

- Are you really interested in this job?
- Are you really motivated by this kind of activity, or are you merely attracted by the pay?
- Are you a shrewd negotiator?
- Do you know how to show flexibility?

How to Answer

It's almost always best to postpone discussions about salary until a thorough understanding of the job responsibilities and tasks has been outlined. If the candidate can find out what the employer is willing to pay, it helps establish the starting point for a negotiation.

Every candidate should do their research before attending an interview so they know the range of their market value. Have a healthy regard for your own value and be able to sell your skills and experience. Show that you have the ability to negotiate and act diplomatically so you aren't perceived as a person who is inflexible. Don't feel shy about redirecting the question back to the interviewer if it is too early to start talking in earnest about salary and benefits.

When asked what you are worth, use the opportunity to sell yourself—your skills, competencies, and experience. If you are asked about your last/present salary and feel things are progressing sufficiently to disclose it, do so, but **do not** lie! If you lie and the employer finds out, in 99.9% of the cases, your candidacy will be over. If you are going out on a limb and asking for a big jump in salary, it's better to make a strong case about why you are worth more at this job than the last. Sell yourself honestly by showing what you can contribute.

Be confident and show that you believe in yourself. Don't be afraid to show your ambition. Let them know you want to make a career with them and you want your salary to reflect your loyalty and value.

Remember, money is important, but if you are not doing what you love and enjoy, no amount of money is enough.

What kind of salary would make you accept our offer? What are your expectations as far as salary is concerned?

✓ Choose the Best Answer

- ❏ I want this job. The salary is secondary.
- ❏ In my last job I earned _____.
- ❏ What amount have you budgeted for this position?
- ❏ There's no limit! I'd rather hear what you can offer. I hope you'll be generous.
- ❏ I'd like to get X% more than I'm currently earning.

? What They Really Want to Know

- How much do you think you are worth?
- Are you a shrewd negotiator?
- What was your last salary?

! Watch Out!

Don't:
- Start off any interview on the subject of salary.
- Give a precise figure.
- Give your last salary.
- Give a narrow range.
- Overestimate or lie about your last salary.
- Ask for the maximum without offering proof of your competencies.

Don't Say:
- I won't cost you much.
- My last salary was _____, and I would like 20% more.
- It's up to you to decide how much I'm worth.
- I don't know what to expect. My expectations are like everyone else's.
- I can adjust to your offer.
- Not under _____.

Try This!

Do:

- Try to find out what their budget is.
- Ask where this job figures on their salary scale.
- Give two figures within a wide range.
- Highlight your achievements first, before ever talking about salary.
- Thank them and ask if there are salary curves.

Say:

- What is someone with my profile worth?
- How much have you planned for this position?
- What benefits come with this position?
- I thank you for your offer. Can you give me an idea of the salary scale?
- If we agree on all the other conditions, I'm sure we can come to an agreement on salary.
- Did I understand you are making a firm offer?

BEST ANSWER ✓

What amount have you budgeted for this position?

SALARY   417

Is salary important to you?

✓ Choose the Best Answer

- ❑ Yes, of course!
- ❑ It is, like for everyone, within reasonable limits.
- ❑ Isn't it for you?
- ❑ Anyone would say that salary is important!
- ❑ These days, we have to admit that money is important. Especially when salaries are low and there aren't many prospects out there.

? What They Really Want to Know

- How much do we have to pay you to work for us?
- Are you interested in the responsibilities of the job?
- What are your deepest values and motivators?

! Watch Out!

Don't:

- Be awkward and reply arrogantly that you are worth _____.
- Pretend to be surprised by this question.
- Bring up financial difficulties in an effort to soften the interviewer.
- Suggest that salary is the determining factor for this job.

Don't Say:

- If you double my last salary, I'm sure we can come to an agreement.
- As a matter of fact, salary is not so important. My spouse works, and _____.
- I'm not a fan of the consumer society, and for me salary is _____.
- I think, without a good salary, I won't be happy here.

Try This!

Do:

- Stress that salary is important and figures in your decision-making process, but is not the single determining factor.
- Avoid bargaining, in the false belief that lowering your expectations will raise your chances of getting hired. It usually happens the other way around.
- Put the salary into perspective with the job responsibilities/the opportunity for promotion/the hierarchical system/training opportunities.
- Ask the interviewer if they have salary curves.

Say: 🗨

- Do I understand correctly that you have just made me a firm offer?
- Salary is one of the five items I would like to talk over with you. But maybe we should leave it for the end after we have covered everything else?
- So far, I have always received a salary that corresponded with my contribution. I hope that will always be the case.
- In a good contract, both parties come out ahead. It's a win-win situation.

BEST ANSWER ✓

It is, like for everyone, within reasonable limits.

We offer a choice between fixed pay and merit pay. Do you have a preference?

✓ Choose the Best Answer

- ❏ I have three kids, so I need a fixed salary.
- ❏ I don't like to take risks, so I would probably take a fixed salary.
- ❏ I prefer the merit pay option, as I believe in myself.
- ❏ Since you offer me the choice, fixed pay would suit me.
- ❏ Please tell me more about your alternatives. I am interested in hearing about them.

? What They Really Want to Know

- Do you believe in yourself? Do you think your abilities will allow you to make more money?
- Are you basically lazy?
- Do you imagine yourself taking on responsibilities and risks?

! Watch Out!

Don't:
- Show reservations (even minor).
- Give a negative reply.
- Ask the recruiter/interviewer to explain the advantages and disadvantages of these two kinds of pay.

Don't Say:
- I don't care, as long as the amount is in line with my duties.
- I don't want too much responsibility.
- Fixed pay. I've got to secure my position. I have a family.

Do: →

- Highlight your readiness for responsibilities and challenges.
- Be enthusiastic.
- Demonstrate your ease with different possibilities.
- Figure out in advance what amount of money you must make so you can make an informed choice when the time comes.

Say: "

- At [my present/previous company] I exceeded my goal to _____ .
- I have a large client base in your area.
- I like challenges and organizing my work independently.

BEST ANSWER ✓

Please tell me more about your alternatives.
I am interested in hearing about them.

What is the minimum salary you are willing to accept?

✓ Choose the Best Answer

- ❏ As long as my basic needs are met, I am open to negotiation.
- ❏ When you say "minimum," what do you mean by that?
- ❏ All work deserves compensation, doesn't it?
- ❏ We haven't even discussed the job description and you're already asking me to make sacrifices!
- ❏ Why are you asking me this question? Is your firm in financial difficulty?

? What They Really Want to Know

- How much are you really worth? Do you know how to negotiate?
- Do you have a positive image of yourself?
- How much do/did you earn in your present/last job?

! Watch Out!

Don't:

- Act embarrassed and show you are ready to accept what they offer without discussion.
- Get on your high horse or explode with anger and end up out of control.
- Bring up living costs and your own monthly expenses.

Don't Say:

- Life is getting more and more expensive so it's hard to talk about minimum pay.
- Minimum pay means minimum efforts!
- When a person is paid too little they don't work hard. I don't think a minimum wage makes sense.
- A low salary is never motivating.

Do:

- Keep the door open and act flexible.
- Find out tactfully what the interviewer is offering as the starting point for a salary discussion.
- Highlight your experience, your know-how, and your achievements from previous jobs. List your experience, your know-how, and your achievements in terms of pay and say what minimum remuneration would correspond with your future collaboration.
- Suggest a reasonable amount [smile] and say you hope to be compensated with lots of additional perks/benefits.

Say:

- I am confident that if I start with a lower salary, in short time I can make money for you and then ask for more compensation.
- Speaking of minimum pay, do you have a salary scale I can see?
- I'm ready to start low, as long as my salary is adjusted when I have proven myself in three to six months.

BEST ANSWER

As long as my basic needs are met,
I am open to negotiation.

What was your last salary?
What is your present salary?

✓ Choose the Best Answer

- ❑ That is strictly confidential. I can't tell you.
- ❑ It wouldn't be very smart of me to tell you.
- ❑ I'm afraid I'll have to have state a figure that is going to seem much too high/low for you.
- ❑ Where I'm working now, there's a gentleman's agreement not to reveal it. I will disclose a range to you, however, once we have talked a bit more about the responsibilities of the job.
- ❑ I don't think I should tell you. I've always been told a good negotiator does not speak first.

? What They Really Want to Know

- How much are you going to cost us?
- Are you as good as you look?
- How much can I get you for? Are you a good deal?

! Watch Out!

Don't:

- Blatantly announce some figure, arbitrarily chosen.
- Appear uncomfortable with the question.
- Go into long, complicated explanations trying to justify your situation.
- Pity yourself or say you are changing jobs because you consider yourself underpaid.

Don't Say:

- They exploited me! My salary was ludicrous.
- I'll tell you, but I want to earn more. I earn _____ a year.
- The least I'm willing to work for is _____.
- Everybody knows my boss always underpaid his staff. And he comes out smelling like a rose!

Do:

- Keep calm and avoid jumping to an answer or hesitating too long.
- Ask questions to clarify the responsibilities of the job.
- Brush the negotiation aside tactfully and gracefully, saying you will come back to it later.
- Smile and say with your eyes, "I'm not going to tell you!"

Say:

- Am I right in understanding that you have just made me a firm offer?
- What I was earning before is in range with what I'm after now.
- I will gladly tell you, after we have negotiated my salary.
- What's your firm's salary scale?

BEST ANSWER

Where I'm working now, there's a gentleman's agreement not to reveal it. I will disclose a range to you, however, once we have talked a bit more about the responsibilities of the job.

What ratio between salary and fringe benefits would you like to have?

✓ Choose the Best Answer

☐ I just want a salary, because you rarely come out ahead with perks.

☐ The highest. I have no top limit.

☐ Personally, I am open to negotiate, but what really matters most to me are the job responsibilities.

☐ What do you mean by "fringe benefits"?

☐ If that includes a house, a car, school fees, vacations, and a new wardrobe, I'm willing to discuss salary.

? What They Really Want to Know

■ Are you really interested in this job?

■ Do you know how to show flexibility?

■ Do you have major needs? What are they?

! Watch Out!

Don't:

■ Reveal a rigid or inflexible attitude.

■ Laugh nervously because you are uncomfortable.

■ Look at the interviewer with shock and remain tongue-tied.

■ Immediately go into detail and start quibbling.

■ Act like you don't know what they mean by "ratio."

Don't Say:

■ I don't know. I have no idea.

■ Your question takes me by surprise. How is it possible that I never thought about that before?

■ I only want a salary. Perks never make you come out ahead.

■ What's a ratio?

■ If it means that I pay less in taxes, I'm interested.

Do:

- Show that you are open and that it's the responsibilities you remain focused on, not the salary.
- Get the recruiter/interviewer to tell you what kind of perks the firm usually offers. Be clever and make sure you suggest those that most interest you if the recruiter/interviewer does not bring them up.
- Ask the recruiter what ratio is most common: 50/50, 40/60, 30/70, 20/80, etc.

Say:

- Thank you for giving me this opportunity. I find the concept very interesting. What fringe benefits do you usually offer your employees?
- A ratio of _____ would suit me. Nevertheless, I am open to other formulas.
- I need a minimum of $_____ to cover my obligations. The rest is completely negotiable.

BEST ANSWER

Personally, I am open to negotiate, but what really matters most to me are the job responsibilities.

Have you ever been asked to accept reduction in pay? Why?

✓ Choose the Best Answer

- ☐ Of course! At my age nobody wants to pay me what I'm worth!
- ☐ An employer does not have the right to do this. There are salary scales.
- ☐ Yes, because I didn't achieve my annual goals.
- ☐ Why on earth would they have done that?
- ☐ No, because I've always made sure my employers linked my contribution to my pay.

? What They Really Want to Know

- Are you aware of the crisis in our sector/field?
- Are you willing to accept a smaller salary than previously expected?
- Are you really motivated by this kind of activity, or are you merely attracted by the pay?

! Watch Out!

Don't:

- Act as if you don't understand the question.
- Show you're ready to make any sacrifice because you're desperate for a job.
- Cling to an expected salary that is much higher than current market salaries.
- Remain stuck on your past experience and feel any reduction in pay is out of the question.
- Underestimate yourself.

Don't Say:

- I understand their point of view. But I don't like it.
- No, but if it's your case, of course I'll accept. I really need this job.
- No, and if I were asked to, it would be out of the question.
- Yes, but I flatly refused.

Do:

- Explain what added value you bring to the company.
- Find out what the recruiter's/interviewer's intentions are in asking this question.
- Justify your own value so a reduction will not be necessary.
- Show yourself ready to negotiate.

Say:

- Taking into account the responsibilities and goals defined for this position, my salary expectations seem justified. But I'm open to discussion.
- Yes, I was once asked to lower my salary expectations, and the company compensated me by covering the costs of a prestigious and costly training program. This seemed more than fair to me.
- What is the range of salaries you have budgeted for this job?
- Do you find my expected salary too high?

BEST ANSWER

No, because I've always made sure my employers linked my contribution to my pay.

17

Trick/Delicate Topics

T HIS CHAPTER DISCUSSES questions about "trick" or "delicate" topics. These
are the questions you dread most and pray the interviewer won't ask you.
But we all know at least one or two of them will probably pop up in the interview. They're the questions that have to do with getting fired, reasons for leaving your last job, being overqualified or under qualified, and that old favorite,
"Why should I hire you?"

In and of themselves, it's not so much that they are "trick" questions, meaning there is some hidden and surprise answer that would be right if you could
only discern it; it's just that sometimes an interviewer will ask you a question
that throws you entirely off track because you would rather not talk about the
subject. These questions just don't always lend themselves to easy (and neatly
tied up) answers.

It's true that an interviewer might ask you something just to try to trip you up,
but their real goal is to find out if you can be creative, show some maturity, and
think on your feet. This lets them gauge how you handle yourself under pressure. Some of these questions seem almost ludicrous (and have nothing to do

with the job)—so you can decide if you would rather just say, "Are you serious?" or try for an answer that shows you understand the silliness of the question but will play along. It's your call, but choose wisely. No one ever said sitting in an interviewer's chair made a person rational or fair 100% of the time.

Sometimes an interviewer will try to rattle you because they think there is something you are hiding or would rather not talk about (and nothing is quite as alluring to an interviewer than digging deep to find hidden skeletons in their candidates!) If they think you haven't been honest and forthright with them, they may ask probing questions to see if they can find inconsistencies in your responses.

Trick/delicate questions included here are:

- Do you need anything else?
- Do you have any objection to taking tests?
- Have you ever been laid off/fired? Why?
- What do you like to be called?
- Should I hire you?
- What would you say if I said it appears that you don't have the qualifications/experience required for this job?
- Why did you leave your last job?
- Why did you leave your last employer? And the employers before that?
- Why are you out of work?
- Did you ever consider quitting your job sooner?
- Why were you fired from your last job?
- What would you say if I said you were overqualified for this job?
- What is your opinion of your last employer?
- What question would you prefer me not to ask you?
- If we were to swap roles, what would you ask me?
- Do you want to ask me some questions?

- Have you ever been asked to hand in your resignation?
- If you were going to the moon, what would you take with you?

What the Interviewer Wants to Know About You

By asking trick or delicate questions, the interviewer is trying to find out:

- Have you thought about the questions I'm going to ask you?
- What area would you rather not go into? What are you afraid of?
- What questions bother or worry you?
- Are you fully prepared for this interview?
- Do you need any more information?
- Are you satisfied with what I am offering you?
- Can you do a quick analysis of where this interview is going?
- Do you dare ask me something? Have you done your homework?
- Have you ever been accused of professional misconduct?
- Have you ever had problems with former employers?
- Have your bosses always been satisfied with your work? If not, what are the areas of concern?
- Did you quit your job or were you asked to leave? If you quit, why didn't you find a new job first?
- What did you do to get fired?
- Do you learn from your mistakes?
- Were you in conflict with your previous employer?
- Are you a job hopper?
- Do you act on a whim?
- Do you know to manage delicate situations diplomatically?
- Will you lose your motivation in six months and quit?
- Will you cost us too much?
- Are you sure what you're worth?
- Are you aware of this firm's customs?

- Is there a cultural issue we should be or you are sensitive about?
- Are you available right away?
- Are you truly interested?
- What makes you think you fit this job?
- Would you like to add anything? What didn't we cover which you think is important?
- Have we figured you out correctly?
- Should we ask you more questions?
- Are you quick on the draw?
- Do you have a sense of innovation/creativity?
- How do you deal with the unexpected?
- Are you flexible and willing to entertain ideas that might be a bit farfetched?

How to Answer

First, when asked a question you dread, act like there is no other question you would rather be asked! If you look at these questions and embrace the opportunity to answer them, you will fare well. Whenever possible, relate your answer back to the job in question. The only way you are going to be able to pull this off, however, is if you have anticipated the question and practiced an answer to it. It doesn't take much now to get lists and lists of possible questions that will be asked in an interview (especially the ones we dread!). Look to see what in your background might cause a problem and figure out what you can say to positively offset it. You might not be able to anticipate every question you will be asked, but you can certainly prepare for the obvious ones.

If you've been fired, don't act surprised when you are asked this question. Surely, you knew it would come up! If you were the interviewer, you wouldn't pass up the opportunity to ask this question—you would need to know the reasons and circumstances for the firing. Not all firings are because the employee was a lazy slob with personality problems. Sometimes it's as simple as a mismatch situation where communication wasn't good on one or both sides. Or your company was going through financial problems, or they were downsizing and found your position expendable. Events beyond their control can cause people to lose their jobs. Explain your situation quickly and succinctly and move on. If you were the one really at fault, take responsibility for it and show what you have learned that will keep you from making the same mistake again. Whatever you do, do not lie about this one. The lie, when found out, does more damage than being fired could ever do. So, play by the rules when asked about the circumstances of your firing.

When asked why you left your last job (or want to leave your current one), frame your answer in positive terms. Do not ever, ever speak badly of people you worked with. There is no way for you to win if you do this. Even if an interviewer sits and shakes their head like they totally understand what you are saying (and even make noises that they agree), the bad taste stays in their mouth later when they go to review each candidate. After all, if you can say that about other people, you might one day say it about them.

When asked about your qualifications (either too many or not enough), emphasize your interest in establishing a long-term association with the company. Talk in terms of being "well qualified" and relate your experience to the job. Companies can never have enough talent or energetic workers who love what they do. Show how you will be one of those workers, even if deemed under- or over-qualified.

When asked if you have questions for them, for heaven's sake, have some questions! Before the interview, write out a list of questions you might like to ask (bring the list with you—it's okay to show you cared enough to prepare a list). Some of them will no doubt be covered during the interview, as you learn details about the job, but some may not. Don't let your shyness or a feeling that asking a question is stupid keep you from making sure you understand everything you need to know to make an informed decision about whether you want the job or not (you haven't forgotten this is a two-way street, have you?). So, ask some thoughtful questions; just don't ask what already been covered or what you should have known before stepping into the interviewer's office.

Now, for the final question, "*Why should I hire you?*" You are going to have to walk a fine line here between boasting and having confidence in yourself. You need to be able to say, honestly, that you think you are the best candidate for the job because (list your reasons as they apply to the job tasks, duties, and responsibilities). It's great if you have a pleasing personality or a terrific smile, but those qualities won't be enough to convince them that you are the right person. Use specific examples to demonstrate your skills and qualities that match the job requirements. Pick the three top ones that you have gleaned from the discussion with the interviewer (and that you have researched ahead of time), and go with those. Make your case with a positive attitude and a belief in yourself.

Do you need anything else?

❑ Actually, my wife is also looking for a job. Do you think you might have an opening in Production?

❑ Thanks, I have everything I need. But, from your perspective, is there anything more I can tell you about my background?

❑ No, but could I call you if I find I've forgotten something?

❑ Yes. I need some coffee, some paper, and a pencil.

❑ I'd like to know the salary.

? *What They Really Want to Know*

▪ Do you need more information to make your decision?

▪ Is everything okay?

▪ Are you satisfied with what I am offering you?

! *Watch Out!*

Don't:

▪ Ask something totally inappropriate.

▪ Ask a question on a subject that has already been covered.

▪ Renegotiate the salary.

▪ Answer with only "No."

▪ Freeze or pause too long for a reply.

Don't Say:

▪ Well, in fact, how long have you been in business?

▪ No, I don't think so.

▪ Yes. I think the salary could be adjusted.

▪ Yes. There are a lot of things I'd like to have, but sometimes you just have to know how to get along without them.

Do:

- Show your interest and enthusiasm and ask questions about the job.
- Ask one last question about the job (one you have prepared in advance that has not been covered already).
- Ask about the follow-up to the interview. Who will contact whom, and when?
- Express your thanks and assure them that you have taken all the questions into consideration. Use the opportunity to summarize the key aspects of the job.

Say:

- I see on your bulletin board that _____. When I came in, I noticed _____ [show you've got your eyes open].
- What's the quality you appreciate most in an employee?
- Is there something that might keep us from signing the contract right now?
- What are the decisive criteria for you in choosing a candidate?
- Would it be possible to do a quick tour of the grounds/building?

BEST ANSWER

Thanks, I have everything I need. But, from your perspective, is there anything more I can tell you about my background?

Do you have any objection to taking tests?

✓ Choose the Best Answer

- ❏ No, but I don't think a test can give you precise answers. Tests aren't bad, but they have their limits.
- ❏ No, but the last time I took one I didn't get the job.
- ❏ Yes, I do. I don't believe in them.
- ❏ I'm open to any tool that helps to define my job profile.
- ❏ I'd appreciate it if we could avoid it.

? What They Really Want to Know

- Do you have confidence in yourself?
- Are you afraid of being evaluated? Do you have something to hide?
- Have you mastered your area of work?

! Watch Out!

Don't:
- Appear to be afraid of taking tests.
- Laugh as if to say, "This is a joke, right?"
- Appear awkward when faced with this possibility.

Don't Say:
- Is that just a way to eliminate me?
- I don't like being questioned or having people snoop behind my back.
- I don't see any use for tests.
- I would resent having to take a test as an invasion of my private life.
- I think an entry test only serves to unnerve a candidate, so I would refuse.
- I've already taken several. I can send you the results if you like.
- No, I do not want to pass any tests!
- Exactly what kind of test are you talking about? If it's a drug test, I refuse.

Do:

- Agree to take any tests they need you to take.
- Ask for the results (a copy and/or interpretation) of the tests.
- Answer spontaneously that it is okay with you.
- Suggest taking them at another time. Ask for another appointment.
- Inquire, in a positive tone, about the type of tests they would like you to take.

Say:

- Of course not. It's always a good challenge.
- I suppose these tests will tell me even more about my skills.
- Not at all. I'd just like to know more about what this test measures.
- Not at all. Could we plan to do that later?
- What kind of tests are we talking about? I am always interested to have more information.
- Who will have access to the results?
- Who is going to interpret these tests?

BEST ANSWER

I'm open to any tool that helps to define my job profile.

Have you ever been laid off/fired? Why?

✓ Choose the Best Answer

- ❑ No. I've been lucky so far.
- ❑ I was laid off when my company downsized.
- ❑ So far, never. I am dependable and forthright and don't see why that would be necessary.
- ❑ Several times, because I've got a strong personality. But in one case I sued and won.
- ❑ Once, for a serious matter. Only once, and it won't happen again.

? What They Really Want to Know

- ▪ Have you ever been accused of professional misconduct?
- ▪ Have you ever had problems with former employers?
- ▪ Have your bosses always been satisfied with your work? If not, what is the area of concern?

! Watch Out!

Don't:
- ▪ Criticize the firm if you were laid off/fired.
- ▪ Lie or misrepresent what happened.
- ▪ Acknowledge it without citing why it happened.
- ▪ Justify yourself by criticizing your boss.
- ▪ Whine and play the victim.

Don't Say:
- ▪ No dialogue was possible.
- ▪ I was fired for personal reasons.
- ▪ I got in their way because I did things differently.
- ▪ I did not like my former boss.
- ▪ I don't like change, and that was the name of the game every day.

- I couldn't get along with my colleagues.
- I don't understand why I was fired. I never did anything wrong.
- Because I used to drink. But that's not a problem any more.

Try This!

Do:

- Describe how an eventual restructuring took place.
- Tell the truth.
- Give a positive reason for the separation.
- Justify your dismissal by negotiating with the firm.
- Mention the closing down of activities of your department/firm.
- Present the situation in a positive light.
- Stay calm.
- Show respect for your former job and boss.

Say:

- After 17 years, it was time to make a change.
- I tried to work out the disagreements over _____, but we never found common ground.
- The dismissal was negotiated in mutual agreement.
- No, I quit in order to get some professional training.
- Yes, because the company closed.
- Yes, because of restructuring.
- I have, but the decision was based on budget cuts.

BEST ANSWER

So far, never. I am dependable and forthright and don't see why that would be necessary.

What do you like to be called?

✓ *Choose the Best Answer*

- ❏ Why do you ask this?
- ❏ I am comfortable with either my first or last name being used. Whatever's the custom here is fine with me.
- ❏ I don't like to be called by my first name. In my country, first names are only used by close friends.
- ❏ I like my title to be used.
- ❏ People usually call me "Momo."

? *What They Really Want to Know*

- ▪ Are you aware of this firm's customs?
- ▪ Is there a cultural issue we should be or you are sensitive about?
- ▪ Do you feel comfortable here?

! *Watch Out!*

Don't:

- ▪ Be overly familiar.
- ▪ Act rigid about this.
- ▪ Avoid expressing your preference.
- ▪ Get involved in long explanations.
- ▪ Appear to be aloof.

Don't Say:

- ▪ What do people call you?
- ▪ Your Highness!
- ▪ I don't like being called "the new kid on the block."
- ▪ I don't know. Why?
- ▪ "Sir."

- By my nickname of _____ .
- I don't really like informality too much.

Do:

- State your preference.
- Show that you appreciate friendliness, but respect as well.
- Be flexible. Leave the door open to the name that is most comfortable for them to use.
- Find out what the company's policy is.

Say:

- By my last name.
- By my first name.
- I'm used to being called "[first name]" or "[last name]."
- What is the custom in your firm?
- You addressed me as "Mr." when I arrived. Is that the custom here?
- I don't have a nickname. I like _____ .

BEST ANSWER

I am comfortable with either my first or last name being used. Whatever's the custom here is fine with me.

Should I hire you?

✓ Choose the Best Answer

- ❑ Yes, you should, and I was going to ask you to do just that.
- ❑ It's up to you.
- ❑ I desperately need this job.
- ❑ That's a funny question. Do you always ask that? I've never been asked such a thing.
- ❑ You'll be sorry if you don't. I'm really good at what I do.

? What They Really Want to Know

- ▪ Are you quick on the draw?
- ▪ Are you available right away?
- ▪ Are you truly interested?

! Watch Out!

Don't:
- ▪ Just stare wide-eyed because you are so surprised by the bluntness of this question.
- ▪ Cross your arms or shrug your shoulders like you don't care one way or the other if they hire you.
- ▪ Act dumfounded and say, "Well, I hope so!"
- ▪ Become too embarrassed and say nothing.

Don't Say:
- ▪ Of course! I'm just the person for you.
- ▪ It's up to you!
- ▪ Yes, but _____.
- ▪ Oh, thank you. You're the only one who has offered me a job.

Do:

- Keep a positive and open attitude and say "Yes."
- Say "Yes" and ask a question about the job that shows you are committed to accepting an offer from them.
- Say "Yes" with your eyes. Lean slightly toward the interviewer to show through your body language that you are fully committed.
- Smile and look the interviewer straight in the eyes and say "Yes."

Say:

- Yes, of course! Let's talk business.
- Yes, you should! And, in return, I can _____.
- Absolutely. I want this job. May I ask you _____?
- Yes. This job is a good fit for both of us and I am ready to accept your offer.
- [If you are unsure you want the job, you must remain positive and say] Before we talk of a specific job offer, I would like to discuss _____ in further detail to be sure we are on the same page.

BEST ANSWER

Yes, you should, and I was going to ask you to do just that.

What would you say if I said it appears that you don't have the qualifications/ experience required for this job?

✓ Choose the Best Answer

- ❑ Everyone has his or her own opinion. But I am confident in myself and in my diplomas.
- ❑ What was it in my file that made you want to meet me?
- ❑ I offer you what I have, and I accept what you have to offer.
- ❑ If, after all these years of experience, this isn't good enough for you, then what is?
- ❑ You must be joking. I am overqualified for this job and you know it.

? What They Really Want to Know

- ▪ Help me think of ways to convince the higher-ups I should hire you!
- ▪ What qualities do you have over the other candidates?
- ▪ What makes you think you fit this job?

! Watch Out!

Don't:
- ▪ Contradict the recruiter/interviewer (outright) or deny the possibility he/she is right.
- ▪ Lose confidence in yourself or simply give up.
- ▪ Make excuses and oversell yourself.

Don't Say:
- ▪ This is what always happens.
- ▪ You have to know how to take risks.
- ▪ Unfortunately it's the only experience I have. I don't know what else to say.
- ▪ You haven't even tested my skills yet.
- ▪ You're making a mistake.

Do:

- State your case by presenting additional skills, not by trying to justify yourself because you feel emotionally threatened.
- Demonstrate your motivation and interest.
- Give examples of your ability and willingness to learn.
- Prove that you know how to recover from a setback.
- Ask the recruiter/interviewer what interested her/him about your candidacy.
- Describe a situation where you managed to adapt easily.
- Expand on the criteria that you meet, and ignore those you don't.
- Highlight any experience that would be useful for the job.

Say:

- I am more than ready to invest in your in-house training in order to meet the criteria for this job.
- I picked you in order to acquire new skills and to advance along my career path.
- My strong point is my perseverance, and I can work at the same time I'm taking courses.
- To convince you, here are three of my other skills that are needed for this job.
- Why not offer me a trial period to test my ability to fit in?
- What was your incentive for contacting me?
- What seems to be missing? I'd like to talk about it.
- You are right about my experience but just let me demonstrate my skills in this area.

BEST ANSWER

What was it in my file that made you want to meet me?

Why did you leave your last job?

✓ Choose the Best Answer

- ☐ I had a nervous breakdown, then I was on sick leave for over six months.
- ☐ I was only earning _____ a month!
- ☐ The hours were too strict.
- ☐ For personal reasons.
- ☐ I needed a new challenge and wanted to take on more responsibilities in my next job.

? What They Really Want to Know

- ■ Have you been accused of professional misconduct?
- ■ Are you stable/trustworthy? Do you act on a whim?
- ■ Were you in conflict with your previous employer?

! Watch Out!

Don't:
- ■ Look down.
- ■ Try to evade the question.
- ■ Lie and find yourself in an uncomfortable position.
- ■ Get upset and answer abruptly.

Don't Say:
- ■ I didn't have the right job profile.
- ■ I don't like to be stuck in the same place.
- ■ The expectations were out of proportion to the available resources.
- ■ I wasn't given the means to do my job.

Do:

- Give a succinct answer, and then go on to another question.
- Briefly explain the situation factually.
- Show that it was a professional step in your career.
- Smile. Resist rationalizing!

Say:

- I reached the goals that were set for me and wanted to have a new challenge.
- I think it's time my career took another direction. This is why I have approached you.
- Although the company's means were limited, the job was very instructive.
- I left after _____ years to increase my responsibilities and reach my career goals.

BEST ANSWER

I needed a new challenge and wanted to take on more responsibilities in my next job.

Why did you leave your last employer? And the employers before that?

- ❏ I can explain that. Everything went wrong.
- ❏ When I don't get along with my bosses, I prefer to move on.
- ❏ I've always learned something with each employer, but I had reached my goals and felt like moving on to something new and challenging.
- ❏ My chief was a perfectionist. I could never satisfy her. And besides, it's one of my principles to change jobs often. It's good for the career and good for the salary.
- ❏ We had some little differences of opinion.

? *What They Really Want to Know*

- Did you run into problems or were you in conflict with your boss or subordinates?
- Have you built a solid career path?
- Why weren't you satisfied? Are you a job hopper?

! *Watch Out!*

Don't:

- Admit you tend to get bored easily.
- Say you are hard to satisfy, which explains the frequent moves.
- Suggest that all your bosses were incompetent.
- Show a lack of tact/diplomacy.
- Give details about your conflict with your last employer.

Don't Say:

- I always have a hard time adapting.
- I was bored.
- I was in over my head. It was just too difficult and the stress was unbearable.
- I rarely get along with my boss.
- The people I worked with were all idiots!

Do:

- Point out the coherence in your career path up to now.
- Show that you can make your new employer benefit from your versatility.
- Add that you recover quickly from setbacks and never give up after a failure.
- Prove that all situations, even the difficult ones, provide wonderful opportunities for learning.
- Look back at past achievements that illustrate your need to grow/evolve.

Say:

- I have always felt the need to evolve toward a different kind of company—bigger, smaller, national, international.
- I liked that job a lot—the company, the manager—but I needed to do something else/set new goals/breathe new life into my career.
- I was never in conflict with my boss. You are free to contact him at _____ .
- I have always wanted to move to a job like this, and each step along the way has given me the necessary tools to be able to do it now.

BEST ANSWER

I've always learned something with each employer, but I had reached my goals and felt like moving on to something new and challenging.

Why are you out of work?

✓ Choose the Best Answer

- ❑ Things weren't going well in my last job—no responsibility, harassment, and so forth.
- ❑ The financial crisis affected everyone—even the best of us.
- ❑ I asked for a raise, which I deserved. But it was not granted, so I left.
- ❑ The experts say that you should change employers every five to seven years. It's already been 10 years since I've been in the same company and four years since my last promotion.
- ❑ I left my previous job when I had met all my goals. I am now looking for a new challenge.

? What They Really Want to Know

- Did you quit your job or were you asked to leave? If you quit, why didn't you find a new job first?
- What did you do to get fired?
- Do you know to manage delicate situations diplomatically?

! Watch Out!

Don't:
- Say bad things about your last boss.
- Go into long explanations that place blame on others.
- Feel sorry for yourself or play the victim.

Don't Say:
- I'm just not lucky. They had to get rid of 10% of the staff and I was one of the ones to go.
- I lost my job over an internal dispute, and I'm not involved in politics.
- I requested a raise/promotion, and it wasn't given to me so I left.
- Because it's better to be without a job than to be in the wrong job!

Try This!

- Say you wanted to commit yourself entirely to your job hunt.
- Present things calmly, taking less than 20 seconds.
- Suggest to your recruiter/interviewer that she contact your last employer for references, if you left on good terms.

Say: 🙺

- The decision was made by my employer and myself that I would look for another job.
- The decision to leave my employer was very difficult. We had a mutual appreciation. What a dilemma it was for me.
- I was expecting an important contract that never materialized. My employer had to reduce his business expenses.
- I have decided to change direction and needed some time to reevaluate my priorities and goals. I am now determined and energized to go!

BEST ANSWER

✓ *I left my previous job when I had met all my goals. I am now looking for a new challenge.*

Did you ever consider quitting your job sooner?

✓ Choose the Best Answer

- ❏ I waited for my boss to fire me. I'm not a quitter.
- ❏ I thought about it, of course. That was my first idea. But I didn't because I would have lost out on my benefits.
- ❏ I had wanted to quit for a long time but couldn't make up my mind if I should or not.
- ❏ No, I fulfilled my contract and we left each other on good terms.
- ❏ No, because I don't like to rock the boat…and then, I didn't know what else I would do.

? What They Really Want to Know

- Are you impulsive?
- Are you stable (loyal)?
- Did you get fired? Why?

! Watch Out!

Don't:

- Criticize your former boss or colleagues.
- Suggest you are easily bored.
- Bring up relationship problems you had at your job.
- Say your job was terrible but you don't like to quit on things.

Don't Say:

- I quit after a fight with my boss.
- I had no choice.
- My wife kept telling me I should quit.
- No. I quit after a nervous breakdown.
- You can't always do what you want.
- Yes, I did, but I kept hoping things would get better.

- I did, but my family situation kept me from making such a decision.
- I'm not a quitter, so I stuck it out.

 Try This!

Do:

- Explain you were waiting for the right opportunity to make a fresh start.
- Mention your participation in a professional program/say you were already in touch with several headhunters/recruiters.
- Speak well of your former boss.
- Talk about what the job offered you that can be transferred to this job.

Say: 🙶

- Tough situations always leave you a little smarter.
- I was determined to stay as long as I felt there was room to grow.
- I was hired to direct a specific project. I knew from the very beginning the job would be over when the project was completed. My boss was very up front about that.
- In fact, I hadn't. It's your ad in the paper that moved me to contact you.
- No, but at this moment in time, it seems like a logical step, in line with my ambitions.
- No, I liked my work, but I couldn't go any further with them.
- No, I was hired for a two-year contract and I fully intend to live up to this commitment, which is over in another month.

BEST ANSWER ✓

No, I fulfilled my contract and we left each other on good terms.

Why were you fired from your last job?

✓ Choose the Best Answer

- ☐ I didn't get along with my director any more and he decided to fire me. Anyway, I didn't want to work for him any more. My conscience is clear.
- ☐ I wanted to change jobs.
- ☐ It was a great experience. In four years, the department had increased its activity by 35%. An internal promotion was not in the cards, so I decided to try to join a major firm like yours.
- ☐ For lack of motivation.
- ☐ Because I didn't get what I wanted when I asked for a higher salary.

? What They Really Want to Know

- ▪ Do you have relational problems?
- ▪ Are you reliable and motivated?
- ▪ Do you know how to recognize your faults? Do you learn from your mistakes?

! Watch Out!

Don't:
- ▪ Openly criticize your ex-boss, your ex-colleagues, or your ex-company.
- ▪ Be taken aback/surprised/embarrassed by this question about your firing.
- ▪ Be evasive.
- ▪ Explain in detail all the difficulties and injustices you have had to face.
- ▪ Suggest your incompetence played a part in your firing.
- ▪ Show your bitterness.
- ▪ Forget to prepare for this question.
- ▪ Justify yourself.
- ▪ Play the victim.

Don't Say:

- I have not had much luck.
- I didn't want to leave but I was fired anyway.
- Sometimes I wonder. I did nothing wrong.

 Try This!

 Do:

- Demonstrate how this situation gave new life to your career.
- Bring up the question of restructuring/redefinition of the job.
- Point out the advantages of this change.
- A large multinational firm bought my company and many jobs were eliminated. I held one of the eliminated positions.
- Show that you have come out stronger and more motivated.
- Talk about your evolution and what you learned.
- Give a brief answer and ask a question that leads the discussion to another point.

 **Say:**

- I used the occasion to take stock of my situation and redefine my professional goals.
- We left each other on good terms.
- Several jobs were done away with, including mine.
- A large multinational firm bought my company, and many jobs were eliminated. I held one of the eliminated positions.

BEST ANSWER

It was a great experience. In four years, the department had increased its activity by 35%. An internal promotion was not in the cards, so I decided to try to join a major firm like yours.

What would you say if I said you were overqualified for this job?

✓ Choose the Best Answer

- ❏ That would surprise me.
- ❏ That would be the first time I've heard that!
- ❏ Take advantage of me. I have to work!
- ❏ I would say, "Pay me accordingly!"
- ❏ Where do you see that my experience might hinder the smooth operation of this job?

? What They Really Want to Know

- Will you lose your motivation in six months and quit?
- Are you going to cost us too much?
- Are you going to try to take over?

! Watch Out!

Don't:

- Make a case against over-qualification.
- Admit that the recruiter/interviewer is right and defend your position.
- Suggest lowering your salary demands.
- Belittle yourself by suggesting this is the only job you can get.

Don't Say:

- I've often been told this. It must be true!
- I need a job with much more routine than before.
- I've had my share of responsibility!
- I know, but there's nothing I can do about it!

Try This!

Do: →

- Accept and request additional responsibilities to make the job equal to your expertise.
- Ask the recruiter/interviewer what criteria were used for judging you as over-qualified.
- Give an example of a past achievement that matches the job in question.

Say:

- I gladly adapt to the demands assigned to me.
- The joy of working means reaching new goals and accepting new challenges.
- The tasks are simply different from my last job. I think I certainly possess the skills do to this job well.
- Over-qualified? I don't think so!

BEST ANSWER ✓

Where do you see that my experience might hinder the smooth operation of this job?

What is your opinion of your last employer?

✓ **Choose the Best Answer**

- ❑ In my opinion he could manage the company better. He has assets that have not been put to use.
- ❑ I have a good opinion of my boss, and we are still on good terms. Would you like to contact her?
- ❑ He lied to me about the financial situation of the company.
- ❑ I don't have an opinion. I'll let you decide. All you have to do is have a look at her.
- ❑ We didn't have the same ideas on _____.

? What They Really Want to Know

- ▪ Did you have relational problems with your last boss?
- ▪ Why did you leave?
- ▪ Do you know how to be discreet?

! Watch Out!

Don't:
- ▪ Criticize your last boss/company.
- ▪ Hang on to your anger if things turned against you.
- ▪ Find yourself with no opinion.
- ▪ Go on and on about a problem you had with your boss.
- ▪ Suggest you and he/she were best friends.

Don't Say:
- ▪ They have a lot of financial/profit/personnel problems.
- ▪ I don't really know her. She didn't check on me much.
- ▪ I find his sense of ethics lacking.

Do:

- Keep a positive attitude the whole time.
- Give some positive aspects of your relationship with your last boss.
- Offer a reference.
- List something important you learned from him.
- State you liked and respected her.

Say:

- The company is admirably well organized and efficient. I like my boss very much.
- I learned a great deal thanks to their procedures and methods. For example, _____.
- I have good memories and learned a lot from him/her, particularly _____.
- We always had an excellent rapport.

BEST ANSWER

I have a good opinion of my boss, and we are still on good terms. Would you like to contact her?

What question would you prefer me not to ask you?

✓ Choose the Best Answer

- ☐ Do you really love your husband/wife/son/daughter?
- ☐ Do you really want to work? My answer might get me into trouble!
- ☐ What I don't like about this job. Since I like everything about it, I couldn't begin to answer!
- ☐ How about you?
- ☐ How old are you? I find this question entirely too personal and I think it may even be illegal.

? What They Really Want to Know

- Have you thought about the questions I'm going to ask you?
- What area would you rather not go into? What are you afraid of?
- Are you fully prepared for this interview?

! Watch Out!

Don't:

- Talk about money, as it is a subject you should avoid.
- Answer this question too seriously!
- Be offended and say nothing.
- Tell them what you really don't want to talk about!

Don't Say:

- There are areas of my private life that are none of your business.
- I have no idea. I'm an open book.
- I don't have to tell you everything.
- I have nothing to hide.
- Don't ask me about my last salary.

Do:

- Give a knowing look and play the game. Show that you understand the intent of this question is to shake you up.
- Appear at ease.
- Answer with humor.
- Smile knowingly.

Say:

- This very question!
- I'm perfectly comfortable answering your questions.
- I'm not afraid of any question.
- Can I have a moment to think about this?
- What is it you'd really like to know?
- Personal or professional?

BEST ANSWER

What I don't like about this job. Since I like everything about it, I couldn't begin to answer!

If we were to swap roles, what would you ask me?

✓ Choose the Best Answer

- ❏ I'd like to take you up on your suggestion! My question would be, "Do you want this job?"
- ❏ Different questions altogether!
- ❏ Do you have a happy life?
- ❏ What sports do you like?
- ❏ All the things you didn't ask me about!

? What They Really Want to Know

- Would you like to add anything? Did I cover everything you think is important?
- Have we figured you out correctly?
- Should I ask you more questions?

! Watch Out!

Don't:

- Ask the recruiter/interviewer awkward questions.
- Use caustic humor.
- Be caught so off-guard that you don't use this opportunity to get across some point about your candidacy.
- Stammer or sit there tongue-tied.

Don't Say:

- I'm not in your position. It's up to you to ask me the questions.
- What do you think of me? Do I fit?
- That's a funny question!
- I wouldn't like to be in your position. I wouldn't have the foggiest notion what to ask you!

Do:

- Reply coherently and ask something thoughtful.
- Be careful not to box yourself into a corner.
- Use the opportunity to find out more about the job.
- Use humor.
- Project yourself in the company as if the decision has been made in your favor.

Say:

- Do you adhere to our values and goals?
- Does the salary scale satisfy you?
- Do you think you are the one for this job? Why?
- Do you want this job?

BEST ANSWER

I'd like to take you up on your suggestion!
My question would be, "Do you want this job?"

Do you want to ask me some questions?

✓ Choose the Best Answer

- ☐ Is there available parking?
- ☐ How many weeks of vacation time do you propose?
- ☐ Do you think I have a chance for this job?
- ☐ Yes indeed! Can we decide to work together?
- ☐ How shall we proceed for the question of salary?

? What They Really Want to Know

- Can you do a quick analysis of where this interview is going?
- Do you dare ask me something? Have you done your homework?
- What questions bother or worry you?

! Watch Out!

Don't:
- Bring up the question of salary at this time.
- Restrict your questions to details about vacation, hours, salary.
- Act surprised and stammer and say no.
- Show that you haven't prepared any questions.
- Ask questions that have already been dealt with during the interview.
- Resort to a trivial question you already know the answer to.

Don't Say:
- I would like to ask you about the salary that has been allotted for this position.
- I had planned to go on vacation on ____. Will that still work?
- I need to think about all the information you've given me.
- I do not have any questions, thank you. Everything is clear.

- Questions will come up with time.
- Yes, I have two children. Could I start a little later in the morning?

Try This!

Do:

- Ask for details on the goals and responsibilities of the job.
- Ask questions about the company's organizational chart and primary concerns.
- Ask about the hiring date.

Say:

- When do you hope to hire your new associate?
- Might I ask you the reason behind the opening for this position?
- Could you explain your organizational chart?
- When do we start?
- When we talked about _____, I wanted to know more on _____.

BEST ANSWER

Yes indeed! Can we decide to work together?

Have you ever been asked to hand in your resignation?

✓ Choose the Best Answer

- ☐ Sure, several times! Just like everyone else!
- ☐ They didn't dare because I'm a fighter. They know good and well I won't let them walk all over me.
- ☐ No. I've always left on my own accord.
- ☐ Yes, for a nice sum of money. I know how to negotiate and how to sell myself.
- ☐ So far, I've never been in this situation. I've always given my best.

? What They Really Want to Know

- ▪ Have your skills ever been questioned?
- ▪ Have you been in conflict with an employer?
- ▪ Have you always carried out your tasks and assignments?

! Watch Out!

Don't:
- ▪ Confirm this outcome.
- ▪ Describe in minute detail what happened.
- ▪ Get emotional or react too strongly.
- ▪ Lie.
- ▪ Show your embarrassment.

Don't Say:
- ▪ It wouldn't be in my interest to answer this!
- ▪ Yes, and it didn't work out well.
- ▪ Yes.
- ▪ No.

Do:

- Admit it and point out the results you achieved before you left.
- Describe the context and show what you learned.
- Minimize your responsibility for it and point out how things beyond your control were contributing factors.
- Point out that it was done with mutual agreement.

Say:

- It was all in all a positive experience. I learned ____.
- I learned a lot of things. For example ____.
- The job no longer met up to my expectations. So, as it turned out, it was a good set of circumstances.
- When the company underwent a reduction in the workforce, I had to resign. However, they helped me find another job at ____.

BEST ANSWER

So far, I've never been in this situation. I've always given my best.

If you were going to the moon, what would you take with you?

✓ Choose the Best Answer

- ❑ Now, that's an interesting question!
- ❑ It doesn't tempt me. Not in the least!
- ❑ A huge dose of enthusiasm, an open mind, and my camera!
- ❑ Trips don't interest me and certainly not to the moon.
- ❑ I'd take my girlfriend so I wouldn't be lonely.

? What They Really Want to Know

- ■ Do you have a sense of innovation/creativity?
- ■ How do you deal with the unexpected?
- ■ Are you flexible and willing to entertain ideas that might be a bit farfetched?

! Watch Out!

Don't:
- ■ Be put off-balance or be afraid to answer.
- ■ Make a long list of trivial things you would take.
- ■ List items without explaining why you wanted them.
- ■ Remain silent or admit you don't know.
- ■ Raise subjects that are too sensitive or in contradiction with the firm's activities.
- ■ Present your values as generalities.

Don't Say:
- ■ I can hardly see myself going to the moon!
- ■ What makes you think I would go to the moon?
- ■ Not a thing!
- ■ Everything but the kitchen sink!
- ■ My resume!

Do:

- Let your humor come through by showing you know what's important but can remain light about the topic.
- Make a choice based on the qualities you want to highlight and explain these choices.
- Mention objects and people to take with you that would serve as evidence of your expertise and personal qualities useful for the position.
- Think before answering and list three to five precise things.

Say:

- Books on such subjects as _____ so I would know what I was seeing and be able to enjoy it even more.
- My family and friends to share the experience with and compare notes.
- A laptop with an Internet interstellar connection!
- A pair of binoculars to see everything up close, my writing journal to keep my notes, and a pair of pliers so I could fix things if I needed to!

BEST ANSWER

A huge dose of enthusiasm, an open mind, and my camera!

18

Social Status

W E'VE INCLUDED THIS SECTION so you will know the type of question(s) you may encounter from an inexperienced interviewer. No interviewer in a large organization that interviews hundreds of people a month, or any trained Human Resources person would ever ask you these questions as they are all illegal. However, since the bulk of jobs are to be found in small businesses (under 20 employees), it likely that sometime during your career you will be interviewed by a person who doesn't fully understand that certain types of questions cannot legally be asked. We include these questions to help you recognize when an interviewer has either knowingly or unknowingly stepped over the line so you can be prepared with how you want to proceed.

Most interviewers are not knowingly trying to discriminate; they are just ignorant of the law or they are nervous and phrase their questions in unacceptable ways. Many interviewers will ask just such a question in a misguided attempt to be friendly. Some interviewers even realize, once they have asked this kind of a question, that they have made a mistake; when that happens, both sides should try to be gracious, overlook the error, and move on with the interview in more positive ways.

It is not legal in the United States to ask any question for the purpose of discriminating on the basis of race, color, religion, sex, national origin, birthplace, age or physical disability.

Here's a list of what an interviewer cannot ask you:

- If your social title is Miss, Mrs., or Ms.?
- To give your maiden name or any other name you have previously used.
- Your age or age group (i.c., 25-35).
- To provide your birth certificate (before hiring you—only legal after you are hired).
- Your birthplace or the birthplace of any of your relatives (parents or spouse).
- Any question that would indicate your race/color.
- Any question that would indicate your gender (unless the gender is job-related).
- Any question about your religion, religious customs, or religious holidays.
- If you are a native-born or naturalized U.S. citizen and the date of your citizenship (they can ask you if you are a U.S. citizen but not how you became one).
- Any question about your marital status (only after hiring, for tax purposes).
- Any question about the number or age of your children, childcare arrangements, or if you are planning to have children (only after hiring, for tax purposes).
- Names of any relatives who might work at the same company.
- To provide your military records, disclose your type of discharge, or if you have served in the military of any other country.
- Any question about the nationality, racial, or religious affiliation of any school you attended.
- Any question about how a foreign language ability was acquired (they can ask about the level of language proficiency if job-related).

- Any question about whether you have been arrested (they can ask for a listing of your convictions however).
- To provide specific references from clergy or any other person who might reflect race, color, religion, gender, national origin, or your ancestry.
- To provide a list of all clubs you belong to or have ever belonged to.
- To ask for or take your picture before you are hired.
- Your willingness to work any particular religious holiday.
- Your height, weight, or any other physical impairment that is non-job related.
- Any non-job related question that presents information that could permit unlawful discrimination.

An interviewer can also not exclude candidates with disabilities as a class on the basis of their type of disability. Every case must be determined on its own individual basis by law. The burden of proof for non-discrimination lies with the employer, not the employee.

Social status questions included here are (these questions are all phrased so they are illegal to ask in this form):

- Do you have people at home for whom you are responsible?
- This job requires long hours. Will that create problems for your spouse?
- Are you planning to have children?
- Are you married? What will your spouse say/think if you accept this job?
- Where were you born?
- What is you family situation? What does your spouse do? And your children?
- Won't your children be needing you from time to time?
- I like your accent. Where are you from? Where were you brought up? Where are your parents from?

What the Interviewer Wants to Know About You

By asking questions about social status, the interviewer is trying to find out:

- Will your personal life get in the way of your professional life?
- Are your home obligations going to get in the way of you doing your job?
- Do you have a partner?
- Do you talk over big decisions with your partner?
- Are you willing to do overtime?
- Do you have any constraints? How available are you? How flexible are your hours? Would you be willing to travel?
- Can we count on you when we really need you?
- What are your priorities?
- Are you a foreigner? Where are your roots? Where did you get your education?
- Where are you originally from? Are you familiar with our customs?
- Do you have a work permit? What kind?
- Have you integrated enough to enjoy living here, or do you need more time?
- Are you planning to have children soon?
- Are you going to be out for a long time on maternity leave?
- How do you see your life evolving in the future?

How to Answer

You can see there is a broad range of topics that cannot be asked outright in an interview. If they are asked, does it mean you should run screaming from the room and head to the nearest Equal Employment Opportunity Commission (EEOC) office to file a complaint? Probably not. It isn't easy to prove that an interviewer meant to break the law and that by finding out some piece of information about your military service or family background, or figuring out your age by asking when you graduated from high school, means they would discriminate against you and not offer you the job because of that information.

So, how should you react? You can go one of three ways:

1. You can answer these kinds of questions honestly and run the risk of revealing information that may cost you the job offer. If you choose this option, answer briefly and then quickly move the discussion back to something relevant to the job.

2. You can refuse to answer the question. Depending on what you say and how you say it, you may appear defiant, hostile, and contrary. If you choose this option, better to go with, "I'm wondering in what way that is relevant to the job?" than "You can't ask me that question—it is illegal!" You can also try, "That question makes me uncomfortable and I'd really rather not answer it." This kind of an answer isn't usually perceived as overly hostile and may keep the discussion open until you can decide if the job is one you want to consider.

   If you get too many inappropriate/illegal questions in one interview, it's a pretty clear indication the job environment probably won't work for you. The best strategy, however, is to try and sidestep these questions altogether and redirect the discussion to a new job-specific topic area. If you just can't do that, it may be time to politely excuse yourself to leave and focus your energies on another job/company where the workers don't dwell on arbitrary and illegal issues. You may have to ask yourself if you would even be happy working for a person/company that openly discriminates against people. Only you can make that call.

3. Finally, you can try to discern the intent of the question and provide an answer that will satisfy both you and the interviewer. Part of the reason these illegal questions are sometimes asked is that the interviewer is afraid of some underlying assumption they have made, whether it's true or not. If an interviewer asks you if you plan to have children, they are worried that if the answer is yes, it could mean that you might not be around when they need you. Or if you are asked if you were born in this country, they may be worried that a person who isn't native-born will not understand or accept the customs of this

country and will cause problems for them. It's okay to ask the interviewer for more information about his or her underlying concern so you will understand how to reassure the person with your answer. In terms of the "Do you plan on having children?" question, you might respond, "I don't have any plans at this time. I can tell you that I'm very interested in developing my career. Now, I'd like to call your attention to my experience and expertise in," or, "I try to balance my work and my personal life. I can guarantee you that I have always been focused on and committed to my job responsibilities, and my personal life has never interfered with my performance."

We don't mean to suggest that every person who asks illegal questions is just misguided. There are highly prejudiced and bigoted people out there. Discrimination is ugly and it does occasionally happen. If you are certain that an interviewer asked you an illegal interview question with the intent of using your answer as a basis for making a hiring decision, you can make a charge with the EEOC. Remember, however, just because an illegal question is asked doesn't necessarily mean a crime has been committed. It is up to the courts to determine whether the information was used in a discriminatory manner. However, if you feel you have to do something to pursue such a matter further, contact the EEOC to find your local branch and file a report.

Finally, it won't come as a surprise that an experienced interviewer will find legal ways to ask what they need to know. For example, instead of asking, "What language do you speak? How did you learn it? What kind of accent is that?," the interviewer will say, "This position is in our international office and we are seeking someone who speaks . . . Do you?" Totally legal with a direct correlation to the job duties. Your best hope is that you get an interviewer who knows how and what to ask, and when you find yourself someday (perhaps) in the position of interviewing others, you become an interviewer who knows not to hit below the belt!

Note: For the following questions, we have listed as the answers possible things that might be said to keep the interview moving along, rather than to say "That is illegal and I won't answer it." You, of course, are free to refuse categorically to answer any illegal question asked of you.

Do you have people at home for whom you are responsible?

✓ Choose the Best Answer

- ❏ With our three children, my husband and I make a nice little family—we balance our lives and are well organized.
- ❏ I have two small children and three cats, and I take care of them all. It's not always easy, but I manage.
- ❏ My family situation is private. I don't think I should have to talk about it.
- ❏ We have children and an "au pair." But you know what? You can't always count on them.
- ❏ Yes, five children and they're all just great. Everybody takes care of everybody else.

? What They Really Want to Know

- ▪ Are your home obligations going to get in the way of you doing your job?
- ▪ Are you willing to do overtime?
- ▪ Can we count on you when we really need you?

! Watch Out!

Don't:
- ▪ Mention all the members of your family or all the responsibilities you have at home.
- ▪ Give too many details.
- ▪ Lie about your situation.
- ▪ Talk about your pets.
- ▪ Complain about your situation.
- ▪ Become indignant and refuse to answer because you don't think this question is legal to ask [you run a great risk if you become vitriolic about this].

Don't Say:

- Yes, and it's not easy with the childcare system available.
- Yes, and it takes a lot of time, as I have to take my elderly mother to the doctor often.
- That's just it! Is it possible to do part of the work at home?

 Try This!

Do:

- Show that the system in place at home includes emergency solutions.
- Use the occasion to demonstrate your sense of organization and foresight.
- Reassure the recruiter/interviewer of your availability without directly answering the question.

Say:

- I know how to make myself available as long as I'm needed.
- Yes, but I've always managed. My previous jobs never suffered from my personal obligations.
- I have four children and have an effective system in place that works even when they're sick.

BEST ANSWER ✓

> *With our three children, my husband and I make a nice little family—we balance our lives and are well organized.*

This job requires long hours. Will that create problems for your spouse?

✓ Choose the Best Answer

☐ It all depends.

☐ My spouse supports me in my career and is ready to accept the constraints of my profession.

☐ How much overtime will I have to do? If it's reasonable, I don't mind. If not, I might have problems with my spouse.

☐ It should be all right. Even though I'm hard working, I don't want to be exploited.

☐ Not as long as I let her know a week ahead.

? What They Really Want to Know

- Do you have family obligations?
- Are you willing to work overtime? Are you flexible?
- Do you know how to organize yourself?

! Watch Out!

Don't:

- Go into detail about your family situation.
- Show that long hours would bother you or would not be possible for you.
- Bring up all your outside activities.
- Show that you flatly refuse to consider longer hours.

Don't Say:

- It all depends. How are the extra hours accounted for?
- I don't really know. Haven't talked to her/him about it yet.
- Obviously! Our family life comes first.

Do:

- Accept the constraint by negotiating something in return.
- Ask for clarification on the short- and long-term objectives of the position.
- Be open and flexible about the possiblity of longer hours, especially in the beginning if you take the job.
- Find out about the frequency and number of extra hours.
- Show your ability to adapt, giving examples.

Say:

- I am flexible and realize that extra hours are part of the job.
- My spouse supports my application for this job. By the way, if you are talking about overtime, how often might that be?
- That's not a problem for my spouse. By the way, what are the long- and short-term goals of this job?
- Neither my spouse nor I see any problem. By the way, how is overtime accounted for? What system do you use?

BEST ANSWER

My spouse supports me in my career and is ready to accept the constraints of my profession.

Are you planning to have children?

✓ Choose the Best Answer

- ❑ Normally, you don't have the right to ask me that question, and I have the right not to answer.
- ❑ I'm sure I don't know. We shall see.
- ❑ Not for the moment. What's important for me now is to invest myself totally in my profession.
- ❑ We are actually trying now. It's not easy but we've seen some experts on the subject.
- ❑ In two or three years, yes.

? What They Really Want to Know

- Are you going to be out for a long time on maternity leave?
- How do you see your life evolving in a couple of years from now?
- What are your priorities?

! Watch Out!

Don't:
- Point out that this question is indiscreet.
- Mention the fact that you already have four children.
- Lie or misrepresent yourself.
- Be offended and reply aggressively.

Don't Say:
- That's private. It's none of your business.
- That's a point I only discuss with my husband/wife.
- Why do you want to know?
- You have no right to ask me that.

Do:

- Control your gestures and first response at being asked this question.
- Avoid feeling attacked.
- Find out if there have been other expectant mothers in the office and whether there were problems for the employer because of this.

Say:

- With my spouse, we plan to have a child in three to five years.
- This is not an issue.
- I am on my own and want to concentrate on my career for a few more years.
- Yes, but rest assured that this will not have an impact on my work.
- Have you had many employees who became pregnant after joining your company?

BEST ANSWER

Not for the moment. What's important for me now is to invest myself totally in my profession.

Are you married? What will your spouse say/think if you accept this job?

✓ Choose the Best Answer

- ❑ That's beside the point, since I have no intention of asking her/his advice and will just announce my decision.
- ❑ There's work and there's family—two very different things.
- ❑ My spouse will ask me one question: "How much are they going to pay you?"
- ❑ My husband/wife/partner will undoubtedly be delighted.
- ❑ My spouse knows nothing about this interview. I'm keeping it a secret!

? What They Really Want to Know

- ■ Do you have a partner?
- ■ Do you talk over big decisions with your partner?
- ■ Will your personal life get in the way of your professional life?

! Watch Out!

Don't:

- ■ Act defensive or use aggressive body language like crossing your arms.
- ■ Give the impression that you never make decisions on your own.
- ■ Get overly exuberant at the mention of family issues.
- ■ Appear irritated at the mention of domestic life issues.
- ■ Give the impression your domestic life is more important than work.
- ■ Act like you never discuss important issues with your partner.

Don't Say:

- ■ He/she has nothing to say about it. It's my own decision.
- ■ He/she thinks it's not a job for me.
- ■ I'd rather not say.

- I don't think the question has anything to do with the job.
- We do not agree on the subject.

Try This!

 Do:

- Assure the interviewer that you have his/her support.
- Make a positive reply about how excited you are to have the job.
- Assure the interviewer that your spouse will not be a problem, and then bring the conversation back to professional issues.

Say:

- He/she will support me in my choice.
- He/she thinks I have the right profile for this job.
- I am not married, so I make my own decisions about my career.
- He/she will be delighted that I have found a job that I am enthusiastic about and which suits me.
- I've discussed the possibility with my wife/husband/partner. He/she feels the same way I do.

BEST ANSWER

My husband/wife/partner will undoubtedly be delighted.

Where were you born?

✓ Choose the Best Answer

- ❏ Now, what importance does this have in recruiting me?
- ❏ In a country where the culture is completely different from yours.
- ❏ You probably don't know much about where I'm from.
- ❏ Far from here.
- ❏ I was born in (country/state/town) and came to (country/state/town) when I was (age). I grew up in _____ , and studied in _____, and I speak three languages.

? What They Really Want to Know

- Are you a foreigner? Where are your roots? Where did you get your education?
- Are you well integrated?
- Do you have a work permit? What kind?

! Watch Out!

Don't:

- Spend too much time talking about your country of origin.
- Hesitate in answering.
- Be vague or self-conscious about your birthplace.
- Apologize for your nationality.
- Place too much importance on the question.

Don't Say:

- Abroad.
- In _____, and I plan to go back soon.
- In _____, and it's not easy to get used to living in this country.

- I haven't been here long.
- I've had a hard time adapting.

Try This!

Do:

- Assure the interviewer you are happy to be here in this country/state/city.
- Give a few details on where you are from, and then bounce back to stressing your assets.
- Answer precisely and clearly.

Say:

- I studied in (country/city).
- I like it here and plan to stay put.
- I've been here for many years.
- I was born in _____ and have been a citizen of this country for _____ years.

BEST ANSWER

I was born in (country/state/town) and came to (country/state/town) when I was (age). I grew up in _____ , and studied in _____, and I speak three languages.

What is your family situation? What does your spouse do? And your children?

✓ Choose the Best Answer

- ❑ That's a long story. Do you really want me to tell you?
- ❑ I live with my wife and our three children. She has a job she enjoys, and the children are in school.
- ❑ I'm divorced and in charge of two young children.
- ❑ Why do you ask? That's part of my private life.
- ❑ What is it you would like to know, actually? I'm happily married with four children.

? What They Really Want to Know

- ▪ Do you have any constraints? How available are you? How flexible are your hours? Would you be willing to travel?
- ▪ Are you planning to have children soon?
- ▪ Would you have your family's support?

! Watch Out!

Don't:
- ▪ Reveal too much dependency on your spouse.
- ▪ Forget to reassure the interviewer about the child-care arrangements you have in place.
- ▪ Jump in too soon to try to get the recruiter to spell out the working conditions.
- ▪ Elaborate unnecessarily on the subject of your home life.

Don't Say:
- ▪ I'm not married.
- ▪ I've having a hard time paying my alimony.
- ▪ I'm going through a nasty divorce.

- My family expenses are quite high.
- My spouse just left me!
- My spouse works and my kids are still little, and it's not easy every day.
- My spouse has a high-power job, so I have to be home at 5:15 every night to pick up the kids from daycare.

 Try This!

Do:

- Show your ability to maintain a harmonious balance between your family and professional life.
- Show your incentive to involve yourself in a motivating professional project.
- Reassure the recruiter that you accept the notion of mobility and/or a flexible timetable.
- Stay brief and concise with your answer and do not furnish many details.

Say:

- My spouse and I have come up with very satisfactory child-care arrangements for our two children.
- Our kids have been out of the house for two years now.
- I have an understanding spouse.
- I have complete confidence in my spouse.
- I don't have children and don't plan to for another four or five years.
- My spouse takes care of our three children during the week, and I take an active part on the weekend.
- We have a good family setup.
- My spouse and I share in the family chores and upbringing of our two children.

BEST ANSWER

I live with my wife and our three children. She has a job she enjoys and the children are in school.

Won't your children be needing you from time to time?

✓ Choose the Best Answer

- ❑ That's something I worry about a great deal. But things usually end up working out.
- ❑ I'm not quite set up yet. You know, I've been out of work for over a year.
- ❑ I have a good set-up. I am lucky to have an "au pair," parents, parents-in-law, neighbors, a daycare center, and an excellent family doctor in place. I've never had a problem before.
- ❑ My kids will just have to fend for themselves. They're big enough.
- ❑ As a matter of fact, yes. I have three kids, the youngest being 15 months and the oldest is nine. I really have to do gymnastics getting them off to the daycare center, school, and all their extracurricular activities. And, on top of that, I am in the middle of a divorce! I absolutely have to find a job.

? What They Really Want to Know

- ▪ Do you have family obligations? Might you be absent for personal reasons?
- ▪ How are you set up with your family?
- ▪ Do you have children?

! Watch Out!

Don't:

- ▪ Say it's a problem and reinforce the recruiter's/interviewer's fears.
- ▪ Stammer, look down, and try to avoid replying.
- ▪ Describe your family in an effort to sensitize the recruiter on this issue.
- ▪ Talk about your kids' most recent misfortunes/blunders/feats.
- ▪ Show your anxiety or that you are alone to deal with the situation.
- ▪ Show pictures of your children with the hope of sweetening up the recruiter/interviewer.

Don't Say:

- Do you know of a good babysitter? Mine just left.
- That shouldn't concern you. It's my own business.
- Are you in favor of big families?
- The daycare center closes at 5 PM, so I won't be able to stay late.
- Do you get maternity/paternity leave here?

 Try This!

Do:

- Assure the recruiter/interviewer that you have a network of people you can depend on, that you are well organized.
- Convince the recruiter/interviewer that everything is under control, and prove it by telling about a couple of past situations.
- Talk about the arrangements you have managed to set up.

Say:

- My current goal is a serious career, and I don't plan on starting a family in the near future.
- My children are grown.
- I can always find help because I've a large network to draw from.

BEST ANSWER

I have a good set-up. I am lucky to have an "au pair," parents, parents-in-law, neighbors, a daycare center, and an excellent family doctor in place. I've never had a problem before.

I like your accent. Where are you from? Where were you brought up? Where are your parents from?

✓ Choose the Best Answer

- ❑ Accent? I haven't got an accent!
- ❑ I apologize. I don't speak your language very well.
- ❑ I come from _____ and am having a lot of trouble learning your language.
- ❑ I know I have a strong accent. I hope you can understand me, though.
- ❑ Thank you. I've been working here since 2001 and studied at _____.

? What They Really Want to Know

- ■ Where are you originally from? Are you familiar with our customs?
- ■ Have you integrated enough to enjoy living here, or do you need more time?
- ■ What is your educational background? Is it of a good quality?

! Watch Out!

Don't:
- ■ Be ashamed of your origins.
- ■ Say you come from a country with an entirely different culture.
- ■ Exaggerate your difficulties with English.
- ■ Dwell on your origins.
- ■ Remain vague about where you are from/were brought up.

Don't Say:
- ■ With my language and my origins, it's not easy to adjust here.
- ■ English is a difficult language.
- ■ I haven't been here very long.
- ■ They used to treat me as a foreigner even at school!
- ■ And you? Where are you from?

Do:

- Say that you have been working in this country for some time.
- Show pride in your country of origin.
- Mention any courses you have taken in English, or since you have been in this country. Mention the schools you have attended.
- Express your thanks and give a brief answer.
- Take advantage by telling a little story about your country.

Say:

- Well, thank you. I've been in this country for seven years and my parents come from Vietnam.
- I was born in _____, but raised in _____ since I was five years old. I am very familiar with the customs here in the United States.
- Thank you. I like English. I'm from _____.
- Thank you. My mother tongue is German. I learned English during my studies here in this country.

BEST ANSWER

Thank you. I've been working here since 2001 and studied at _____.

19

Behavioral Interviewing

F OR THE LAST 20-PLUS YEARS, some employers have been using a different style of questions when they interview candidates for jobs. Instead of asking "traditional" questions, which tend to allow for more subjective answers on the part of the candidate (which often cannot be verified as fact unless some kind of very specific example is included in the answer), they are asking behavioral questions which demand that a candidate provide an example of a job-related behavior they have demonstrated in the past.

Some studies show that conducting a behavioral-based interview improves hiring reliability up to about 75 percent when compared with using only traditional questions to elicit information from a candidate. Most interviews are now a combination of both types of questions.

You might ask, what's the difference between a "traditional" type question and a "behavioral" type question?

Traditional interview questions are straightforward and open-ended, asking the candidate to provide information about themselves, their goals and values, their likes and dislikes, their past bosses and co-workers, and so forth. Candidates can respond with a short answer (especially if they are shy or unprepared). Sometimes a mere "Yes" or "No" would suffice, even though that would not give the interviewer much to go on!

Typical traditional questions are:

- Are you creative?
- Are you tenacious; do you persevere?
- Tell me about yourself!
- How do you judge yourself? What are your best qualities and your biggest limitations?
- What is your working style?
- How well do you accept hierarchy?
- What kind of person manages you the best?
- Why do you want to change jobs?
- What are your long-term goals?
- Is salary important to you?
- How would you describe the direction your career is presently taking?
- What do you wish to become in our company?
- How long are you going to stay with us?
- There seems to be a six-month gap in your resume. What did you do during this time?
- How do you relate to others?
- How long have you been looking for a job?
- Can we contact your present/last employer for information about you?
- Can you describe a typical day in your last job?

These questions often ask for an opinion or feeling on the part of the candidate that may not always be based on fact or evidence. Anyone can say they are creative or tenacious or can talk about long-term goals (that may or may not reflect the person's real desires). Anyone can say they relate well to others and have never had a problem with their co-workers. The problem with these kinds of questions (and hence their answers) for many interviewers is that there is no empirical proof that shows what a candidate is capable of. They force the interviewer to make a gut instinct decision as to whether or not the candidate is the person who can best do the job.

Behavioral interview questions, on the other hand, are more pointed and probe more deeply into actual experiences or situations the candidate has been in. They ask for very specific illustrations of how the person has behaved in the past.

In a nutshell, the whole premise of a behavioral-based question is this:

The most accurate predictor of future performance is past performance in a similar situation.

Behavioral questions are designed to elicit objective facts from a candidate that allow the interviewer to base employment decisions on past actions with the assumption that how a person has acted in specific employment-related situations indicates how he/she will act at a new job if faced with the same or similar situations. Behavioral questions are designed to pinpoint certain characteristics and skills that employers have predetermined are necessary to do the job they offer. The interviewer will outline situations similar to those that might be faced on the job, and will compare the candidate's answers to the actions of successful employees. There is no "right" or "wrong" answer per se to a behavioral question, but you are judged and may be scored as "demonstrated the skill" or "didn't demonstrate the skill". Employers find these kinds of questions a more useful way to get very pointed, verifiable, and comparable information from a candidate.

Instead of asking how you would behave (which at best is only theory) in a certain circumstance, they will ask how you did behave in a certain circumstance. Answers must show exactly how you handled a situation that they have determined is congruent with the job in question. The interviewer will want to know how you actually handled a situation, instead of a hypothetical guess of what you might do in the future.

Behavioral questions are usually framed as statements and begin with the words:

- Describe . . .
- Tell me about . . .
- Give me an example of . . .

When a candidate hears these words at the beginning of a statement, they should know they are being asked to provide a very specific example from their past. Not only do these behavior-based "questions" elicit more specific and relevant information, but they are often followed up with more questions that allow an interviewer to drill down and gain even more information and clarity based on what the candidate says.

Typical behavioral questions are:

- Describe a complex situation/problem that you had to deal with.
- Describe a team you were on. How did it function? What did you bring to it?
- Describe a time when your work was criticized.
- Describe a time when you were not able to obtain your objective.
- Describe a situation in which you felt you proved your competency in the area of _____.
- Describe a time when you had to make a quick and basically intuitive decision.
- Describe a situation where you needed an outside opinion. How did you go about getting it?
- Describe a time when you had to excel as a leader.
- Describe a time when you succeeded in inspiring team spirit.
- Tell me about a situation in which you had to make a very difficult or painful decision.
- Tell me about a situation where you had to work under pressure/ against the clock.

- Tell me about a time when you had to communicate an idea in writing.

- Give me an example of a time when you had to persuade people to do something they really didn't want to do.

- Describe for me the most unique solution you've ever developed to a problem.

- Tell me about a time when you had to deal with conflict at work.

- Give me an example of a time when you took the initiative to lead a project.

- Tell me about a time when you had seemingly too many deadlines approaching at the same time and you needed to prioritize your work.

When asked a behavioral-type question, a candidate must give detailed and specific examples. You can either describe a complex situation you faced, or you can't. You can either tell of a time when you overcame a conflict at work, or you can't. There isn't room for generalities when answering behavioral questions. Bluffing or supposing how you would behave doesn't work. You either answer with an example from your past (which is unlike any other candidate's experience) or you fail to answer the question satisfactorily.

How To Prepare for Behavioral Questions in an Interview

It sounds like it might be almost impossible to prepare for an interview where behavior-based questions are going to be asked. How can a candidate ever anticipate all the questions that might be asked and prepare for them? Most people feel intimidated and overwhelmed just to think about this.

First, don't let the word "behavioral" make you nervous and cause you to throw your hands up in despair. You can be ready for these questions. We've said it before and we'll say it again. You must do your homework if you are going to be ready to answer interview questions, whether traditional or behavioral. You must be familiar enough with the job to know most of the skills and personal characteristics needed to do it well, and you must evaluate and reflect on your past to make sure you can demonstrate that you possess these skills, abilities, and characteristics by the examples you give. The good news is that there are a limited number of competencies for each job and if you have done your homework, you will be ready for most of the questions you will be asked.

What You Can Do

1. **Become familiar enough with the job to know what is likely to be needed to prove you are the best candidate.** Carefully review the job description, if you have it, or the job posting or ad. You should be able to get a sense of what skills and behavioral characteristics the employer is seeking from reading the job description and position requirements. Research the company's website and any other information about them you can find on the Internet or at the library. If you do not have a job description for the exact job in question, use the Internet to find a job description for a position that is similar. It's not that big a leap to surmise that there will be many common areas between the two. Even if the jobs are a bit different, you will still be ahead of the game by having anticipated what is likely to be asked, and prepared yourself for it.

2. **Make a list of at least 5 to 15 skills, abilities, knowledge, personal attributes, and other factors important to do the job.** Pretend you are the interviewer and write down what kind of information you would want to elicit from the candidates to find out their suitability for the job. Be sure you frame these as behavioral questions that call for a specific example to demonstrate each aspect of the job. Once you have made your list of questions, write down two or three examples from your past that demonstrate your suitability for each of the factors.

3. **Take your examples from a variety of experiences that demonstrate your skills and abilities.** It's good when you can combine work experience with a non-work experience to show you have used the skill in a variety of settings. Examples may be from your work experience, your personal life, or some social or other situation. Give priority to your work experiences the majority of the time, as they will be of most interest to the interviewer. Be expressive but remain as succinct as possible when you tell your story. Remember the interviewer will likely

ask you for more detail, especially on the things that capture his/her interest.

4. **Use recent examples.** Refresh your memory regarding your achievements in the past year or two. You can do this by referring to your resume as a starting-off place. Your examples can be drawn from many areas in your life: internships, hobbies and leisure activities, team involvement, community service, and work experience. In addition, you may use examples you are especially proud of, such as running a marathon, holding a political office, exhibiting work at an art show, climbing a high mountain peak, or biking across the country. It's best to stick with more recent examples, as they will be fresher in your mind. If you are asked for more details, it's easier to remember something from the last 12-18 months than something that happened 10 years ago. Even though it's acceptable to use examples from outside of your work experience, it's best to keep at least 95% of your answers on work-related experiences.

5. **Talk about your results.** Be as specific as possible about your contribution and the quantitative results achieved. It's better to talk in facts and figures when possible and show how your measurable results affected either an increase in productivity, a decrease in costs, or the elimination of errors. If you find that specific measurable results don't apply to your example, try to explain how it streamlined processes, empowered others, or resolved communication difficulties.

6. **Let others speak for you.** It's perfectly reasonable to occasionally use quotes from others (bosses, customers, or co-workers) to illustrate something about yourself. You can say, "My boss particularly liked the way I took the initiative to get the job done, without being asked to step forward."

7. **Use a structured approach to your answer.** There are many acronyms to help you organize the way you present your information to an interviewer when asked a behavioral question. The most common of these are STAR and SAR. Using either of these formulas, your answer will always have at least three or four distinct parts to be complete.

The STAR formula is organized this way:

- **Situation:** give an example of a situation you were involved in that resulted in a positive outcome.
- **Task:** describe the tasks involved in that situation.
- **Action:** talk about the various actions involved in the situation's tasks.
- **Results:** give the results that directly followed because of your actions.

The SAR formula is organized this way:

- **Situation:** the description of the task, situation or problem.
- **Action:** the action you took in either in discovering the problem or resolving it.
- **Result:** the final measurable result(s), using facts and figures to illustrate.

Either way of remembering how to organize your information is fine to use. When you answer using either of these formulas, the interviewer is better able to envision and link your specific behavioral responses to specific duties and characteristics of the job he is interviewing you for.

Prepare at least one response using the above formula for each skill or personal attribute you may be questioned on. Prepare stories that illustrate times when you have successfully solved problems or performed memorably. It won't hurt you to develop specific STAR responses to demonstrate your teamwork abilities, initiative, planning, leadership, commitment, and problem-solving skills. These are used in most jobs, and thinking about them ahead of time will only benefit you in the long run, even if you aren't asked about them specifically in every interview. Be prepared to provide examples when results were different than expected. Be sure to vary your examples, so you don't use the same one twice.

8. **Practice your stories until they are clear and concise, and from one to three minutes long.** You will not be able to answer behavioral questions well unless you have practiced. It is imperative that you boil down your answers and "separate the wheat from the chaff." It is too easy to ramble on and on if you haven't thoroughly pared down your stories to the basic information that needs to be shared. We're not suggesting you memorize your answers, but do put together a cohesive answer ahead of time that you can recall when needed. It's often a good idea to review your responses immediately before an interview to refresh your memory and give you a feeling of confidence that you are ready to handle any question asked of you.

9. **Be prepared for follow-up questions.** The interviewer will likely want to know more if they are interested in what you say. Typically, an interviewer will probe deeper into a story to try to get at the specific behavior(s) they are interested in. They might ask:

- What were you thinking at that point?
- Tell me more about your meeting with that person.
- Lead me through your decision process.
- How exactly did you do that?
- Tell me exactly what steps you took to resolve that.
- What was the basis for that decision?
- How exactly did your role evolve?
- How did you handle time deadlines, pressures, and unexpected situations?
- How did you handle adversity?

When you are asked follow-up questions, listen carefully and then answer. Supply the necessary details. It's vitally important you are honest. If you omit or try to embellish parts of your story, the interviewer will likely suspect it and will begin to distrust other things you say.

10. **Ask to come back to the question.** If you are stuck for an answer to a particular question, it is reasonable to ask the interviewer if you may move on to the next one and you'll come back it. Don't do this more than once or twice, or you will damage your position. If you don't understand a question, ask for clarification and, when you understand what is being asked of you, make sure you answer the question completely.

A Final Thought

It helps to keep in mind that there are no right or wrong answers to these questions. There is only "what you did." Your experience is different from the experience of anyone else. You must be honest as you tell your stories. Don't try to make yourself a superhero and suggest that without you the company would have fallen into wreck and ruin. Don't underplay your part either and leave the interviewer thinking you are only a follower and incapable of making decisions. Tell your stories truthfully, clearly, and succinctly and trust that you are unique.

If you talk about how you behaved in a specific instance and later decided that you should have behaved differently, explain this to the interviewer. Show what lessons were learned. The interviewer will be far more interested in knowing that you have learned from the past and won't repeat behaviors that don't work well. You will be judged fairly if you show growth and maturity.

Tell me about a time when you had to plan and coordinate a project from start to finish.

BEST ANSWER

When I worked for _____ I was in charge of a project which involved providing better training for the customer service personnel by utilizing the expertise of our technicians. I organized a meeting to bring both teams together to discuss and brainstorm how we could improve our support to customers. After this meeting, using the information we had gathered I drew up my plan using the best ideas. I organized four teams, balancing each team with technical and non-technical people. We had a short deadline so I did periodic checks with the teams. After only three weeks, we were able to implement the plan and saw immediate results in improved customer service satisfaction. I was very proud of the spirit or cooperation and teamwork by everyone involved. Management commended me for my leadership role, but I know without the dedication and hard work from all parties, we would not have had such tremendous success.

Describe a situation where you had to deal with a difficult person.

BEST ANSWER ✓

I was asked to work on a new project when I worked at ____, and I had to join an existing team and replace someone who had to leave because of illness. This person was highly respected and valued and I think the team leader somehow resented me for having been asked to step in. I was left out of important and vital meetings and communications. After a few weeks of this, I took the iniative to set up a one-on-one meeting with her to try and resolve the problem. I showed her I understood the key objectives of the project and that I would be able to meet those objectives with the same, if not more, dedication than the employee who had been forced to leave. I was able to talk with her about some of her underlying issues with management, which, when clarified, helped her to realize that she had been placing some of her anger with them onto me. In the end, we came to an understanding and the morale of the entire team improved. We were able to exceed our goals and the company became more profitable because of this increased performance on everyone's part.

Answering Behavioral Questions

Don't:

- Try to bluff your way through a behavioral interview question.
- Lie about your experience.
- Describe how you would behave. Describe how you have actually behaved in the past.
- Use pat answers that interviewers are adept at spotting.
- Try to portray yourself as a person who never makes mistakes.
- Try to portray yourself as a person whose only failings are that you work too much, are too dedicated, too loyal, etc. This is transparent to an interviewer.
- Expect that you can just "wing" it with behavioral questions. If you do nothing to prepare, you will stumble during the interview.
- Ramble on and on because you didn't organize your thoughts ahead of time.
- Be vague or say too little.
- Use examples that are 20+ years old, unless specifically asked about something from that time in your life.

 **Try This!**

Do:

- Use the STAR or SAR technique to organize your answer. Describe the **Situation** you were in or the **Task** you needed to accomplish; describe the **Action** you took, and the **Results** obtained.
- Be specific, not general or vague.
- Give concrete examples of difficult situations that actually happened at work, showing what you did to solve the problem.
- Keep your answers positive.
- If you don't understand what is asked or you are not sure how to answer the question, ask for clarification.

- Prepare stories that illustrate times when you have successfully solved problems or performed memorably. This is the only way to respond meaningfully in a behavioral interview.
- Review the job description, if you have it, or the job posting or ad. You should be able to get a sense of what skills and behavioral characteristics the employer is seeking from reading the job description and position requirements.
- Refresh your memory about your achievements and highlights of your school activities (if new to the workforce) or career over the past few years.
- Think about challenging problems or obstacles you faced and come up with a STAR statement about them.
- Make a list of at least 5 to 15 skills, abilities, knowledge, personal attributes, and other factors important to do the job and prepare answers for them.
- As you think about how to prepare, use your past experiences from all walks of life: internships, classes and projects, activities, team and sports participation, community service, and full or part-time jobs.
- Concentrate on the areas of decision making, leadership, organizational, problem solving, initiative, planning, commitment skills and teamwork abilities, as these areas are important in most jobs, regardless of the field.
- Vary your responses. Don't use the same job or example every time.
- Be prepared for follow-up questions from the interviewer as they try to elicit more details. They will often ask clarifying questions when they want more information about something you have said.
- Be honest about your mistakes since the experienced interviewer will be looking for "progress" and "growth," and not perfection. Show what you have learned from your mistakes and how those experiences have benefited you in the long run.
- Practice, practice, practice! It's the only way to make sure you will do well when answering behavioral questions.

Keep in Touch...
On the Web!

www.impactpublications.com
www.ishoparoundtheworld.com
www.exoffenderreentry.com
www.veteransworld.com